LATIN AMERICA
The Dynamics of Social Change

LATIN AMERICA
The Dynamics of Social Change

Edited by
STEFAN A. HALPER
& JOHN R. STERLING

CONTRIBUTORS
Gino Germani, Helio Jaguaribe,
Irving Louis Horowitz, John Gerassi,
Andre Gunder Frank, Ivan Illich,
Anthony F. C. Wallace,
Richard R. Fagen

ST. MARTIN'S PRESS   NEW YORK

AFFILIATED PUBLISHERS: Macmillan & Company, Limited,
London – also at Bombay, Calcutta, Madras and Melbourne –
The Macmillan Company of Canada, Limited, Toronto

Contents

Acknowledgements

The editors wish to acknowledge the assistance of the following organizations in making this collection possible: The Committee of Latin American Studies, The Committee for International Studies, and The Institute of International Relations, all of Stanford University. In addition, we would like to express our gratitude to John J. Johnson, Richard Fagen, Gabriel L. Kaplan and Robert Rosensweig for their early help and encouragement, to Dennis Sullivan for his criticism, to K.I.S. for her general assistance, and to Nancy Halper for her critical suggestions and continuing support.

Introduction

In the past two decades social scientists have introduced several new approaches to the study of political, social and economic modernization in developing areas. The contributors to this volume explore some of these theories with critical reference to Latin America's current and historical problems. Of central concern is the fundamental conflict in Third World development: violent structural change or gradual reform of the archaic institutions which have inhibited the development of a modern secular society.

Despite dramatic advances in some sectors and some countries, Latin America remains an underdeveloped region. Widespread poverty remains and, in many cases, is increasing along with inequitable social stratification and unequal opportunities for education and advancement. The growing potential for social and political upheaval has made it clear that the pace of change must be accelerated, that Latin American economies must be diversified and that basic changes must be effected in the social structure, not simply because they are necessary for the societies to prosper and progress but because a fundamental regard for social justice makes them imperative.

Latin American political systems, while formally democratic, have been slow to lose their élite bias. The lower strata, largely illiterate and unknowledgeable of political affairs, have traditionally been manipulated, misled and excluded from the political process. Those groups conscious enough to vote, and sufficiently experienced to perceive their more enduring interests, have often had limited effect because they have lacked the necessary resources and skills to form institutions capable of channeling their views into the political system. A lack of cohesion, moreover, has effectively prevented them from influencing the political élite or even directing the political parties established in their name. In a word, democracy in most of Latin America (with some notable exceptions) is underdeveloped.

The initial obstacle to a discussion of development in Latin America is the lack of a generally accepted definition of the word "development". Problems of confusing and idiosyncratic terminology have plagued social science literature in this area and, as one of the contributors to this volume suggests, may be regarded as a real barrier to the emergence of a unified theory of Latin American development.* Political development, narrowly defined, concerns the institutionalization of the processes of governing and representation in patterns consistent with the principles of secularity and rationality which guide modern social action. However, in a larger sense *political* development cannot be divorced from *national* development; for as a nation modernizes, responsibility for reorganizing and readjusting traditional institutional patterns in the economy and the society falls increasingly on the political system as the legitimate arbiter of conflicting interests and claims. The transformation of the economy from traditional-subsistence to modern-industrial brings crucial importance to the government's power to tax and regulate while the concurrent transformations in the social structure (the rise of the middle class, the spread of universal education, etc.) produce greater demands from previously marginal sectors for participation in the political decisions which affect their lives.

The various aspects of national development are perhaps more clearly viewed as factors in the process of *modernization*, which, as Gino Germani illustrates in his table of the "Stages of modernization in Latin America", may serve as a viable general framework for analysing social change in Latin America and other developing regions. Positing the "modern industrial state" as a generic type characterized by secularity and other specific features, Germani sets out the analytic tools necessary for studying the diffusion of modernization from the more modern centers to the peripheries: internationally, from the more modern nations to the less advanced, and internally, from the more developed geographic regions or political, social and economic

* See I. L. Horowitz, "The Norm Of Illegitimacy . . ."

sectors of each country to the less developed. The process of transformation may be viewed as consisting of three analytically distinct parts (economic, political and social) which display reciprocal causality. Each process may, by its stage of advance or retardation, facilitate or inhibit the progress of the other components. It may be said, moreover, that within a given cultural and historical framework, there may exist certain minimum degrees or thresholds of development in any one particular sphere which must be reached in order to allow further advances in other spheres.

While not always explicit, the idea of diffusion underlies many of the more traditional analyses of the development process. Generally the economic system has been credited with a clearly primary role; growth is spurred through investment and trade from the more developed centers (nationally and internationally) to the less developed areas. In the beginning the basic trade consists of exchanging raw materials and unprocessed agricultural products for the manufactured goods of the more advanced areas. As natural resources are developed, along with the infrastructures necessary to exploit them, local labor is employed, secondary industries arise, and a self-sustaining internal market emerges. The resulting economic development is credited with promoting modernization in the social and political spheres by creating the resources for increased education and communication, an open system of status mobility, and a general shift in the organizing principles of the society toward more "modern" principles of social action.

However, as many observers have come to recognize, high rates of modernization in one sector of the economy, such as the primary export market, will not necessarily lead to rapid or balanced development in other sectors of the society's economy. While there may be a rise in the Gross National Product, this may actually represent only an increase in the income of certain limited portions of the population with a correspondingly limited impact on the processes of social and political modernization. Large portions of the population may remain outside of the dynamic sectors of the economy and thus be unaffected by its modernizing trends. Furthermore, such growth cannot truly be considered economic *development* because it is not self-sustaining: its continuation is clearly contingent on factors external to the national economy, i.e. the world market in which the essential primary exports must be sold.

Many of these same factors can be seen throughout the course of Latin American economic history. Early growth was stimulated by colonial and post-colonial trade of raw materials for finished products; foreign investment played an important role in the development of the national resources, particularly agricultural and mineral, and their accompanying infrastructures. However, the specialized import-export trade which resulted, while achieving considerable growth and modernization with some significant effects in other spheres, has not yet produced balanced national economies characterized by self-sustained development. Limited industrialization has taken place and the modern economies which have grown up among the upper and middle strata of society have in many cases advanced to the point of producing domestically the consumer goods previously imported. However, due to continuing inequalities in income distribution and hence, buying power, few countries have achieved the mass internal markets necessary to move successfully into adequate domestic production of capital goods. As a consequence of their continuing need to finance imported capital goods through primary exports their economies remain dependent on the unstable world commodity markets. Economic stagnation, inflation, and balance of payments deficits have frequently been the result.

Unbalanced economic development naturally resulted in unbalanced modernization in the social and political spheres. Failure to achieve dynamic internal mass markets has corresponded in many cases to a partial continuance of the legacy of the post-colonial social structure with its high status differentiation and limited mobility. While the upper strata enjoyed the benefits of the economic advances, there could hardly be equal participation in the elements of social modernity – education, communication, transportation – for those who remained marginal to the modern economy.

Varying degrees of social and political modernization, however, have taken place and are continuing. The industrialization process has incorporated some portions of the lower strata into the modern society and created avenues for upward mobility. Developments in mass communications and the gradual extension of "urban" features to the rest of the country have tended to draw increasingly larger segments of the population away from their traditional ways of life.

As the modernization process advances, so does the ability of the lower strata to organize and express themselves. There has been an increasing tendency toward popular participation in the political system, frequently expressed through intervening structures such as labor unions or peasant leagues or directly through political fronts or parties. Popular elements have at times captured national office and attempted to introduce measures aimed at reforming the social structures, but usually with limited success. Reform is seldom neutral and any government which undertakes it must carefully assess its resources and bases of support. The political history of Latin America reveals few real examples of popularly-oriented régimes which possessed the stability and organized support necessary for effective determination of controversial development policies, frequently opposed by those sectors with vested interests in the *status quo*.

Great hopes have often been placed in the emerging middle classes as an influence for stable democratic government and reformist national development policies. As supposedly non-élite members of the modern society, middle-class citizens might logically be expected to be inclined toward popular participation in government and to possess the necessary political skills to effect it. At the same time their interest in the progress of industrialization would naturally lead them to support national policies favorable to economic development. To date, however, such tendencies have not been clearly displayed. In many cases the emergent middle classes have tended to adopt the values of the upper classes to which they aspire and have been ready to condone the disruption of orderly democratic processes in order to protect the economic establishment from attacks by reformist governments.

In this regard the example of Brazil is particularly relevant.

Three presidents in recent times, Vargas, Quadros, and Goulart, have each in his own way attempted to institute basic reforms to correct the imbalance which has divided Brazilian society since its colonial beginnings into a rural-urban, traditional-modern duality. Brazil had achieved a considerable rate of industrialization through import substitution; however, she could not move into self-sustained development and true economic independence without undertaking basic reforms of her social structure and income distribution. Too great a portion of the population still lay outside the modern sector, lacking the buying power to support the further spread of industrialization. However, as Helio Jaguaribe observes, neither the upper nor the middle classes were willing to pay the price of reform: (1) increased efforts at saving and investment and (2) redistribution of income, education, and power. The middle and upper classes formed a tacit pact of mutual interest and self-protection against the lower classes and ultimately the two were able to utilize the military to protect their positions by effecting the removal of the threatening reformers. President Kubitschek, on the other hand, accepted the limitations of his situation and concentrated on further development of the industrial sector in hopes of indirectly affecting the rest of the society. He managed to achieve a relatively impressive rate of growth, but the basic imbalances remained and by the end of his term it became clear that further development of industry would be impossible until greater portions of the population were effectively included in the modern economy as producers and consumers. The needed reforms, however, were apparently impossible within the existing political framework. As shown by the coup of 1964 and the military régime that followed, the Brazilian economic and military élites were willing to allow the democratic political processes only a limited degree of sovereignty. The ultimate arbiter of inter-class interests remained the military.

The unstable nature of popular democratic régimes in Latin America has been viewed more generally by Irving Louis Horowitz in terms of a lack of *legitimacy*: that is, a lack of universal recognition and acceptance of the political system as an appropriate and inviolable set of procedures and rules which govern men in their political actions. The concept of democracy, while closely tied in its operational aspects to the modernization process (for example, the development of popular participatory institutions), is essentially a statement of value which certain societies have adopted for measuring the performance of their political systems and justifying, or rendering legitimate, their exercise of authority over their citizens. The concept of legitimacy refers not only to the government and its exercise of power, but also to the manner in which the government is selected and judged fit to continue in office. Hence, repeated interventions by the military would suggest that they, or the élites which they represent, are the determining factor in establishing a régime's "legitimacy" rather than any process of popular elections. Since each of the non-Communist republics of Latin America espouses democratic principles of popular sovereignty, such a pattern of military/élite intervention would render the political system itself fundamentally *illegitimate* for violating the essential values which justify its exercise of power.

If one accepts the relevance of this analytic framework, it becomes easier to understand the dismissal by Frank and Gerassi of electoral politics ever leading to basic reforms in Latin America. Since the political instability stems from a distorted economy and society, where particular sectors have developed far more than, and indeed at the expense of, other majority groups, it is essential to examine the causes of the initial unbalanced economic development. Many traditional interpretations have emphasized the erroneous decisions taken by native businessmen who favored the commodity export trade rather than manufacturing goods for the home market. Frank and Gerassi both dismiss this argument and point to the role of foreign powers, principally the United States. Both writers seek to show that far from the boon to development it has been called, American economic investment in Latin America has helped to perpetuate the region's backwardness. It is suggested that the American presence has "co-opted" the potentially nationalist middle class, directed resources and energy into the development of materials for extraction and export, and created American controlled import-substitution businesses.

One may dispute the precise motivations and goals of American investment in Latin America, but one can hardly deny that American businessmen have been primarily motivated to increase their capital and profits, and not necessarily to develop balanced national economies. As Gerassi illustrates in his article, the United States has a long history of overt and covert involvement in the political and economic affairs of Latin America on behalf of American interests. To the extent that the United States continues this involvement it is liable to the charge that it is encouraging patterns of economic growth inimical to the balanced national development of these countries.

The day may not be far off when North American involvement will no longer be accepted in Latin America. Events in Peru, Chile, and elsewhere provide evidence of the popular appeal of positions taken in defiance of American interests and influence. It is not simply the objective conditions of economic underdevelopment that are changing, but rather people's awareness of them and the conceptual framework within which they are viewed.

In modern society, an individual's self-image, particularly as influenced by his perception of the status of the social group with which he identifies, is critical in determining his attitudes toward the social order as a whole. And yet, traditionally, large sectors of Latin American society have tended to be insular in their life styles and limited in their contacts with the greater society. As the effects of social and cultural modernization spread, inevitably men in backward societies begin to question their traditional positions and social roles as they see new potentials for themselves and their children in the ostensibly open and status-mobile modern economy. Through the mass media people not only learn new frameworks of thought for explaining their deprived position in society, but also for the first time come to identify more closely with the status of their class on a national scale, and with status of their country on the international level. And these perceptions reflect on their own social and personal identities.

As Monsignor Illich points out, it can be a genuinely new and emotionally charged experience for a Latin American peasant to learn that his own identity as a peasant or laborer is socially determined and that he as an individual has the capacity to play an active role in shaping the society that defines him. The dynamics of this crisis of identity are key to understanding the explosive potential of rapid social modernization in developing societies. Interpretations of history in economic terms are clearly inadequate to explain fully the complex motivations which drive men to revolution. More than simple economic inequity, the ways in which men regard one another socially, the identities and values which they attribute to themselves and others may be the most crucial factors in creating violent discontent within a society.

Anthony F. C. Wallace in his essay provides a theoretical structure which captures the emotion described by Illich and views it as a social dynamic. He delineates two major types of revolution in developing areas: revolutions of *appetite* and revolutions of *identity*. Although not directed specifically at Latin America, his paper offers a theoretical framework for analysing the thought patterns of persons brought into revolutionary activity through continued denial of their human worth as manifested by the social system. Wallace discusses the relationship between identity and social change, illustrating, through the revitalization concept, the individual's effort to work toward that society whose values are commensurate with his own concept of identity.

The implications of the revitalization concept relate directly to the concept of legitimacy; a political or social system is adjudged legitimate by each individual to the extent that it manifests values which allow him to fashion a personal identity consistent with his expectations. In this respect, an illegitimate social order that tends to restrict non-élite participation and denies the ambitions of increasingly large politically aware groups, induces anxieties in these alienated sectors similar to those described by Wallace in his typology for a revolution of identity. In the sense that the society's actions are inconsistent with the individual's personal moral code, the established order ceases to act as a legitimate arbiter of personal conduct. Such a situation is ripe for the emergence of a revolutionary code placing blame for the society's ills on the abandonment by its leaders of the most cherished traditional values of the national heritage. Calls for necessary revolutionary action are expressed in terms more moral than economic or political.

It is intriguing to transfer this analysis to the pattern of illegitimacy in Latin America where the fundamental values of the democratic system are constantly denied, large sectors of the population are relegated to inferior status, and the sense of an independent national identity is impeded by what is perceived as North American hegemony. It would not be difficult to imagine situations in which the stress between value system and reality could provide the basis for a revolution of identity. Indeed, Wallace's quotations from Fidel Castro would suggest that the case of Cuba may provide one such example.

In general terms, the economic, political and social structures of Batista's Cuba were similar to those in the rest of Latin America and presented many of the same development problems. But whereas the other republics, for the most part, have followed programs of gradual reform, the Castro régime opted for a revolutionary solution and has forcedrafted a reorganization of Cuban society at an astonishing rate. The central question is how Castro has managed to effect such a profound transformation of Cuban society and how, aside from the obvious ideological realignments, the Cuban authoritarian model differs from other Latin American nations in terms of participation, mobilization and myth.

Pre-revolutionary Cuba presented all the characteristics of a society in fundamental conflict with the identity aspirations of the great mass of the population: the politics were corrupt, dominated by the very rich, and subservient to the United States. The social and economic structures were dominated by an urban-based élite, predominantly light-complexioned, while the great mass of the people, black and poor, did not enjoy access to schools, hospitals and other social services readily available to the rich. The resentments and frustrations created by these conditions provided the setting for a revolution of identity – one that would, in theory, reaffirm the common man's dignity as a human being and his right to participate honorably in the political and social institutions of a modern Cuba, as well as to share in the benefits of a revitalized and equitable economy.

In setting out to transform Cuban society, the Castro régime has clearly recognized the central importance of realigning the identity perceptions and value orientations of the great mass of the people. The government's efforts have focused on the creation of the myth of a new society which emphasizes change, participation, and pride in a new Cuba. So often in the case of "reformist" régimes of other Latin American nations the élites have violated their own democratic ethos, thereby undercutting the legitimacy of their governments and belying the social myths of equality of economic and political opportunity. Hence they have been unable to mobilize their populations around any programs for reform within the existing political structure. The Cuban élite, on the other hand, has been able to legitimate its abrupt and authoritarian re-ordering of the society and economy by reference to a core of coherent and familiar symbols backed by the charismatic feeling of "Fidelismo". By interpreting social change in terms that are meaningful and understandable to the Cuban people, Castro has been able to re-order the domestic structure by attacking the beliefs thought to sustain the former institutional framework.

The intent has been to re-socialize the mass of the population – to introduce a new status structure, a new system of rewards, new economic and political priorities and a new concept of the individual, linking his destiny with that of the state. In contrast to the other Latin American societies where the mass has perceived a limited vested interest, material or emotional, in the political régime, the Cuban myth has been designed to create a fully participating citizen. Thus, for example, while the régime has increased spending for public health services to record levels, it has also placed heavy emphasis on individual contribution and sacrifice – through work in the literacy campaign or cutting cane for the sugar harvest – without distinction as to class or occupation. Participation in "revolutionary" peer group activities re-inforces the individual's commitment to the régime and his feelings that it represents his own notions of a just society. In official papers and public speeches reference is made to the central myth of an ideal society attainable only through collective sacrifice and the creation of a "new" Cuban individual and social identity. In Wallace's terms, the myth of the new Cuban man in a revolutionary society reduces frustration by providing specific guidelines which allow the individual to reach widely accepted social goals.

To what extent Castro's efforts have been truly successful in their aims is still very much open to question. It should be clear, however, that the kind of considerations taken into account by the régime must be heeded by any reformist Latin American government in the coming years if it is to succeed. As the modernization process continues in Latin America, diffusing into the more underdeveloped sectors of each society, it appears certain to place an ever greater strain on the political system as a focal point of national consciousness and an arbiter of the path modernization is to take. A history of uneven, prejudicial development favoring particular interest groups within each society is now being contested by a growing awareness on the part of the disadvantaged sectors of the population of new realms of possibility and new avenues for personal and group advancement, opening the door to increasing social discontent in Latin America in the coming years. The forms of expression this discontent will take will inevitably be political, and those who hope to manage the societies in a representative fashion can only attempt to provide the moral leadership required of political figures in the midst of a continuing social revolution.

I

Stages of Modernization in Latin America*

1. THE TOTAL TRANSITION AND ITS COMPONENT PROCESSES

"Modern-industrial" society as a *generic* category is defined here in terms of "secularization", that is: (a) change in the predominant normative structure regulating social action and in the related internalized attitudes and propensities (an extension of "action by choice" over "action by prescription"); (b) growing specialization of institutions and emergence of specialized and autonomous value systems in relation to each institutional sphere; (c) growing institutionalization of change (over institutionalization of tradition). The minimum universal requirement for the existence of any "modern-industrial" society consists in the "secularization" of scientific knowledge, technology, and economy, in such a way as to lead to the ever-increasing use of "high energy" and to the maximization of efficiency in the production of goods and services.[1]

These traits may be regarded as a basic (although generic) core of any industrial society, and also as universal requirements for its existence and maintenance. However, beyond the institutional setting required for the attainment of an increasing use of high energy and an increasing efficiency in productive technology, allowance must be made for a wide range of structural and cultural variations, that is, for many divergent types of industrial societies. Whether the future evolution will bring increasing homogenization or increasing diversity is a question still open to discussion.[2]

* by Gino Germani.

Although a certain degree of secularization (which again may vary under different historical and socio-cultural conditions) is a necessary condition for "high energy" use and high efficiency in the production of goods and services, *it is not a sufficient one*. In fact there are various instances of secularization not followed or not accompanied by high energy use, or increasing technological efficiency. In the "Great Transition", instead, the association was an historic fact to be explained in terms of a unique and very long historical process which, *once it had taken place*, originated a new cultural complex: "modern-industrial" society. As it is obvious, the process leading to the emergence of the first historical case of this new type of society must be distinguished from the great variety of forms of transition which occurred later in the process of its diffusion, adaptation, and transformation, first in some Western societies, then in the rest of the world.

I am not concerned here with "*the* great transition" prior to the emergence of the first historical instance of industrial society, but with the *many* transitions produced by the universal diffusion of the new "modern-industrial" complex. From the point of view of its empirical or historical occurrence, each of these processes is a concrete totality. The complexity of the process and the variations it has assumed under different historical, cultural, social and economic conditions require that its analysis be conducted in terms of various component processes. In this sense I shall distinguish here three main component processes: *economic development, social modernization,* and *political modernization.* These distinctions are currently employed but the definitions implicitly or explicitly used are not always clear, and in any case are far from uniform among social scientists. For this reason, some indication will be given as to the meanings assigned to the distinctions in the present context.

Again, for the same analytic purposes each of the three main processes should be perceived as composed of a series of partial processes. In the present paper, however, though mention will be made of some components, this series of distinctions will not be pursued further.

The main processes and their component sub-processes are interrelated, as is shown by the statistical correlations usually observed among them. But such correlations are far from being perfect, and should be interpreted as no more than the expression of a tendency for certain indicators to be associated. What can in fact be inferred from the historical experience is that the various sub-processes may occur at very different *rates*, and in different *sequences*. Differences at what may be considered the "point of departure" of the transition and in the various internal and international conditions under which the transition takes place may be responsible for such variations in rates and sequences.

Economic development and social and political modernization are defined here primarily as processes of *structural change*, with the total transition being conceived as a *cumulative* process, into which at any given moment the *results* of its previous course become incorporated as determining factors in the further course of transition. In each process the definition is based on the application of the basic principles characterizing the "modern-industrial complex".

Economic development is tentatively defined as a *structural transformation* of the economy, through which the mechanisms functionally required for "self-sustained growth" are permanently incorporated into it. The ideal type of a developed economy may be characterized by the existence of a series of main traits: (i) use of high energy and high-efficiency technology in all branches of economic activities (including primary); (ii) existence of appropriate mechanisms (institutional and human resources) for the permanent creation and/or absorption of technological and organizational innovations (such mechanisms should ensure the continuous rise of new dynamic sectors, to compensate or to replace those whose dynamic role in the economy is decreasing, or which have reached their maximum possibility); (iii) proper diversification of production; (iv) predominance of industrial over primary production; (v) adequate "mix" of capital and consumer goods industries (a different mix according to the situation of the individual country and its stage of development); (vi) higher ratio of capital investment to national product; (vii) high per capita productivity; (viii) predominance of capital-intensive over labor-intensive activities; (ix) greater independence from (or less dependence on) foreign trade (in terms of its proportion to GNP at given population levels, of its strategic importance to the maintenance of growth and its diversification as regards types of goods and number of countries); (x) more equalitarian distribution of GNP, both in terms of socio-occupational strata, sectorial activities, and geographical areas.[3] The *process* of economic development is defined as the transition towards an empirical economic structure described by the traits mentioned above in the "ideal type".

A distinction should be made between *economic expansion* and *economic development*. The first may be defined as a process exhibiting steady growth in per capita GNP over a relatively long period of time, but lacking some of the strategic traits required for "self-sustained growth", that is, some of the structural components of economic development enumerated in the preceding paragraph.

This does not mean that economic expansion does not involve structural change. In fact, it is also a process of structural change, *but this change is not sufficient for "self-sustained" development*. Economic expansion may (and such is indeed the more frequent case) take place on the basis of the modernization and expansion of some specialized primary production, its integration into the international market, and the accompanying commercial and financial expansion with all its further repercussions on the economy, and its "modernizing effects" in other sectors of the society. Economic expansion may eventually originate, or be transformed into, a process of economic development. Perhaps it may constitute at least one of its preconditions. While there is no agreement about considering it a *necessary* precondition, it can be said with more certainty that it is not a *sufficient* precondition. The re-orientation of the economy and the introduction of the structural changes required for economic development cannot, in fact, be assumed as automatically induced by a certain degree of economic expansion. Only under certain conditions may economic expansion become a step – perhaps an important one – in the process of economic development.

The concept of *political development* is even more controversial than that of economic development. Perhaps three major traits may be singled out: (i) the "rational organization of the state" (in Weberian terms), including high efficiency in performing the expanding and increasingly diversified, specialized, and centralized functions of the state in an industrial society; (ii) the capacity of *originating* and *absorbing* structural changes in the economic, political, and social spheres, while maintaining at least a minimum of integration; (iii) some sort of political participation by all or the great majority of the adult population. Other components which are usually included may be conceived as consequences or aspects of the three traits enumerated. This is the case, for instance, of "nationhood", which could be considered one aspect of total participation; or "stability", here subsumed in the capacity of leading and absorbing change, without disrupting the social system.

Finally, *social modernization* is largely conceived of as a residual category, best illustrated (rather than defined) by a series of component processes: (i) the "social mobilization" of an increasing proportion of the population;[4] (ii) urbanization, i.e. increasing demographic concentration in urban areas (often one of the most typical expressions of mobilization); (iii) other demographic changes, such as decline in death and birth rates, and subsequent changes in the age structure; (iv) changes in the family structure and in the internal relations of the nuclear family, as well as in kinship groups; (v) changes in the local community of political participation; (vi) changes in communications; (vii) changes in the stratification system: modification of the stratification profile (first a reduction of the traditional intermediate strata, then an expansion of the modern middle strata); modification of the nature of the cleavages between strata, with the final emergence of a "stratification continuum"; increase in "exchange" mobility; increase in "structural" (transitional) mobility; emergence of a form of permanent mobility by "growing participation" (based on a mechanism of "self-sustained mobility") consisting in the continuous occupational upgrading and the continuous transference of status symbols from top to bottom; (viii) changes in the scope and forms of participation, particularly extension of civil and social rights to the lower strata (similar to the extension of political participation); extension of modern forms of consumption to the same groups; extension of education and the resulting extension of feelings of participation and increasing identification with the community; (ix) other important changes in such institutions as church, voluntary associations, forms of leisure, etc.; (x) decrease in differentials (demographic, economic, socio-cultural) between strata, social groups, rural-urban, and regions (while decrease in differentials may affect the great bulk of the population, some higher cleavage may persist or even increase at the top of the society, especially with the concentration of power, or at least certain forms of power).[5]

The distinctive trait of modern society is its permanent incorporation of appropriate mechanisms to originate and to absorb a continuous flow of change, while maintaining an appropriate degree of integration. In this respect, one can introduce an analogy with economic development: social and political modernization is a transformation of the social structure involving mechanisms of "self-sustained social and political change". In fact, given the basic unity of the process of transition, "self-sustained economic growth" and "self-sustained political and social change" are different ways of perceiving the same concrete process. Failure to establish such mechanisms for continuous change may lead to a "breakdown" of the process of social or political modernization, in the same way as failure to establish the corresponding mechanisms in the economic structure is conducive to a "breakdown" of the process of economic development. Finally, it must be stressed that the essential trait defining modernization is not the *fact* of continuous change, but the capacity of *originating* and *absorbing* it.[6]

2. VARIATIONS IN RATES AND SEQUENCES AMONG THE COMPONENT PROCESSES

The interrelation between component processes must be conceived as one of *reciprocal causation*. That is, they affect one another, and such reciprocal effects will determine the orientation and rate of the total transition, and may also produce inhibiting or facilitating effects on any single component process. In other words, processes of economic development (and, under given conditions, processes of economic expansion) condition processes of social and political modernization *and vice versa*. It may also be suggested that there exist minimum degrees (thresholds) of economic development (or economic expansion) which are required for the attainment of given degrees of social or political modernization, *and vice versa*, given minimum degrees of social or political modernization constituting the requirements for the attainment of given degrees of economic development or economic expansion. But a theoretical model suited for the analysis of such reciprocal relationships, and even an acceptable conceptual scheme, are still lacking. It may only be suggested that the types and forms of the interrelations and the various "thresholds" will vary according to the historical circumstances in which the transition of each nation occurs. Such historical circumstances cover a considerable range of factors – cultural, social, economic. And – most important – they concern not only the internal conditions of the society in transition, but also its external conditions, especially its relation to other societies. This is one of the reasons for the differences in rates and sequences among the various partial processes of economic development and modernization. This approach suggests that economic expansion may generate effects on the social structure similar to those induced by economic development: it is in this sense that economic expansion may have a "modernizing effect".

The nature and consequences of this interrelationship between component processes are deeply affected by the historical and social circumstances under which the transition is taking place, including sociocultural differences at the "point of departure" for each nation or region. As already noted, one of the main sources of variation in the paths followed by the total transition is the variations in *rates* and *sequences* in which the component processes take place. And the variations themselves should be explained in terms of the different contextual conditions (economic, cultural, political and social), both at the national and at the international level. Taking the historical experience of Western earlier transition as a baseline for comparison, we see that there have been cases of different *rates* (i.e. *acceleration* or *deceleration*) as well as differences in *sequences* (*retardations* or *anticipations*). Well-known illustrating cases of acceleration and anticipation (with regard to the "equivalent" degree of industrialization) are provided by the increase in urbanization (strictly defined as demographic concentration in urban areas) or decrease in mortality rates, which tended to *precede* rather than *follow* or accompany economic development. Less universal, but often observed in different countries, are cases of acceleration of social mobilization, of political participation and diffusion of aspirations, which in the Western model have tended to occur at a lower rate and have advanced considerably only *after* the economy had reached a higher degree of economic development (especially in terms of structural change). But contrasting phenomena of *slower* rates and *retardation* are also very common. It must be noted that acceleration and/or anticipation in certain processes may well coexist with retardation and/or deceleration in others.

This lack of synchronization or unevenness is of course a well-known aspect of social change in general. One of the crucial consequences is the coexistence of more "archaic" and more "advanced" (speaking in relative terms) sectors within the same countries, the same institutions, the same social groups and the same individuals. In the latter case, for instance, "modernized" attitudes and behavior in some fields of social action may coexist with "archaic" or less modernized attitudes and behavior in other fields. While generalizations in this respect are very hard to verify, it may be suggested that basic values (especially those internalized in the early life of the individual) may remain unchanged and may coexist with other values and attitudes acquired through the contact with more modern environments and influence. Taking an illustration from the Latin American scene, one may note that "manifest" acceptance of the modern technology (and even its actual use) may be accompanied by a persistence of more "archaic" value-orientations that are not very favorable to modern science; or extremely "advanced" political and social ideologies may be accompanied by traditional values and behavior in concrete every-day life, in the family, in interpersonal relations, in personal aspirations, and in the image of one's own life. The phenomenon of coexistence originates particular effects of "fusion" of the "modern" and the "traditional". One illustration here is the fusion of the emphasis on consumption which characterizes the more advanced stage of development and the ideal of leisure and consumption of the traditional seigneurial way of life. Breakdown of modernization and economic stagnation may perhaps be partly explained by the persistence of "non-modern" value orientations beneath the surface of accelerated processes of modernization occurring in different sectors of the society.

An important aspect of the discontinuity and unevenness in the process of transition is the differentiation of a "center" and "periphery", both *within* each nation and, at the international level, *among* nations. The relation between the "advanced" and the "backward" areas (at the internal and at the international level) is not always one of coexistence, but in many cases it may turn into one of superordination, of hegemony of the center over the periphery. "Dualism" may tend to be a self-reinforcing process, and to increase instead of withering away.

It may be useful at this point to enumerate briefly other factors which are likely to intervene and to condition the nature, orientation, and rate of the component processes and of the total transition.

(1) The nature and availability of human resources in each country (the country's "viability" and the necessary conditions for economic development according to its resources). These may originate different types of development and modernization, such as the *expansionist* or *intrinsic* development suggested by Hoselitz;[7] or may impart a particular dynamics to the economic process, as in the case of the "economy of the open spaces" in Argentina and other Latin American countries.

(2) The relative position within the center-periphery dimension of the country in relation to: (i) the international stratification according to political and economic power and consequently according to degree of political and/or economic dependence; (ii) the specific (and

changing) circumstances created by the international situation at the moment and during transition.

(3) Historical and cultural traits and social structure of the country when initiating the transition (i.e. type of society at the "point of departure". It may be observed that the concept of "traditional society" has often been used as a residual category including a great variety of social structures and cultural conditions. In fact, a typology of "points of departure" would be necessary).

(4) The state of knowledge in the *natural* sciences and the nature of the available *technology* at the initial moment of the transition and their combined evolution and changes *during* the transition. (In many developing countries these changes are originated elsewhere; their exogenous nature will exercise a particular impact on the form of transition in the receiving country.)

(5) The state of the *social* sciences, especially in relation to the process of modernization and economic development. This is dependent not only on the development of the social sciences, but also on the degree of accumulation of historical experience – at the international level – at the initial moment and during transition.

(6) The degree of "spontaneity", "awareness", "deliberation", and "planning" which characterize the social actions generating the partial processes of economic development and social modernization.

(7) The nature and the proportion of the *exogenous* or *endogenous* factors determining the transition.

(8) The different types of elite that lead, or in one way or another participate in, the initiation of the transition and its further stages.

(9) The changes which took place in societies which developed and modernized earlier and the types of advanced industrial society which have emerged. These societies (especially the "central" and hegemonic nations) serve as models of transition and as such provide alternative goals for modernizing groups in developing societies

and, more generally, exercise the well-known "demon-stration effect". It may be noted that this is how the different *ideologies of development* are originated. Such ideologies may turn out to be powerful factors in shaping the transition.

Some other general observations must be added: (i) these categories of factors are not clearly separable; in fact, there is considerable overlapping among them; (ii) the various factors are not independent, but are intercorrelated to different degrees; (iii) all the factors operate within an international system which moves towards greater unification and interdependence. While analyzing the process in a given national unit, it must always be remembered that such a process cannot be separated from the global context at the international level; (iv) finally, as indicated above, all factors have a dynamic nature. In other words, they change continuously through time, thus originating at any given moment different configurations of circumstances affecting the transition while it is taking place.

An interesting example of the consequences generated by the variations in rates and sequences is the "modernizing effect" of economic expansion: an acceleration of a *certain* process of social modernization (often accompanied by retardation in others), in comparison with the rate of economic development (as defined here). This variation is particularly important in the case of many Latin American countries and it will depend on the extent and the nature of the "backward", "forward" and "lateral" linkages on the rest of the economy, and their repercussions on other sectors of the social structure.[8]

3. STAGES IN THE TRANSITION

One basic question which has not been theoretically solved as yet is the definition of the "equivalencies", in comparing sequences and rates of the partial processes in different transitions. That is, some independent criterion for comparison is required in order to define the "equivalent" or "expected" degrees reached by the different partial processes. Two different procedures are usually followed: (i) the historical experience of the Western model may be assumed as a general criterion or base-line for comparison (as in the examples given in the preceding paragraph); (ii) equivalencies based on statistical averages and correlation of the indicators of the various processes in many countries may be used. Both procedures are useful, but are theoretically inadequate to the extent in which the criterion is assumed as a universal model of transition. There is no reason to believe that the "Western" model should be repeated; in fact, the contrary is more likely. Statistical procedures are very necessary in order to discover correlations and associations between processes, but they cannot explain their causes, nor the existence of both statistically normal or deviating cases. Another problem with the statistical definition of "equivalencies" is that usually it is obtained in countries where *transition has occurred at different historical periods, under rather divergent international conditions,* and which find themselves at very different levels of transition.

The answer to this problem should be a theory of stages of modernization. This attempt however has not been successful so far.[9] In fact, the differences in rates and sequences of the component processes as well as the other variations generated by the different sources already mentioned are likely to generate such a variety of "paths" as to eliminate or greatly restrict the validity of any general or universal scheme of succession of fixed stages. Or perhaps the scheme of succession should be based on a theory able to integrate many relevant determinant and contextual factors, and to generate a *whole typology of transitions* (with "equivalent" stages along "divergent" paths) applicable to a great variety of historical processes. The social scientist is confronted here with a dilemma. On the one hand, he lacks such a theory, at least at the moment. On the other, the use of notions of "levels", "degrees" and the like is very hard to avoid in any analysis of the transition. In fact they are implicit in it, and unless each case of modernization is considered as a unique instance and all comparisons (even implicit ones) are discarded, these notions are likely to be reintroduced in one way or another. That is why conventional and arbitrary external criteria (like the "Western" model or statistical correlations) maintain their usefulness, despite their obvious theoretical shortcomings. Another possibility can be suggested as a partial remedy to the lack of a satisfactory theory. I am referring to *descriptive* schemes of succession regarding a limited group of countries, perhaps a region, relatively more homogeneous in terms of their initial cultural and social structure and the historical conditions under which the transition has occurred (or is occurring). It may be suggested that more valid generalizations could be formulated for limited geographical-cultural areas and for specific historical periods. This type of scheme would be no more than a convenient way of presenting a simplified overview of a series of similar (but not identical) historical processes. On the other hand it could have some analytical use in illuminating particular clusterings of traits and types of succession. In fact the use of stages could be linked to the idea that in the course of the transition the variations in rates and sequences of the component processes and the impact of the other determining and contextual factors (at the internal and the international levels) may tend to crystallize in specific structural configurations. These in turn are likely to be incorporated into the process itself and to be transformed into key factors in explaining its further course. Perhaps this might offer a more objective basis for the selection of stages and the periodization of the transition.

Two main criteria may be suggested for the identification of stages: (a) emergence of a configuration of traits (in the economic, social and political structure) endowed with a certain degree of *stability* and *durability*, and clearly differentiated from the preceding and the succeeding structural arrangements; (b) the configuration's causal weight in shaping the further course of the transition.

From another perspective the stage may be perceived as a "turning point" in the transition. Certainly any historical process is a concrete continuous flow and the notion of a "turning point" is always, to a great extent, an arbitrary or conventional device. However, its use may help to restrict a purely deterministic model of the transition. In this sense a "turning point" may be defined as a particular moment (of variable duration under different conditions) in which a re-orientation *may* (or *may not*) occur. Its actual occurrence as well as its nature – positive or negative – from the point of view of successful modernization and economic development, will be determined by the particular interrelationship of social and economic processes, that is, by the particular configuration of social and economic structural traits originated by the previous course of the transition, *and* the "decisions" taken by the social actors (individuals and groups in key positions). It is suggested that the breakdown of modernization, economic stagnation or (vice versa) further progress towards *higher* degrees of modernization and economic development could be explained in terms of such "configurations" and "decisions".

Two important points must be noted here. In the first place, it is understood that configurations or traits not only regard the *internal* structure of the society, but also the *external* and *international* situation. Secondly, it is recognized that while the notion of "decision" is particularly difficult and theoretically imprecise, it is frequently used implicitly or explicitly in the analysis of historical processes and especially economic and political policies. In any case, the meaning of "decision" must be defined in terms of the range of "choices" concretely available to actors. Such a range will vary under different internal and external conditions (i.e. under given "configurations" of structural traits).

Another important factor is the degree of scientific knowledge and technology (both in the natural and in the social sciences) available to actors. As mentioned earlier, the degree of "spontaneity", of "awareness", of "planning", under which the transition occurs, is an important factor to be taken into account. Such a degree has been increasing with time, and from this point of view the situation of the countries which initiated their transitions earlier must be considered in a completely different way from that of the presently developing nations.

4. ELEMENTS OF A STAGE SCHEME IN THE CURRENT DISCUSSIONS ON LATIN AMERICA

Latin America seems to offer the conditions suggested earlier as capable of insuring certain limited validity to a scheme of stages:

(a) relatively similar cultural, social, and economic settings *at the beginning* of the transition and (b) similar external and internal historical circumstances *during* the process. In fact, though there have been few attempts to present an explicit theory of stages, most if not all of the historical and theoretical analyses of modernization or its component processes tend to assume in one way or another a succession of stages valid for the whole region. To a certain extent, however, the perception of Latin America as a unit is based not only on theoretical historical and socio-cultural factors, but also – to use an obsolete term in reference to a condition which still exists – on "geopolitical" and ideological causes: Latin America's common political status *vis-à-vis* the international political power structure and the allocation of "spheres of influence". It is also true that the intellectual tradition contributed quite a bit in creating the "field" of Latin American studies, with the result of pushing it too far, often transforming it into a mere stereotype and in any case bringing the theoretical productivity of this generalization to the point of diminishing returns.

Some contribution to a scheme of stages may be found in relation to the analysis of partial processes. The Argentine urbanist Hardoy, for instance, has suggested a succession of six stages to describe urban history in Latin America:[10] the pre-colonial urban culture of the Aztecs and the Incas, then the Spanish colonial foundational stage, followed shortly by a third stage essentially completed by 1580 in which the Spaniards and the Portuguese established the settlement pattern of the region. The fourth stage, a rather long one, covering nearly two hundred years, was characterized by the consolidation of the urban pattern, along with the institutions of the colonial society. Independence did not bring many changes, but instead a fifth stage, marked by European immigration and by the "europeization" of the main Latin American cities. Finally, the present stage is characterized by internal rural-urban migrations and a fast rate of urban growth. In the same field of urban history another writer sees two broad stages: the first centrifugal, out of the towns, and the second centripetal, tending to urban concentration, especially towards the primate or cosmopolitan city.[11]

The centrifugal phase is characterized by the *hacienda* (or the *fazenda* in Portuguese America) which is usually recognized as one of the central institutions of traditional society in Latin America, endowed with political, social, military and judicial functions; it has been compared with the Roman *villa* during the decay of the empire.[12] The development of the hacienda system involved a weakening of the role of the cities, and the "decentralization of the New World society around the landed estate" in a fashion not dissimilar to post-Roman Europe. The contrary stage, towards centralization in cosmopolitan cities, was a direct expression of the relationship with the outside world, and most of all of the political, economic and military dependence of the colonial society on its European metropolitan centers. The idea of two phases, however, more than providing a scheme of succession of stages, suggests a very interesting and synthetic view on two of the most important forces operating in colonial times and later (Morse's second urban centripetal stage extends through the nineteenth century and is continued into the present one).

Implicit in the analysis formulated by economists, both in regard to specific countries and in relation to the transition in the region as a whole, is the use of broad stages of development. Perhaps the more popular form is the distinction between "outward" and "inward" growth (*crecimiento hacia afuera versus crecimiento hacia adentro*). These two forms of growth correspond to those found in an economy based on international export (outward growth), and an economy based on industrialization (inward growth). The "turning point" when the change in direction of growth took place in Latin America is usually given as 1930, that is at the time of the Great Depression. The change from "outward" to "inward" expansion means to Latin American social scientists much more than an economic change. Rather, the structural change in the economy marked also the beginnings of a series of other changes in the social structure, in politics, in ideology, and in degree and nature of national identity. However, these distinctions are implicit, or in any case lack a precise formulation. Furthermore they are not designed as a theory of stages, even if this is in fact their role in the analyses. Often the "outward"-"inward" distinction is interpreted in terms of change in degree of foreign dependence and national alienation, the outward phase corresponding to dependence and to an "alienated national consciousness", in contrast to the "inward" phase, marked by a growth in the level of self-determination. In fact, the underlying concept in this approach is that of increasing self-determination: from a complete absence of it (or absolute dependence) in colonial times to a "semi-colonial" or "informal colonial" situation during the phase of outward expansion (with a very low degree of self-determination), to the third stage of "inward" development which involves for the first time a deliberate attempt to lead the developmental process in terms of national interests.[13] Writers with different ideological leanings, especially those inspired with extreme left orientations, do not usually agree on the degree of self-determination in the last "inward" stage. For them, imperialistic hegemony and national alienation are linked to the power structure prevailing in the Latin American nations. They consider that true national liberation can come only through revolutionary change. In that sense, "inward" development under the leadership of the national bourgeoisie is doomed to failure. In fact, they do not have any faith in the bourgeoisie and in its ability to lead a process of really autonomous national development.

Despite the manner in which these broad phases of modernization outlined above may be ideologically used or abused, they are based on the perception of drastic changes which have occurred in the region and tend to emphasize the role of external or international factors, which often fail to receive full consideration in studies made by foreign social scientists.

In this search for schemes of stages in Latin America, other valuable though indirect contributions may be found. For instance, the drastic change introduced in the social structure of Latin America by the rise and growth of the "middle sectors" could be interpreted again in terms of a succession of stages: the first characterized by the hegemony of semi-feudal and semi-capitalistic "oligarchic" élites, closely linked to the primary export economy; and a second, more advanced stage in which the participation of the new middle strata introduces a powerful component of modernization and may become a factor for further economic and political development. The rise of the middle classes is seen as an aspect of a series of changes which have occurred since the second half of the nineteenth century, in the expansion of the primary export economy, foreign investment, foreign immigration, better and more rational organization of the state, improvements in communication, transportation, education, and living standards. It is usually recognized that the growth of the "middle sectors" took place in the twentieth century, especially in its first three decades, although the new – and more decisive – wave of industrialization after 1930 contributed too to its further expansion.[14] Though the role of these sectors in the process of modernization has become highly controversial in recent years, nobody is likely to deny that their appearance involves a major change in the process itself, through a relatively stable modification of the structural configuration of the society.

In the foregoing discussion I have only considered some partial schemes of stages as well as some of the more common implicit *assumptions* about stages' succession in Latin America. As indicated earlier, there are very few attempts at constructing *explicit* comprehensive schemes: in fact I know only two, and of these one is still unpublished. Although the main purpose of both is to analyze the political process, they may be considered comprehensive insofar as both take into account, at least to some extent, social and economic changes. The first one was presented some years ago by K. Silvert and the present writer. It was based mainly on an analysis of the process of political mobilization and the successive expansion of political participation. This process was perceived as an aspect of social mobilization and social integration and closely related to the underlying total transition. In the present paper, the "political" stages have been maintained (with various modifications), but the economic and social components have been added, according to the theoretical approach suggested earlier.[15] Another attempt has been presented by Helio Jaguaribe.[16] He distinguishes three main stages: the *colonial*, the *semi-colonial* and the *transitional*. In this scheme we find an excellent presentation of the idea of increasing self-determination. In fact its more important variable (though by no means the only one) seems to be the degree of *dependence* and the corresponding degree of authentic national autonomy. In the first stage, which does not end with the collapse of the Spanish or Portuguese colonial régime but with the beginnings of the expansion of the primary export economy as a result of the industrial revolution (that is, at the middle of the nineteenth century), the degree of dependence is at its highest point. In the semi-colonial stage the dependence continues, though in a different form, while the internal transformation of the society originates an "initial capacity for self-induced growth". This capacity is further reinforced with the breakdown of the primary export economy after 1930, during the third "transitional" stage, which is also characterized by the rise of new groups and classes and the appearance of new tensions.

Finally, an important contribution to the idea of common stages may be found in the discussions among historians on the possibilities of a comparative history of the Western Hemisphere. In this regard it is relevant to mention here that during the consideration of "The History of America Program",[17] Charles C. Griffin in reporting the discussions on the national period of American history (both Latin and non Latin) stated that, "strange as it may seem", there *was* "considerable agreement on the important problem of periodization". In consequence he suggested a common framework, distinguishing four periods:

> I. *The Break with the Old World* (1770–1820)
> II. *The Development of New Nations* (from 1790s to 1860s)
> III. *The Adjustment to Industrial and Financial Capitalism* (1860s to the First World War)
> IV. *The Reaction of America to the Impact of the Twentieth Century Tensions in Western Civilization* (1941 to present).[18]

In this brief review I have omitted any references to the application of stages to single nations, as well as to the more abstract and general formulations such as, for instance, the well known "folk-urban" model developed by Redfield.[19]

STAGES IN THE ECONOMIC, SOCIAL AND POLITICAL MODERNIZATION OF LATIN AMERICA

External Factors	Main Stages	Economy	Society	Politics
Discovery Conquest Colonization	I *Traditional Society*	*Isolated regional economies.* —Subsistence economy predominant. —Export sector: small but important in shaping the further course of dependent development.	*Traditional structure.* —*Stratification:* dual system. (With some internal differentiation: the local traditional intermediate strata.) —*Hacienda* system (as an economic and social unit and as a center of authority). —*Demography:* death and birth rates high; natural growth: none or very low; urban concentration: very low.	1 *Colonial rule.*
American and French Revolutions	II *Beginnings of breakdown of traditional society*	*Transition towards dependent economic expansion.* —Persistence of subsistence economy and regional isolation with some beginnings of a limited internal market. —Free trade and, in some cases, first wave of growth of primary export.	*Subsistence of the traditional order (but release of disrupting factors).* —*Stratification:* little or no change in the dual system but substitution of Spaniards by Creole, rise of a very small — but dynamically important — urban élite. Some "exchange" mobility caused by revolutions and liberation and civil wars.	2 *Attempts and failure at establishing a modern national state.* (2, 3, 4). *Revolutions and Independence Wars.* —Formal independence and attempts to organize a modern national state, under the rule of the urban élites. *Anarchy and Caudillismo.* 3 —Enlightened urban élites (civilization) vs. caudillos and lower uneducated strata ("barbarism");

External Factors	Main Stages	Economy	Society		Politics
	Beginnings of breakdown of traditional society (cont'd)		–Persistence of the *hacienda* as a basic economic, social and political institution. –Local (and regional or provincial) societies: isolation reinforced by breakdown of the colonial administration. –Persistence of the traditional way of life for more than 90 per cent of the population. –Some initial attempts of modernization (in urban centers, by the "independent élites"). –*Demography*: little change from Stage I; natural growth: very slow; urban concentration: very slow.		–"Inorganic" democracy as opposed to "enlightened aristocracy"; –Centrifugal tendencies. Local "peripheral" caudillos and regionalism. *Unifying autocracies.* –Emerging unification under the rule of a "central" caudillo.
				4	
				3	–General traits of substages 3 & 4: (a) Formal independence, but no national identification, except for the élite.
				4	(b) "Oligarchy" (landed interests and associated sectors): maintaining and increasing economic and social power; (i) in most cases through the caudillos; (ii) in some cases through direct political rule (see stage 5). –Beginnings of "traditional" political parties (parties of "families" and "notables"); Conservative vs. Liberal; Federalists vs. Unitarians, etc. (All "oligar-

External Factors	Main Stages	Economy	Society	Politics
				chic" parties with restricted or no ideological differentiation)
				—No political mobilization and participation of the masses, except "traditional" participation under popular caudillos or the "Clientele system".
Impact of the industrial revolution.	III *Dual Society and "Outward Expansion"*	*Primary export economy and "outward" dependent expansion.*	*Limited "modernizing effects" of "economic expansion".*	*National organization and middle classes participation crises.*
—Technological innovations in transportation, communication, production.		—Different degrees of modernization of the primary production (plantation, agriculture, cattle breeding, mines).	—First wave of limited social modernization (rate and extent depending, in each country, on the type of "economic expansion"). Resulting "dualism".	(4, 5, 6)
—Advanced industrialization of "central" countries.		—Evolution of the traditional paternalistic *hacienda* towards modern forms of modern enterprise.	—*Primate cities* (foci of "limited modernization").	(i) *General traits.*
—Mass European emigration.		—Gradual extension of the internal market.	—*Urban changes:*	— Rational-bureaucratic organization of the state. Centralization and increasing control of the national territory.
—European capital investment overseas.		—"Economic expansion" (increase in GNP).	Appearance of a modern middle stratum; decrease of traditional "intermediate" strata.	—Professionalization of the army.
		—In some countries:	First wave (in some countries) in the formation of an urban modern proletariat.	(ii) *Variable traits.*
				—Characteristics of the political regime and level and nature of participation: three possibilities according to extent of social modernization (varying cases of slow transition from 4 to 5

External Factors	Main Stages	Economy	Society		Politics
					and 6; or sudden leaps, overpassing intermediate stages including directly to sub-stage 7 c or d).
Ideologies Political & economic liberalism.		*first wave of industrialization* – closely linked to primary production.	–Beginnings of *social mobilization*, and "modern" participation (large variations among countries from very slow to very fast rate; from very small to large proportion of population).		*Continuation of the unifying autocracy pattern* (interrupted by crises of succession, attempts at democratization – relapse into autocracy).
	Dual Society and "*Outward Expansion*" (cont'd)	–"*Dual*" economies. Strong *internal cleavages*: (i) urban-rural; (ii) center & periphery. –Foreign capital. Foreign immigration (few countries). Alliance landed interests – foreign interests.	*Demography.* –In most countries: persistence of traditional high fertility and beginnings of decline in death rate. Slight increase in rate of growth. –In some countries: faster advance into the demographic transition; higher decline in mortality followed by decline in fertility. –In some countries: mass foreign immigration. –Increase in urban concentration and high urbanization (in countries of foreign immigration).	4	–"Modern" political participation nonexistent or effectively impeded. –Military interventions as quasi-institutionalized mechanism for political succession. (type "a").
Models "Western" *Foreign Influence* Western European (mostly British)		–British influence. –Investment in social overhead capital (railroads, communication, and primate cities' urban services; education and health in more advanced countries).	*Duality.* –Coexistence of "modern" and	5	–"*Representative democracy with limited participation*" (political power monopolized by the oligarchy). –"Modern" limited participation in the "central" area; beginning of mass parties (populistic, with strong middle-class component). –Stability or (in some cases) possible continuation of the pre-

External Factors	Main Stages	Economy	Society	Politics
	Dual Society and "Outward Expansion" (cont'd)		(modified) "traditional" patterns (at the geographical, social, cultural and psychological levels). —Coexistence of "modern" and "archaic" groups and sectors of the social structure. Coexistence of archaic and modern traits within the same institutions, groups or categories of population. Coexistence of archaic and modern attitudes and behaviour within the same individuals. —Strong differences and contrasts between a "center" and "periphery" *within* each country. *Center*: highly urbanized – usually primacy of the capital city – modern, developed; and *periphery*: underdeveloped and archaic. Increasing contrasts between *country* and *city*. —*Marginality*: large sectors of the population in the periphery and (partially) in cen-	vious ("a") type of military intervention, sometimes changing into intervention in middle-class participation crisis ("b" type of military intervention). —Middle-class participation crises (striving for enlarged participation). —"Oligarchic" national consciousness. *Representative democracy with enlarged participation"* (middle classes régimes—but coexistence and often implicit alliance with oligarchy). —Increase in "modern" "enlarged" political participation (extension to first wave of urban modern proletariat, in "central" areas); rise of modern mass parties. —Ideologies: pre World War I: "old" populistic parties with national-liberal ideologies; post World War I: beginnings of

6

External Factors	Main Stages	Economy	Society	Politics
			tral areas in a state of social, economic and political marginality. Different degrees and types of marginality. "Internal colonialism".	"new" populistic parties: emphasis on social justice. –Stability, save for middle classes participation crises. –Military intervention becoming ideological and playing essential role in middle classes participation crises (on both sides). (Type "b" military intervention) –"Middle classes" national consciousness.
Great Depression (1930) Second World War (1939) *Ideologies* Liberalism Marxism Nationalism Fascism	IV *Mass Social Mobilization*	*Industrialization and "inward" development.* –Breakdown of primary export international market. –Breakdown of primary economy. –Decline of terms of trade. –Unplanned (sometimes unwanted) industrialization changing into (after World War II)	*Increase in rate and extent of social mobilization.* –Widespread and increasing urbanization. –Mass *internal* migrations (before 1930, some countries; after 1930, all countries). –Further enlargement of middle strata (still urban), importance of white collars. "New Generation" industrial entrepreneurial sector. –In some countries: new	7 *Transition to total participation and lower classes participation crises.* –Political mobilization of urban lower strata (rural-urban migration; rise of "new proletariat", availability of emerging sectors). –New populistic parties: "national-popular movements". –Unionization with intervention or leadership of the state. –Extension of social rights –

External Factors	Main Stages	Economy	Society	Politics
Models "Western" "Eastern" "Chinese" Foreign Influence USA Cold War	Mass Social Mobilization (cont'd)	deliberate industrialization. –First phase: import substitution and emphasis on consumer goods. (In some countries beginnings second phase: capital goods.) –Further extension of the internal market. (Predominance of a unified national market with surviving "pockets" of subsistence economies.) (Different degrees of extension according to countries.) –Economic stagnation (after development of consumer goods industry and advanced replacement of imports). –Inflation. New economic bottlenecks. –Persistence of latifundia and problems related to the land tenure system.	"second generation" urban proletariat. –In others: beginnings of a modern urban proletariat. –Demographic transition (in some countries decline of the death rate persistent or increase of birth rate; in more advanced countries: decline of birth rate). In most countries: *population explosion.* –End of foreign european immigration. –Some *international migrations* (within Latin America). –"Internal Colonialism" (*decrease* in relative terms, *increase* in absolute numbers). –Spread of social mobilization (with varying degrees and extension of "marginality" still persisting; coexistence of "mass society" and marginality).	minimum wages, social security, etc. to urban workers (only partially implemented). –Predominance of "social justice", "national-development" over "liberal-national" ideologies. –Decline of "oligarchy" but increasing ambiguity and absorption of middle classes (especially higher bourgeoisie, but also white collars) into the *status quo.* –Decline (and/or) failure of social reform attempts by middle-class régimes. –Reformist tendencies (and lack of radicalization) among *participant* urban workers. –Changing nature of military intervention (type "b"). Increasing ideological role of the army ("the ideological frontier") mostly as a barrier against extension of participation and social reform. "Pseudo-Nasserist" and "pseudo-

External Factors	Main Stages	Economy	Society	Politics
	Mass Social Mobilization (cont'd)	(Some limited efforts for an agrarian reform under representative-democratic régimes.) –Revolutionary agrarian reforms connected with "national-popular" régimes. –Problems related to distribution of income. Problems related to entrepreneurship and local investment. –First experiment in socialist economy. *Ideologies.* "Desarrollismo" "Economic national-ism"		developmental" military coups. –Increasing fragmentation of all relevant political groups: church, military, middle classes, mobilized lower strata. –Appearance of "new radical left" and leftish nationalism. –*Participation crises*: four possibilities: (a) "Representative democracy with total participation" (highly unstable because of persistent rigidities in the system); (b) Open or disguised military dictatorships (equally unstable); (c) "National-popular régimes" (alliance of "new industrialists" and urban proletariat, with some military support); (d) "Socialist dictatorships" (unlikely in most advanced countries but possible given a repetition of the a-b cycle).

5. A TENTATIVE SCHEME OF STAGES OF MODERNIZATION IN LATIN AMERICA

The table presented in this paper does not pretend to offer a "theory of stages". Its purpose is more modest: it is an attempt to provide a highly simplified overview of the transition, which may be useful in illustrating some of the main characteristics of the process. Certainly the table can be regarded as no more than a highly condensed common sense summary of the social history of Latin America. Needless to say, because of this condensation, and its level of generality, it does not represent *any* of the specific historical processes which have occurred (and are occurring) in the Latin American countries. Exceptions will be the rule, but precisely by emphasizing these "deviations" the table may be used perhaps as a tool for comparison, and as a means for emphasizing both specific and common traits (if any) in the process of modernization in Latin American countries. Furthermore, by classifying its empirical content in the three main processes of the total transition (and by specifying in a rough way some of its corresponding sub-processes) it may help to highlight both its synchronic and its asynchronous aspects: cases of *acceleration* or *deceleration* of specific sub-processes, or differences in their sequences; or cases in which differences in the rates and sequences have produced *fusions* or *contemporaneity* of stages instead of a *succession*, as indicated in the scheme (and as actually occurred, at least in some empirical instances). Finally the scheme may help to provide at least a provisional answer to the problem of the *implicit* use of some type of succession. As noted earlier, even the mere mention of "more" or "less" advanced, so frequent in all discussions on the subject of modernization, involves the implicit assumption of the idea that some changes usually precede others, or that a given country is located in a different point in the (implicit) temporal succession: the assumption of succession. In this sense, an attempt, as exemplified in the table, may be seen as a step in making *explicit* such assumptions, by suggesting a more specific definition of the succession.

I shall not attempt to describe here each of the stages indicated in the table. For one thing, this would be impossible within the limited scope of a paper; furthermore, the content of the table is well known and self-explanatory, in the light of the current social science literature on the region. But the table seeks to provide a certain ordering of the material in terms of the various component processes, and in terms of turning points and temporal succession. Therefore, the final portion of the paper will be devoted to illustrating the type of analysis which could be attempted on the basis of the suggested framework. The rise and crystallization of "stabilizing effects" mainly in the third (but also in the fourth) stage, will be considered, and a mention will be made of the interplay of endogenous and exogenous factors.

6. INTERACTION OF ENDOGENOUS AND EXOGENOUS FACTORS IN THE PATTERNING OF CONFIGURATION OF STAGES

It will be seen that the main stages are *dated* by *external events*. Now the contribution of similar *broad* characteristics to all countries at approximately the same chronological time raises an important issue (even if allowance is made for large variations in more specific characteristics, as in part suggested in the table). In fact, given the well-known fact of different rates of modernization among the various national units, any given date would find them in different positions or stages. Even if the scheme of succession had the precision of a natural law, the lack of synchronization *between nations* (not to speak of asynchronousness *within* nations) should make obvious the impossibility of initiating the same stage at approximately the same date or within a relatively short span of time. Homology does not involve simultaneity. The answer to this apparent absurdity highlights the dynamic importance of the *exogenous* factors on which the periodization is based. These factors generate in each country – irrespective of their degree of modernization at that moment – a series of processes essentially similar in all of them. It is precisely the common nature and the relative simultaneity of this external impact which contributes so powerfully to giving similar or equivalent broad characteristics to each stage. Needless to say the similarities do not exclude important differences. It is also true that specific structural configurations emerging at a given stage in each nation are the result of both exogenous and *endogenous* factors. Finally, it is very important to note that the release of similar processes in countries located at different stages *has usually accentuated their internal discontinuities*, the asynchronousness between areas, institutions, attitudes and behavior patterns, since the external impact may accelerate some component process while leaving unaffected or decelerating others.

The historical meaning of the external impact is obvious enough but its role in accentuating homogeneity *among* nations and discontinuities *within* them has often been overlooked. And the same may be said of the role exercised in this double effect by the interplay between exogenous and endogenous factors. Perhaps it could be suggested that this effect has been increasing over time or, at least, that it has tended to become more visible in the third and even more in the fourth stage. The suggestion could also be advanced that with the increase in international interdependence in all spheres – and especially with the growth of worldwide power stratification structure – the exogenous factors may have become more powerful. This may have occurred even if the internal strength of many nations was becoming greater because of economic development, increasing social modernity and increasing level of "national consciousness" (or at least decreasing alienation), all of which characterize the stage of "inward expansion". On the other hand, as time elapsed and the lag between countries within the region tended to be widened in certain aspects of the transition, the generalized effects of the external impact may have accentuated the internal discontinuities, especially in all those cases in which such impact induced the acceleration of some component processes, while at the same time blocking or decelerating others.

The combined effect of exogenous and endogenous factors in the third stage are well known: economic expansion on the basis of primary export economy, and inducement of "limited" modernization effects in the social and political orders. The extent of the "modernizing effect" was a function of three main variables: (i) the type of primary export economy; (ii) its degree of success in inducing "economic expansion" (as defined earlier); and (iii) the existence of internal modernizing élites and their effectiveness. It is the type of primary export economy which largely determined the variety and extent of the repercussions on the rest of the social structure. But again these repercussions were limited or expanded, retarded or accelerated by the action and the orientation of the élites.

Economic expansion which was based on a type of primary production, requiring the mobilization of a small part of the population, or with limited economic backward, lateral, or forward linkages, did not exercise a widely diffused impact on the social structure. Such was the case of mining or plantation economies or other economic, foreign-oriented and integrated activities, relatively isolated from the national economy. A typical "dual" society and economy was likely to emerge with strong cleavage between "archaic" and "modernized" sectors. Social modernization could affect some aspects of behavior and institutions in some restricted areas and restricted social groups – usually the higher and middle strata in urban centers or more often in "primate" cities. However, even in these sectors some basic value-orientations would remain unchanged, coexisting with other manifest symptoms of modernization.

In those countries in which the primary export economy required, or at least indirectly induced, the participation of large sectors of the population at both the lower and the intermediate occupational levels, an enlargement of the internal market and/or some other "spreading" effect as well as other processes of social modernization occurred at an accelerated rate and in advance of "corresponding" or "equivalent" degrees of economic development.

Where the élites remained very ineffective or unwilling to go beyond their immediate and shortsighted interests, the modernizing effect was more restricted. The contrary occurred where élites imbued with modernizing ideologies were ready to push the process at least up to the extreme point permitted within the limits of other contextual factors (these limits being usually determined from one side by the "class perspective" of the élites, on the other side by the general historical framework in which their actions took place). As a result different types and extent of modernizing effects could be expected and perhaps a typology could be constructed with various intermediate types ranging from relatively "encapsulated" activities, more or less segregated from the rest of the economy and the society, to more dynamic activities exercising an impact on a considerable proportion of the population and affecting a wider range of social segments, groups and institutions.

The main external impact in the fourth stage was the Great Depression which forced industrialization in all Latin America. This trend was further reinforced by the Second World War, and in the interplay with internal factors emerged important social forces and new attitudes favourable to "inward development" through deliberate industrialization, and perhaps national planning. Industrialization in the thirties, however, began in many cases not only as an unplanned but also as an undeliberate and *forced* process, imposed by the new conditions created after the Great Depression and continued by the outbreak of the war. Industrial growth and a considerable rate of economic development which characterized most Latin American countries in the forties and the first half of the fifties seemed to end in stagnation, or at least in a noticeable slowing down, in the following years. Though in the more advanced countries industrialization went beyond the phase of import substitution in consumer goods,[20] further obstacles appeared which delayed both industrial development and the development and modernization of other sectors of the economy. These obstacles, which in part reflected the new conditions created by the previous industrial growth, have been related by many observers to persisting traits crystallized during the third stage, and the incapacity of the Latin American societies to introduce the required structural changes. This again could be interpreted as directly and indirectly determined by a complex of internal and external factors.[21]

Another important process typical of the fourth stage, widespread and fast rate of urbanization, was the result of another combination of internal and external factors: the population explosion brought about by the modernizing effects of the third stage (introduction of sanitary technology, and some slight improvement in living conditions of the masses) on the other primary export crisis, together with the persistence of highly unequal distribution of land in the rural sector, and (to a limited extent) the new demand for industrial labor. Urbanization was obviously related to mass internal migrations. Now these population movements must be considered an aspect of another crucial process: social mobilization.[22] As indicated in the table, social mobilization had been initiated in the third stage (as one aspect of the "modernizing effects"), but it tended to acquire massive proportion in the fourth stage. The environmental changes mentioned above (population explosion, primary economy crisis, emerging industrialization) were part of their causes. But the process also required changes in attitudes, and these were induced by a series of internal and exogenous factors: changes in the ideological climate (both at the international and at the national level), and widespread innovations in mass media communication through the period. As new sectors of the population became ready for political participation, a different type of "participation crisis" appeared, in which the middle strata found themselves ambivalent and sometimes opposed to the recently mobilized portions of the lower strata. These internal developments, and other pre-existing internal factors such as the remnants of archaic power structures and the persisting "political-cultural" trait of military intervention, coupled with powerful external factors such as the cold war and the United States hegemonic power in the region, tended to shape political development often involving new rigidities and prolonged stagnation or even apparent relapses into processes similar to the older pattern of unstable democratic rule, alternating with military or non military dictatorial or quasi dictatorial régimes. This was especially evident in some of the more advanced countries. But here the nature of the instability and of the dictatorships was quite different from those characterizing early stages. In some cases they took a new form of "national popular régimes" in which political and social participation was effectively extended to the lower strata, though in different ways than in the conventional "representative democracy" model, while actual or threatened military intervention operated most often as a means of "demobilization" of these strata.

7. THE "STABILIZING EFFECTS" OF MODERNIZATION AS POSSIBLE FACTORS OF DELAY FOR FURTHER CHANGE

Whichever the range and nature of the "modernizing effects" and their consequences in creating a relatively advanced sector in the society, one common feature in the structural configuration emerging during the third stage was that it contained also certain "stabilizing effects". In other words, the "modernizing effects", even when they were more conspicuous and widespread, *failed to incorporate the appropriate and sufficient mechanisms for self sustained change in the economic, social and political orders.* A good illustration of this failure is the tendency to persist within the framework of primary export economy, even at a moment when it was both more rational and feasible to undertake a deliberate attempt to re-orient it in terms of industrialization and diversification of the primary sector, at a higher technological level. The feasibility of such re-orientation was more pronounced in the larger countries and in those where the modernizing effects had been stronger. Still, even in these more favored situations the impulse to industrialize was delayed until the thirties, and it was generated by an external impact: the spontaneous protection created by the breakdown of the international market. Even the impact of the First World War failed to introduce a permanent change in attitudes.[23] In terms of the analytical framework suggested in a previous section, at a certain moment, during the third stage, a "turning point" was reached in which two choices were made possible: either to shift towards a policy of deliberate industrialization, re-orienting in terms of higher productivity and appropriate diversification the primary sector, or just to continue with the old path of the "outward growth" even when such growth had ceased to be viable.

The explanation for this and other similar failures may be found in a complex of interrelated endogenous and exogenous factors which could be called the "syndrome of outward expansion". Among many others I would like to mention two aspects of it. First, though it included important dynamic components they were insufficient to induce change in certain highly strategic features of the social structure, and/or to offset endogenous and exogenous obstacles. Second, some of the modern partial structures introduced in the third stage tended to operate more as *stabilizers* than as *dynamic* factors. Some of the paradoxical features of Latin America stem from this fact, since precisely where the "modernizing effects" appeared to be stronger and more widespread, delay and stagnation tended to affect further progress after a fairly advanced degree of modernization had been attained, sometimes at a very fast rate. Though the consequences, in terms of stagnation, became visible only in the fourth stage, the underlying causes are to be found in the structural configurations which emerged in the third stage, in the "syndrome of outward expansion". In the fourth stage, on the other hand, new "stabilizing effects" were added. One of their common characteristics was that these effects are really part of the integrative consequences of social modernization. They are "stabilizing" insofar as they lead to the incorporation of new groups into the modern sector, in terms of cultural patterns, types of consumption (even if at low level), social relationships, expectations and aspirations, political participation and other aspects of behavior.

How these "stabilizing effects" (or better, "mechanisms") played a role as obstacles to further modernization is difficult to analyze. Oversimplifying the issue, it may be said that they tended to decrease the economic, political, and social innovational potential of the emerging and newly incorporated groups (both at the middle and lower socio-economic level, in urban areas). Sometimes they permitted their virtual or silent alliance with those vested interests most interested in maintaining the *status quo*. In other cases they tended to transform into an incoherent, fragmented and ambivalent political action, what could have been a unified force for political, social and economic change.

It would be beside the scope of this paper to attempt this analysis, and only a brief mention of three, among the most important stabilizing effects, will be made here. In the first place, I will refer to the rise and growth of the urban middle classes.

As shown elsewhere,[24] it can be observed that these groups have expanded in Latin America beyond the size which could have been expected on the basis of the level of economic development and some other aspects of social modernization (this comparison is made taking the Western experience as a criterion). Though the rise of the middle strata was usually considered as a favourable factor for modernization, it is now widely recognized that, once these sectors have attained a certain degree of social and political participation, their reformist propensities are considerably softened as they become increasingly absorbed into the system. It could be observed here that in the European case, these groups had originated in the period between the two wars, the most impressive "breakdown of modernization" as yet to be observed. Obviously, it cannot be denied that the rise and growth of these strata is one of the crucial aspects of social modernization. But the Fascist episodes did demonstrate that under given circumstances they could operate as powerful obstacles to further modernization. It is true, however, that in Latin America, by and large, the middle classes have not originated Fascist-like *mass* movements, although there were several attempts to manipulate them in such direction. But their ambivalence and political inefficiency is nonetheless a reminder of their ambiguous structural position, at least in certain periods during the transition.[25]

A second important illustration of stabilizing mechanisms is provided by mass internal migration. Here, again, we find a process which is not peculiar to Latin America. It is well known how mass oversea emigration operated as a "safety valve" in Europe during the nineteenth century. This "latent" function of emigration as a "substitute for revolution" was not so "latent", since European political rulers did not fail to make a deliberate use of it as a means to decrease lower-class pressure. This important side effect of rural-urban migration (or even any internal migration) is not usually recognized in Latin America. Many, especially the conservatives, perceive the "urban explosion" as a threat to the *status quo*, or as an increased potential for social revolution. But in fact, emigration from the more backward regions is likely to operate in selective terms, giving an outlet precisely to the most active and potentially more "dangerous" (from a conservative perspective) individuals, among the rural population.[26] It may be argued that this revolutionary potential is transferred to the major urban centers, that is, to the very site of political power in the nation. In the new setting they should become far more dangerous to the stability of the social system. The real process, however, is rather different, since in the urban society new "stabilizing mechanisms" are set in motion.

It must be recognized that the new urban sectors, recently incorporated, may become available for political participation (as in fact they did on several occasions), and originate new political forces often threatening the social and political *status quo*. But the experience of the post world war period is that these urban sectors are easily satisfied with partial reforms involving modest improvements in their own standard of living and level of participation in political affairs or the unions. Though these advancements seem threatening to the less enlightened of the conservatives, they operate as integrative factors, in a similar fashion to that which occurred with the middle strata during the third stage. On the other hand many observers coincide in suggesting other similar stabilizing mechanisms. For instance, the transfer to the city usually involves an amelioration of the living conditions, as experienced by people coming from very depressed areas. This may be true even in the case of urban unemployment or poverty. In other cases urban marginality, especially through the transfer of rural patterns into the city, operates as a neutralizer of political mobilization.

Finally, another powerful stabilizing mechanism is social mobility. Though the urban migrant has less mobility opportunities than the city-born, still whatever opportunities he achieves are far superior to the situation in the place of origin.[27] Obviously it remains to be seen how long these mechanisms will remain in effective operation. It is possible that they will wither away with time. But until now they involved an absorption of the revolutionary potential in the recently mobilized lower sectors of the population.

The reason why all these stabilizing mechanisms may become obstacles for further change is that, at the level of modernization reached by Latin America, such changes are not likely to be accepted by the hegemonic groups within the national society (and abroad) without a powerful and highly determined pressure from those who would benefit most by the changes themselves. But if these groups potentially interested in social reform are channelled into petty sectorial improvements the cause of reform itself is seriously jeopardized, at least temporarily. The contradictory effects of partial modernization may be more clearly perceived now. From one side these effects are considered positive, since they involve a real advance and an amelioration of the quality of life for some sectors of the population. On the other hand, however, because this degree of social modernization was achieved *before* other crucial and necessary changes were introduced, they turned out to operate as obstacles for further progress. A particular sequence among component processes is delaying the whole transition.

It would seem that a detailed analysis of the structural configuration emerging during the present stage of "mass social mobilization" should help to identify the nature of the obstacles, old and new, and the meaning of the "turning points" and the possible choices which the present generations are confronting in Latin America.

NOTES

[1] This definition of modernization has been adopted from G. Germani, "Secularización y Desarrollo Económico" in *Resistěncia a Mudanca* (Rio de Janeiro: Centro de Pesquizas Em Cienciais Sociais, 1960). A revised text appears in S. N. Eisenstadt (ed.), *The Protestant Ethic and Modernization: A Comparative View* (New York: Basic Books Inc., 1968).

[2] Among the recent contributions to this discussion, see: A. S. Feldmann and W. E. Moore, "Industrialization and Industrialism" in *Transactions of the Fifth World Congress of Sociology* (I.S.A., 1962), Vol. II; Raymond Aron, "La théorie du développement et l'interprétation historique de l'époque contemporaine" in R. Aron and B. F. Hoselitz, *Développement Social* (Paris: Mouton, 1965); Reinhard Bendix, "Tradition and Modernity Reconsidered" in *Comparative Studies in Society and History*, IX (1967), pp. 292–346.

[3] Some of the elements included in this definition are highly controversial. For instance, a number of economists challenge the idea of the predominance of industrial over primary production as a universal requirement for development; see, for instance, Peter T. Bauer and Basil S. Yamey in *The Economics of Under-Developed Countries* (Chicago: University of Chicago Press, 1957), chap. XV. For an illustration of the opposite view (which is also the most accepted one), see W. W. Rostow, "Industrialization and Economic Growth" in *Stockholm MCMLX. First International Conference of Economic History* (Paris: Mouton, 1960). The Latin American *communis opinio* among social scientists in the region is in favor of industrialization as a condition *sine qua non* of development. Most of them insist also on the key role of production goods industries as a necessary higher stage of industrialization. The "Latin American Thesis" is best expressed by the ECLA document *Toward a Dynamic Development Policy of Latin America* (New York: U.N. e/CN/12/680. Rev. 1). Statistical evidence confirms overwhelmingly the causal association between industrialization and economic development; see H. B. Chenery, "Patterns of Industrial Growth" in *American Economic Review*, 1960, pp. 624–54.

[4] The concept used here differs from the one currently employed. See G. Germani, "Social Change and Intergroup Conflicts" in L. H.

Horowitz (ed.), *The New Sociology* (New York: Oxford University Press, 1964).

[5] On the idea of "self-sustained mobility" in modern industrial society, see G. Germani, "The Political and Social Consequences of Mobility" in Lipset and Smelser (eds.), *Social Structure and Mobility in Economic Development* (Chicago: Aldine Publishing Company, 1966).

[6] Since the notion of "institutionalization of change" is often considered synonymous with "non-conflictive" change, two essential qualifications must be added:

(a) In the first place, by definition, changes occurring at early and at intermediate phases of the transition usually are quite disruptive of the social order. Not only disintegration of the old structures may take place at a rapid rate, but the building of the new order will be characterized by deep cleavages and conflicts (often revolutionary conflicts) between groups. This has been the experience of the past, and it is even more true of the presently developing countries (for an analysis of the conflicts generated by *one* of the aspects of the transition, social mobilization, see Germani, "Social Change and Intergroup Conflicts", *op. cit.*).

(b) Secondly, even in the more "advanced" societies, though change is institutionalized in terms of the *surface value system* of the society (that is, change is legitimized), in fact *all* existing modern societies include *at least* some set of institutions, or sector of the social structure, in which change is likely to be highly conflictive, in some cases to the point of causing important disruption of the social order, and a high degree of disintegration. Though some of the conflict areas are peculiar to specific types of modern industrial structures, and even to specific cultural national settings, it is possible that the general (universal) framework of the modern industrial order *per se* includes intrinsic and unavoidable structural tensions, which under given circumstances may have a tremendous conflictual potential (see Germani, "Secularización", *op. cit.*).

[7] Bert F. Hoselitz, "Patterns of Economic Growth" in *The Canadian Journal of Economics and Political Science*, 21 (1955), pp. 416–31.

[8] See Albert O. Hirschman, *The Strategy of Economic Development* (New Haven: Yale University Press, 1958), chap. 6 (definition and discussion of "backward and forward linkages").

[9] An excellent historical analysis of the use of stage theories in economic history may be found in Bert. F. Hoselitz, "Theories of

Stages of Economic Growth" in B. F. Hoselitz *et. al., Theories of Economic Growth* (Glencoe: Free Press, 1960); W. W. Rostow, *The Stages of Economic Growth* (Cambridge University Press, 1960). On stages of social evolution, a whole library could be quoted, starting from theories of progress, to nineteenth-century evolutionism, to its present-day revival under the form of "neo-evolutionism".

10 Glenn H. Beyer (ed.), summarizing a paper by Jorge E. Hardoy, in *The Urban Explosion in Latin America* (Ithaca, N.Y.: Cornell University Press, 1967), pp. 57–8.

11 Richard M. Morse, "Latin American Cities. Aspects of Function and Structure" in *Comparative Studies in Society and History*, IV (1961–2), pp. 473–93.

12 G. Cespedes del Castillo, "La Sociedad Colonial Americana en los siglos XVI y XVII" in J. Vicens Vives (ed.), *Historia de España y de América* (Barcelona: Vicens-Vives, 1957), p. 508.

13 The distinction between the stage of "outward" and the stage of "inward" development is usually made by ECLA economists. The idea of increasing self-determination of Latin American countries – in the stage of "inward" development – underlies the theories of many Latin American social scientists, as well as of at least some of the ideologies of the "national left".

14 For an illustration of this chronology, see John Johnson, *Political Change in Latin America* (Stanford University Press, 1958), Introduction.

15 G. Germani, "Democratie Représentative et Classes Populaire en Amerique Latine" in *Sociologie du Travail*, III (1961), pp. 96–113; G. Germani and K. Silvert, "Politics, Social Structure and Military Intervention in Latin America" in *Archives Européennes de Sociologie*, II (1961), pp. 62–81. An application to Argentina may be found in "El proceso de transicion hacia una democracia de masas en la Argentina" in *Politica*, XVI (1961), pp. 10–27; a revised English text is published in D. B. Heath and R. N. Adams, *Contemporary Cultures and Societies in Latin America* (New York: Random House, 1965).

16 The scheme of stages is included in the notes of a lecture course at Harvard University (1965), circulated in dittoed form.

17 It was a project initiated by Arthur P. Whitaker in 1947, sponsored by regional and international institutions and widely discussed

at scientific meetings. See A. P. Whitaker, "Introduction to the Project for a History of America" in Lewis Hanke (ed.), *Do the Americas Have a Common History?* (New York: Knopf, 1964). This compilation includes many contributions relevant to the problem.

[18] Charles C. Griffin, "Problems of the National Period" in L. Hanke, *op. cit.*

[19] For an excellent review of the theories of social change in Latin America, see Juan F. Marsal, *Cambio Social en la America Latina. Critica de algunas interpretaciones dominantes en las Ciencias Sociales* (Buenos Aires: Solar-Hachette, 1967).

[20] A sequence of three phases could be observed in the process of industrialization: from a high predominance of manufactures concentrated in food, beverage, tobacco, a minor proportion in textile, and a very small sector of other industries, to the most advanced (within the region) with a very marked expansion of metallurgical, chemical and other industries. See United Nations Economic Commission for Latin America, *The Process of Industrial Development in Latin America* (New York, 1966).

[21] For an analysis of the internal and external economic factors involved in the slowdown and stagnation, see United Nations, *Towards a Dynamic Development Policy for Latin America* (New York: 1963).

[22] See Germani, "Social Change . . .", *op. cit.*

[23] The idea of the "great delay" in industrialization was introduced to explain the Argentinian economic stagnation in the fourth stage. However, it could be extended to other major Latin American countries as well. See Guido Di Tella and Manuel Zymelman, *Las Etapas del Desarrollo Economico Argentino* (Buenos Aires: Eudeba, 1967). Though in some countries the "modernizing effects" involved some degree of industrialization, previous to the Great Depression it still remained well below what could have been possible. For instance, the development of transport infrastructure which elsewhere provided a great incentive for industrial expansion failed to do so in Latin America. See Economic Commission for Latin America, *The Process of Industrial Development in Latin America* (New York: United Nations, 1966), pp. 6–9.

[24] Germani, "The City as an Integrating Mechanism", in Glenn Beyer (ed.), *The Urbanization Explosion in Latin America* (Ithaca: Cornell University Press, 1968).

[25] On the reaction against the "middle-class myth", see the excellent analysis prepared by the UN Economic Commission for Latin America, *El Desarrollo Social de America Latina en la Postguerra* (Buenos Aires: Solar-Hachette, 1963). For an early evaluation of the potential threat of the rising middle classes to political modernization in Latin America, see Germani, "La Clase Media en la Argentina con Especial Referencia a sus Sectores Urbanos" in Th. Crevenna (ed.), *Materiales para el estudio de las Clases Medias en la America Latina* (Washington: Panamerican Union, 1950), vol. 1. Indications on the causes of the failure in establishing a classic Fascist régime based on the middle class in Argentina, Germani, "Fascism and Class" in *Studies in Comparative International Development*, IV (1968).

[26] Unfortunately, empirical evidence relevant to this suggestion is not available, since most studies on internal migrants did not consider the problem of selection at the place of origin.

[27] Among other references, see the review articles by William Mangin, "Latin American Squatter Settlements", in *Latin American Research Review*, II (1967), pp. 65–98; Richard Morse, "Urbanization in Latin America", in the same journal, I (1966), pp. 35–74; on the political effects, see the papers published in the special issue of *Sociologie du Travail* on "Ouvriers et Syndicats en Amérique Latine", by several authors (no. 4, 1961), and the special issue of *Revista Latino Americana de Sociologia* on the working class in Latin America (no. 3, 1967).

2

The Brazilian Structural Crisis*

1. HISTORY AND POLITICAL DEVELOPMENT

The Three Stages of Development
Brazilian history presents a particularly sharp contrast between a fast-moving political picture and a very slowly changing socio-economic structure.

In the course of its more than four centuries of existence as a Western or Westernized society, the country has changed its constitutional régime and its system of government several times. Discovered by Pedro Alvares Cabral in 1500 and settled by the Portuguese, Brazil was ruled by a general governor, later (in the eighteenth century) called viceroy, who was appointed by and directly subordinate to the Portuguese king until 1808, when the country was promoted to kingdom parity with Portugal, to become an independent empire in 1822 (Pedro I, 1822–31; the regency, 1831–40; Pedro II, 1840–89). In 1889 a military coup proclaimed the Republic, which stabilized, after a short-lived military positivist régime (Marshals Manoel Deodoro da Fonseca and Floriano Peixoto, 1889–95), into an oligarchical republic (República Velha) lasting until 1930. A radical revolution led the country first to a radical régime (1930–37) and then to a semi-fascist régime (the New State, 1937–45). This was followed by a democratic republic (1946–64) which fostered economic development and some socio-political change but was finally overthrown by a reactionary military coup in 1964.

In contrast to the multiple political phases, the corresponding socio-economic structure of Brazil passed through only three

* by Helio Jaguaribe.

stages: the colonial until 1850, followed by the semi-colonial up to 1930, and the transitional from 1930 to the present.[1]

The Colonial and Semi-Colonial Stages

It was as a plantation establishment that Brazil was settled, developed, and achieved a high level of success for its ruling class. And this economic system, combined with the peculiar features transmitted by the Portuguese culture[2] in the three formative centuries of its colonial past, decisively conditioned the course of Brazilian evolution.

The colonial establishment was based, internally, on the appropriation of the land and the means of production by a politically powerful patrician minority, assisted by a few urban merchants and supported by a small middle-class military and bureaucratic apparatus. Externally, the colonial establishment led to, and became dependent upon, the country's specialized agriculture which supplied the Western markets with such basic primary products as sugar, hides, and later, coffee, not to mention the short but immensely valuable cycle of gold mining in the eighteenth century. With the revenue from these exports it was possible to import consumer goods for the ruling class and to import the slaves and later the machinery required to keep the economy functioning.

The external success of this system, based on its relatively high productivity (due to its natural advantages) and the continuously increasing external demand for its exports (until the beginning of the twentieth century), made it relatively easy for the colonial establishment to maintain internally the *status quo*. The middle class, then still small and condemned to economic marginality by the master-slave régime of production, was co-opted by a system of "clientele" politics[3] which provided, at the expense of the public treasury, probendarian or semi-useless jobs in exchange for votes for the appointees and representatives of the landowners.

That the transition from the colonial to the semi-colonial stage was a relatively painless and gradual one was due to the formation and expansion of a domestic market. After the Eusebio de Queirós Act of 1850 (forbidding the overseas traffic of slaves), slave labor was substituted by paid immigrant labor, and this generated an internal circulation of income and an increased accumulation of capital which spurred the country's incipient capacity for endogenous growth.

The semi-colonial establishment was even more successful than the preceding one, but not substantially different from it. The economy and politics of Brazil continued to be dominated by the rural patriciate of landowners, aided by the import-export urban merchants, still predominantly of foreign origin, and supported by the military and civil bureaucracy, the latter always formed by the clientelistic cooptation of an expanding marginal middle class. The rural masses, changing from slave to "free" labor (slavery was finally abolished in 1888) under a semi-feudal régime of production, were kept entirely isolated from any level of decision-making either in the economic or in the political field. Coffee production began to expand in the last third of the nineteenth century, experiencing a boom which continued into the first years of this century.

The colonial stage corresponded to the formation of a centralized government, successor of the colonial administration, which was able, after Independence, to maintain the political and cultural unity of the country. The semi-colonial stage corresponded to the diversification and growing complexity of Brazilian society. Its several formerly unconnected centers of production were then gradually united by the expanding domestic market. A Brazilian national identity, still more objectively characterized than self-consciously developed, began to take shape and express itself in the arts (chiefly literature and music), in the legal organization of the country (constitution law, commercial and civil codes), and in its already typical style of life (the "cordial man"), of organization (person oriented rather than functional), and of dealing with its own affairs (the "jeito" technique).

The colonial stage had led to expanded use of the arable lands under the slave régime of production, creating the pre-conditions for an internal market. The semi-colonial stage then formed a large internal market, converting into an effective polity the old plantation society and creating, in its turn, the conditions for the emergence of the middle class to political influence and economic participation.

The Crisis of Transition

Two factors pushed the semi-colonial establishment toward a structural crisis in the course of the twenties: one internal and the other external to the Brazilian society.

Internally, the semi-colonial establishment was disrupted by its incapacity to keep the ever-increasing urban middle class under the control of the patrician landowners. The semi-colonial mode of production, supported by peasants in a semi-feudal régime of dependence toward the landowners, was creating a surplus of a middle-class population, economically marginal, which began to concentrate in the cities, pressing for public jobs. Rio de Janeiro and the major provincial capitals, Recife, Salvador, São Paulo and, later, Belo Horizonte, grew rapidly in a process of accelerated urbanization which preceded the industrialization of the country and which imposed an increasing stress on the "clientele" system of politics and the "cartorial" state. Together with this growth in numbers, the middle class experienced a cultural awakening, which, after some decades of delay, was permeated by the post-Victorian intellectual atmosphere of Europe.[4]

The combined effect of the quantitative expansion of the middle class, beyond the possibility of their incorporation in the Semi-Colonial "cartorial" state, and of their cultural awakening to modernity, made it increasingly difficult for the semi-colonial establishment to keep the middle class under its control. The coup de grace to the system was brought about by an external factor: the growing accumulation of unsaleable stocks of coffee, a product suddenly deprived of any potential value by the Great Depression.

The imbalance between Brazilian coffee production and the world demand had been felt since the beginning of the century. By concentrating the ever-expanding capacity for production, which was practically unlimited due to the abundance of labor and virgin lands, on a single crop, Brazil soon had a supply of coffee that surpassed the relatively inelastic demand for it. By the Taubaté convention of 1906 the coffee planters succeeded in keeping a stable price level, establishing a quota system by which the government would buy and store the surplus of the production while the exports were limited to the actual demand. This system, however, was in itself self-defeating, because, by maintaining the high incentives for coffee production, it led to the accumulation of increasing stocks with decreasing probabilities of future liquidation. The great depression of the thirties gave the system its final blow, dropping the prices from forty cents to eight cents per pound.

The economic, social, and political transformations that led to the end of the semi-colonial establishment were embodied in the revolution of 1930, which overthrew the last president of the Old Republic, Washington Luis Pereira de Souza, and brought Getulio Vargas to power. Summarily speaking, there were two major consequences of the crisis of the semi-colonial establishment. At the political level, it brought the middle class, which had had the short-lived experience of ruling the country in the military positivist republic (1889–95), to power again. At the economic level, it forced the country, no longer capable of financing the import of her required consumer goods, to produce them domestically in a spontaneous process of industrialization by import-substitution.

The Three Roles of Vargas

Getulio Vargas, the man who led the revolution of 1930 and brought the country to political modernity, is still today a very controversial figure in partisan politics. His lasting impact on recent events and the varying political positions he adopted in the course of his life have given rise to many contradictory interpretations of his aims, including the denial by some of any social significance to his political manoeuvers other than the tactics required for absolute personal power.

Actually, while Getulio Vargas was on the one hand a manipulationist of people and symbols for the sheer purposes of power politics, he was also a highly representative man who could understand and respond to changing social expectations. His capacity to sense the direction and the meaning of the prevailing social demands and to embody the image of their fulfilment led him to play three successive roles in power: the radical in the twenties and early thirties; the semi-fascist in the late thirties and early forties; the welfare laborite from 1943 until his tragic suicide in 1954.

These three roles of Vargas corresponded to the different expectations felt and roles performed by the Brazilian middle class in these three decades. The transitional stage of Brazilian development was marked by the emergence, revolutionary rise, conservative shift, and reactionary defense of the middle class in its drive and struggles from marginality to participation in the Brazilian establishment.

Vargas was a radical when the middle class, whose aspirations he embodied and whose revolutionary rise he led in 1930, was of a radical bent. As already mentioned, the revolution of 1930, like the revolution of 1889, led a political group to power which was representative of an economically marginal middle class. In both cases the middle class and its leaders were neither able to understand the necessity for, nor disposed to do something about, changing the economic system which was perpetuating the privileges of the rural oligarchy and therefore marginalizing the proper middle class. Because the former system of rural property and exploitation was kept unchanged, the rural oligarchy easily recovered the political control of the state once the republican government permitted free elections. That the same inaction, after the revolution of 1930, would lead to the same result was clearly understood by Vargas and his supporters as the scheduled date for the elections of 1938 was approaching. This time, however, the middle class could not afford to return to the old patriarchal régime. They needed to share the control of the state in order to keep the way to public jobs open. The solution which conciliated Vargas's own desire to stay in power with the middle-class aspiration for more or less secure public jobs was the coup of 1937 which created, with the New State, a semi-fascist régime based on the military and civil middle-class bureaucracies. The conversion of Vargas from radicalism to quasi-fascism was just an expression of a similar transition of the middle class, once radical liberalism proved to be at variance with their fundamental interests.

The New State period was contemporaneous with two relevant events. One, external to Brazil, was the Second World War, dividing most of the world between the fascist and the anti-fascist coalitions. The second, internal, was the expansion of the Brazilian process of industrialization with the formation of two new social groups: the industrialists and the proletariat.

Economic and geopolitical reasons, among others, led the New State, contrary to its doctrinairian (but never seriously assumed) implications, to join the anti-fascist coalition, to the point of sending troops to fight the Axis in Italy. The rise of the new social groups generated by industrialization, on the other hand, introduced a corresponding change in the internal political balance.

Again giving proof of his perspicacity, Vargas understood, as early as 1943, that fascism was doomed to defeat; that the post-war world would be a world of mass democracy; that his New State régime could not survive the new post-war conditions; and that the Brazilian middle class had lost its revolutionary impetus and could no longer be the basic support of the state. In view of these considerations, Vargas shifted his political position once again, and for the last time. His design was to organize a new political force, based on an alliance between the two new emerging groups: the industrial bourgeoisie and the proletariat. His strategy was to initiate the change himself by calling a Constituent assembly and then manoeuver to influence its formation and to take over its leadership. His tactic was to use the machinery of the New State, apparently in continuation of his own régime, to change its socio-political basis and meaning without changing its outward look. His ultimate purpose, finally, was once again to perpetuate himself in power.

The subtle manoeuvers of Vargas, however, failed because he was overthrown by a military coup in 1945, once the middle class and its traditional political agency, the army, somehow grasped the intentions and the meaning of Vargas's action. But Vargas, for his own short-term purposes, was actually defeated only partially. Because he had correctly understood the new course of events, formulated the right political answer, and adopted the appropriate role, he achieved, in the long run, his objectives. The two parties created by Vargas as the agencies of the new social forces, the Social Democratic Party and the Brazilian Labour Party (better known by their Brazilian initials – PSD and PTB), formed an alliance which actually ruled Brazilian politics from then until the military coup of 1964.

The PSD-PTB corresponded, though very imperfectly and loosely, to the formation of a national front, incorporating the national bourgeoisie (the industrial bourgeoisie and the sector of the commercial bourgeoisie in the trade of the products of the national industry), the progressive middle class (technicians and managers of the new industry and the new intelligentsia), and the proletariat. This national front, composing (loosely) the majority of the Congress, was able to lead the country, albeit with very low consciousness of its role, on the way toward economic development and national emancipation, from the second Vargas government (1950–4) to the Kubitschek government (1955–60), until the new structural crisis of the sixties.

2. PROGRAMMED DEVELOPMENT

The Vargas Plans

Brazilian industrialization, spontaneously started and impelled by the import-substitution process generated by the crisis of the thirties, was severely afflicted in the later forties, once the foreign currency accumulated during the war was inconsiderately spent on non-priority applications. The country had succeeded in changing the structure of its imports, becoming practically self-sufficient in the production of most of its required consumer goods, without achieving, however, a corresponding change in the structure of its exports. With the West's gradual recovery from the depression, the volume and prices of Brazilian exports to the industrialized countries dropped again to the pre-depression levels. In the meantime, however, the Brazilian GNP had increased fifty per cent and the incompressible demand of the capital goods required for keeping the new Brazilian industrial park running had surpassed the country's capacity for importation.

The resulting imbalance of Brazilian balance of trade had to be corrected by a selective use of the scarce foreign currencies. Rather than devaluating the cruzeiro, the Brazilian authorities decided to submit the importation to a régime of physical control, according to a system of priorities devised to favor the importation of raw materials, combustibles, and machinery. This system rapidly brought the government to recognize the necessity for economic planning.

The first systematic efforts at economic planning were made by the second Vargas government. One set of plans (those of Romulo Almeida) was oriented toward developing the country's capacity in the field of energy and combustibles: the oil plan and the creation of Petrobras, a state monopoly for its prospecting, extraction, refining, and transportation; Eletrobras (only much later approved by the Congress because of the vested interests in the foreign-controlled pre-existing power companies), as a state-owned holding for the generation and distribution of electric power; the national coal plan, for developing and rationalizing the extraction, transportation, and use of Brazilian native coal. Another set of plans (Lafer's Re-Equipment Plan) was oriented toward transportation – railways and ports. When Kubitschek, after the interregnum succeeding the suicide of Vargas, took over the government (1955–60), a government committed to a program of intensive economic development, he could start his own planning effort from a much higher level of technical preparedness.

The Target Plan

The Target Plan (Programa de Metas) of the Kubitschek government consisted, basically, of a system of thirty-one global targets, aiming at certain minimal physical goals of production in six strategic sectors: energy, transport, food, basic industry, education, and, a special target, the construction of Brasilia, the new capital. The Plan was based on the assumption that the spontaneous and uncoordinated economic growth of the former years had created an intrinsic imbalance among the main sectors of the economy, so that without a planned attempt to correct the resulting bottlenecks no further development could be achieved.

For correcting these bottlenecks the plan fixed the minimum physical supply of infra-structural and basic goods and services required to fill the prospective demand (in general for 1960–1) and assure, subsequently, the balanced expansion of the national economy. A special agency, the Development Council, was therefore created to coordinate the public and private projects required for the fulfilment of each of the targets of the Plan.

The Target Plan had highly successful results. Taking 1960 as the deadline year, the energy targets were almost entirely reached in electric power generation (96 per cent) and substantially achieved in oil (75.5 per cent for extraction of crude, 71 per cent for refining). In the sector of transport the plan had its targets well approached in railways (100 per cent for engines, 58 per cent for wagons, 80 per cent for rails) and even surpassed in highways. In maritime transportation the average achievement was more than 90 per cent. The intermediate industries presented an attainment of 181 per cent of the target for steel ingot production and 89 per cent for Portland cement. In the sector of capital goods the goal for the automobile industry was more than 90 per cent reached, that for shipbuilding was 98 per cent fulfilled. The industry of equipments, for which no quantified goals had been fixed, increased by 100 per cent, permitting the country to produce, in 1960, two-thirds of its total demand of equipment.

The special target, the creation of the new capital – the advisability and timing of which remains a controversial issue – was also achieved and Brasilia was inaugurated on 21 April 1960, with a capacity of 100,000 inhabitants, but not large enough to permit the full transference of the federal government from Rio de Janeiro to Brasilia. Actually, only the Congress and the Supreme Court could be completely moved to Brasilia; most of the branches of the Executive continue to function in Rio.

The impact of the execution of the Target Plan on the economy of the country was equally great. Negatively, the Plan has contributed to increase the pace of inflation, as revenues of the Union proved to be insufficient to finance its part of the plan. The share of the Union actually proved much larger than anticipated because the federal government had to supply part of the investments which were to have been borne by the private sector (as in the steel industry, for instance) and all of the States, with the exception of São Paulo, also depended on the help of the Union to meet their financial commitments. Given the index 100 to January 1952, August 1956 was 222 and October 1961, 862, in terms of cost of living.[5] But owing to the structural causes of the inflation, the Target Plan failed, as became clear in the subsequent years when the inflationary rate underwent a much sharper rise.

On the positive side of the Target Plan, far more important than the negative one, it should be stressed that the Plan changed the quality and scale of the Brazilian economy. Brazil definitively became – although still insufficiently – an industrialized country. The industrial index jumped from 100 in 1949 and 162.3 in 1955 (beginning of the Kubitschek administration) to 266.3 in 1960, while the GNP passed from 100 in 1949 to 138.4 in 1955 and 183.0 in 1960. The GNP increased from 1955 to 1960, at constant prices, to 41.1 per cent *per capita*. The industrial growth in the same period was 145.5 per cent larger than the increase of the GNP.[6]

3. THE CRISIS OF THE SIXTIES

The Imbalanced Growth

In spite of its exceptional achievements, the Kubitschek government ended in an impasse. It was already evident, in the last year of his term, that Kubitschek's model of development had exhausted its potentialities and that, whoever the successor would be, a second Target Plan, as a simple continuation of the first, would not be feasible.

In fact, the crisis which became obvious in the beginning of the sixties was already incipient in the middle of the fifties. That crisis was the result of the structural imbalance which had affected the whole Brazilian process of development since the thirties: imbalance between the urban and the rural sectors, with the corresponding imbalance between the Center-South and the rest of the country; imbalance between the public and the private sectors, with the resulting disequilibrium between the increasing responsibilities of the former, notably the federal government and its agencies and its proportionally decreasing revenues; imbalance, finally, between the expanding economic process, on the one hand, and the stagnated socio-political process, on the other.

The second Vargas government had already understood the nature of that structural imbalance and attempted to provide a solution. The problems confronting the country were much more complex than the sheer necessity of increasing, through the techniques of economic planning, the efficiency and rationality of Brazilian industrialization, until then impelled by a spontaneous process of import-substitution. The problems were going even beyond the economic sphere and affecting the whole social life of the country. They were, ultimately, an expression of the fact that the original duality of the semi-colonial system, divided between a relatively small (in terms of employment) dynamic export sector and a much larger stagnant sector, at the level of subsistence economy, was persisting in a different and aggravated form. The process of industrialization had not changed that old duality in any fundamental way. It kept it as it formerly was and simply created a new and parallel one: the duality between the modern industrial-urban complex and the archaic agricultural-rural complex. Fundamentally, the problems of the country could be reduced to one single global one: the economic, social, cultural, and political incorporation of the marginal sectors and the marginal regions into the national process of development, until then restricted to the Center-South region and, in that region, to its bourgeoisie and to sectors of its middle class and proletariat.

Ultimately, this had been the purpose of the second Vargas government – to combine economic development with social reform and regional balancing. Such a purpose, however, implied a price that the new Brazilian Establishment did not want to pay: (1) increased efforts at saving and investment and (2) redistribution of income, education, and power. This new Establishment, formed by incorporating the middle class into the old Establishment, had converted the previous antagonism between the patrician landowners and city export merchants, on the one hand, and the formerly marginal middle class, on the other hand, into an implicit alliance against the intrusion of the masses. The fact that the middle class had not yet completely overcome its functional marginality (not only because of the still insufficient industrialization but also because of the remaining skill deficiencies of the ascriptive sectors of the middle class) was a decisive factor in leading the middle class to stick, along with the upper class, to a closed society.

Vargas was finally defeated by the reactionary forces, who once again had mobilized the army against the legitimate civil government. He preferred to commit suicide (24 August 1954) rather than resign and let the military, unopposed, take over the control of the country.

It was in order to avoid the same kind of confrontation that had proved fatal to Vargas that Kubitschek, taking power one year later, preferred to make a tacit deal with the oligarchical forces. He would keep the conditions of the countryside unchanged, thereby preserving the economic and political interest of the landowners, in exchange for their permission to promote the accelerated development of industry. Implicit in this policy was Kubitschek's conviction that a fast and programmed industrialization would inevitably and naturally extend the new forces and styles generated by industry to the countryside, so achieving, by a gradual, indirect, but not less effective means, the indispensable goal of modernizing the countryside.

Facts, however, have not confirmed that assumption, with the partial exception of the State of São Paulo, where the semi-feudal modes of production have really been submitted to a spontaneous process of change, in the direction of capitalist agriculture or rural middle-class family farming. Instead of a spontaneous adjustment of the rural-agricultural complex to the expansion of the urban-industrial system, the implicit Kubitschek pact led to an abysmal differentiation and imbalance.

Highly concentrated (11 per cent of the rural establishment own 70 per cent of the agricultural land) and inefficient, Brazilian agriculture kept the peasants economically, culturally, and politically marginal. While they represent 50 per cent of the population they remain almost completely illiterate, do not vote, and participate in less than 15 per cent of the national income, with an annual per capita income of about $40.00.[7] Corresponding to that imbalance was the regional one. While the North, the Northeast, and the Center-West had 29 per cent of the total national population, they had only 14 per cent of the national income. Correlated to this were also, in one form or another, the other structural imbalances previously referred to: the public-private sectors' disequilibrium and the unevenness between the expansion of the economy and the stagnation of the socio-political process of the country.

The Populist Experiments

In the years succeeding the Kubitschek government (1961–4) and until the military coup which overthrew President Goulart, two governments tried three successive experiments for solving the Brazilian structural crisis.

The first government and the first experiment was that of President Janio Quadros. Quadros's short-lived government (seven months) was one of the oddest political episodes of Brazilian history. Its singularity started with Quadros's campaign and election. Linked by his former position as governor of the State of São Paulo to the conservative anti-Vargas forces, he succeeded in getting both the vote of the masses – led to believe in his electoral promises of social reform – and the vote of the élites – led to believe he was a sound conservative in populist disguise for obtaining mass support. Once in government he showed a conservative concern for orthodox financing and economic stability and, at the same time, a determination to innovate in social matters and in foreign policy. Maintaining and strengthening this determination, he finally adopted – but had not the time to implement – a developmental position in the economic field, which would probably have been incompatible with his intial sound financing commitments. Using the presidential authority with an amplitude and in an autocratic style unparalleled in the Brazilian experience, he tried to promote and introduce rapid and radical changes by the power of his own decisions and will. It was a Bonapartist rule at the service of a reformist design but without the control and support of Bonaparte's armies.

The most striking feature of the new style of government and of the new policies pursued by Quadros was revealed in his foreign policy. Breaking a half-secular tradition of almost automatic and fully uncritical alignment with the United States on international issues, the Quadros government officially admitted the obvious existence of numerous areas of non-coincidence and even of plain conflict between Brazilian and American interests. This fact, moreover, was understood to be due not to accidental and easily removable factors but, on the contrary, to structural long-term incompatibilities between the present interests and policies of the United States and some vital interests of Brazil in particular and of Latin America and the third world in general.

This new realistic approach to the position of Brazil in the international arena led to a clearly formulated independent foreign policy based, ultimately, on a neutralistic approach to the USA–USSR confrontation and on a self-conscious and deliberate effort by Brazil to reach a better understanding and cooperation with the other Latin American countries in particular and with the third world in general.

The Quadros government, however, was doomed to a short life. Understanding, in its fundamental aspects, what had to be done to solve Brazil's problems (acceleration of the national development with and by the incorporation into its process of the marginal classes and regions) Quadros realized neither the political conditions required for implementing his policies (organized mass support, for instance) nor the political limits of viability (the degree of dependability of the army, for instance) of his purposes. Once the magic of his authority was surpassed by the accumulation of frustrations and fears on the side of the ruling classes and their gendarmes, the army, Quadros was confronted with the imminence of his destruction.

Quadros had never had a majority in the Congress, and he had lost the allegiance of his own appointed chiefs in the army. By late August 1961, competently manoeuvered by Carlos Lacerda, both the Congress and the army clearly showed their willingness and preparedness to overthrow him – either by a Congressional impeachment supported by the army or by a military coup endorsed by the Congress. Quadros, subject to great emotional instability, lost his nerve and, rather than try to outmanoeuver his enemies by using the instruments still under his control, decided to quit the government. Preferring to resign rather than risk being deposed, he probably still counted on the possibility of being called back by the pressure of the popular indignation which would arise on his quitting the government. Quadros's unexpected resignation, however, caught the public so much by surprise that, before articulated protest could be generalized, the army had already taken full control of the country and sent him abroad under strict vigilance.

The second government in that period was that of João Goulart, vice-president of the Quadros government. Taking power with the utmost difficulty (September 1961) after counteracting the coup attempted by the former cabinet ministers of Quadros, Goulart spent the first part of his term, until January 1963, in a risky and hard struggle to regain full presidential authority.[8] He then started, successively, his own two political experiments, known, according to definitions by the late San Tiago Dantas, as the "positive left" and the "negative left" experiments.

The positive left experiment, under the leadership of San Tiago Dantas, then appointed finance minister, and under the technical orientation of Celso Furtado, then planning minister, was a fascinating attempt to combine, in a highly sophisticated form and within the framework of representative democracy, social reform with economic development. Never in Brazilian history have national goals been more adequately and clearly formulated and policies for their achievement better designed.[9] And never has a cabinet had two more capable and well-intentioned ministers than San Tiago and Furtado. The positive left experiment, however, was not given an effective trying chance by Goulart. Less than six months after their appointment, San Tiago Dantas and Celso Furtado, together with the rest of the cabinet, were dismissed before they could go beyond the preliminary steps of implementing their policies. Personal resentments, fears of losing popularity among the masses, and the political leadership of the PTB-PSD coalition were probably some of the major reasons which impelled Goulart to the suicidal dismissal of his best men, thus unwittingly bringing about the liquidation of his chances of presiding over a great government and even of simply surviving in power.

The second experiment of the Goulart government, the negative left attempt, although marked by its lack of an articulated formulation, was also oriented, in a certain sense, toward combining reform with economic development. The first experiment, however, was aimed at preserving a simultaneous approach to both goals (not to mention technical qualification and political consistency), to be reached in a consensual and gradualist form and through essentially rational ways. The negative left, on the contrary, was an irrational-romantic-rhetoric process, promising the most radical changes in the direction of goals only vaguely indicated (agrarian reform, economic nationalization, redistribution of income), to be reached by still less clearly explained forms, except that they were supposed to be of a revolutionary nature. Driven to a popularity contest with his brother-in-law, political mate, and rival in leadership, Deputy Leonel Brizola, President Goulart lost the means of keeping under control and maintaining within viable limits the actions and the political image of his government. As a result, before his goals could be properly formulated, let alone implemented, his attempts at social reform were slashed by a military coup which forced him out of power and into exile in the first days of April 1964.

The Military Régime

The events that took place after the military ousting of President Goulart have led to some relevant new political facts and implications. Initially, the anti-Goulart coup, although presenting from the very beginning all the features of a military "pronunciamiento", also had the backing of a rather large section of the public opinion. Practically all the rural and urban bourgeoisie, most of the middle class, and even some sectors of the working class supported or accepted as a minor evil the overthrow of Goulart, while most of the popular forces, although opposing the coup for its extra-constitutional nature and particularly for its reactionary implications, were not prepared to make any strong effort to defend a government whose social promises and meaning had been surpassed by Goulart's lack of consistency and dependability.

Soon after the coup, however, it became clear that the military, long frustrated by their new marginality in the process of national development, did not intend, as most of the people had thought, to give up the control of the government to the civilians this time. Seen from that perspective, a process was started, with institutional act No. 1 (9 April 1964), in which a naked appropriation of power, by the military as a corporation and their leaders as individuals, entered in conflict with the interest of the conservative classes and groups in a military custodianship of the present socio-economic order. These classes and groups have traditionally used the military as their agents for compelling the governments elected by the popular forces to stop short of any measures affecting more fundamentally their privileges and the socio-economic order founded on them. Now they realize that the preservation of that order had to be bought at the price of full military appropriation of political power, with their reduction to subordinate, if economically independent, assistants and followers.

The second fact which emerged out of the military rule was its incompatibility even with the most limited and controlled forms of representative democracy. Institutional act No. 1 forced the issuing of acts Nos. 2 and 3, with the complete exclusion of the people from any effective political decision.

The third fact which was made clear by the military rule, within the conditions above mentioned, was its necessary colonial-fascist tendency. Oriented for stability as its primary goal – that is, preserving the existing socio-economic order by freezing the *status quo* – but interested in achieving economic goals, the military régime is doomed to have a fascist propensity. Independently of other considerations (such as, for instance, the kind and depth of repressive measures in use), the promotion of economic growth without social change is, precisely, one of the three essential features of fascism, as a political model. The two other fundamental features of fascism, as a model, are also to be found in the Brazilian military régime: (1) the middle-class nature of the movement and of its leadership and (2) the monopoly of the whole political and governmental processes by a self-supporting and self-appointed bureaucracy, which is the army, in the conditions of Brazil.

That fascism, however, in an underdeveloped country still maintaining a semi-feudal countryside and incapable of disposing of a convenient market for her growth, had to be, necessarily, a Colonial-Fascism – a fascism of dependence toward the dominating power of the region, the USA. The limitation of the market – both for consuming goods and for capital accumulation – is the typical colonial limitation. All fascist societies tend to limit the capacity for expanding their domestic market by freezing the *status quo*. In the conditions of Nazi Germany, however, to consider the most opposite case, that limitation was doubly compensated: first, because the level at which the *status quo* was frozen was incomparably higher than the Brazilian one; and second, because the market was enlarged by external military conquest, which was an essential aspect of a dynamic industrial fascism.

In Brazilian Colonial-Fascism the *status quo* is frozen at a still very incipient level of socio-economic development. And no external conquests are imaginable. That is why such fascism is above all colonial and must be made the principal basis of the so-called interdependence with the United States, as the planning minister, Roberto Campos, has emphasized from the beginning.

An interesting corollary of this condition is the ultimate non-viability of the right-wing nationalism of the "hard line" faction within the army. It is always possible, of course, that the "hard liners", be they under Costa e Silva (who was supported by this faction during the Castelo Branco government) or under one of the other colonels who dominate that group, could take power. What is not possible, however, is that the hard liners could maintain their nationalist position in any but a simply verbal and propagandistic form. For, the moment they exceed these merely rhetorical forms of expression, they would lose the external support of the United States, which is a *sine qua non* requirement for compensating the military régime for its lack of popular support and socio-economic dynamism.

The fundamental problems confronting the military régime, therefore, are caused by its triple difficulty in matching its own requirements of suitability, in keeping within the limits of its internal socio-economic viability, and in doing so in a mutually compatible form.

The problem of suitability of the régime is the problem of its adjustment to the basic necessities of the internal and external forces whose support it depends on. Scared by what appeared to them as an imminent risk of a communist takeover, in the Goulart government, the Brazilian bourgeoisie and middle class, internally, and the United States, externally, have found their basic interests to be mutually compatible and complementary. They realize they would be better preserved by a military rule than by undependable populist governments. In the long run, however, once the original fears are placated, the natural divergences existing among these two classes and their external ally will reassert themselves. It will be increasingly difficult for the régime to maintain its colonial-fascist features under the pressure of national interests, willing to expand and to increase their autonomy. The military régime, however, will not be able to survive if its essential features have to be altered. In Brazilian conditions, as already observed, a fascist régime cannot afford not to be colonial – because of the loss of United States support – nor can a colonial régime afford not to be fascist – because of its lack of internal support.

The problem of the régime's internal socio-economic viability, on the other hand, is expressed by the increasing difficulty and final impossibility of controlling the effects of the prolonged stagnation and unemployment which tend to be caused by the freezing of the *status quo*. The unemployment of the middle class[10] generates radical leaders who become organizers of the revolutionary impulses of the exploited and unemployed masses, in a process which finally surpasses the repressive capacity of the government apparatus and explodes in an uncontrollable social revolution.

Moreover, matching its requirements of suitability and staying within the limits of its socio-economic viability are already, even separately considered, tasks too difficult for the military régime. Therefore, doing both things at the same time, in a mutually compatible manner, would seem very unlikely. In the last analysis, what tends to strengthen the suitability of the régime, i.e., the firm maintenance of its colonial-fascist features, tends to affect its viability – sufficient economic expansion to provide appropriate employment, chiefly to the middle class.

The precarious line of conciliation of its conflicting requirements consists, for the military régime, in succeeding in keeping the masses under control, but so stagnated as to trigger explosive unemployment. Such equilibrium, by its very precariousness, cannot be maintained for long. With United States assistance and the connivance of the Brazilian conservative forces it is, anyhow, a possibility for some years. The chief significance of the Costa e Silva government, therefore, will be that it represents a chance for a more defined option: liberalization of the régime through some means of returning power to civil authority and reopening the political process (as he has publicly stated to be his firm intention), or stiffening military control and the colonial-fascist features of the system and thereby closing the doors to a peaceful settlement.

NOTES

[1] Cf. Celso Furtado, *Brazilian Economic Growth* (Berkeley: University of California Press, 1964); and H. Jaguaribe, *Desenvolvimento Economico e Desenvolvimento Politico* (Rio de Janeiro: Fundo de Cultura, 1962).

[2] The Portuguese culture, from the Renaissance until modern times, has been mainly characterized by: (a) the immobilism of its basic beliefs centered on a Middle Ages Catholicism permeated by the influence of the Italian Renaissance, but unaffected by the Reformation, the Rationalist philosophies of the seventeenth and eighteenth centuries, and the scientific revolution, and alien to technological innovation; (b) an ascriptive system of fixing values and assigning functions, based on a centralized, authoritarian, military-supported bureaucratic government; (c) a statutorial rather than contractual mode of life, oriented toward the enjoyment of protected incomes and status, as provided by manorial forms of agricultural exploitation or bureaucratic jobs, or by monopolistic or state-guaranteed forms of trade.

[3] On "clientele politics" and the "cartorial" state, see H. Jaguaribe, "Politica de Cleintela e Politica Ideologica", in *Digeste Economico* (São Paulo, 1951), and also in *O Nacionalismo na Atualidade Brasileira* (Rio de Janeiro: ISEB, 1958).

[4] In 1922, under the intellectual leadership of Mario de Andrade and the patronage of an elder writer, Graca Aranha, a "modern art week" took place in São Paulo; it broke away from the current academic style and introduced modern literature, painting, sculpture and music to the scandalized public.

[5] Cf. *Desenvolvimento e Conjuntura* (Feb. 1962), and *Apud Economic Bulletin for Latin America*, Vol. IX, No. 2 (Nov. 1962).

[6] Cf. Fundação Getulio Vargas, *Anuarie Estatistico Brasileiro* (1963).

[7] Estimating, optimistically, the peasants' income to be 50 per cent of the agricultural income, the figures would be, according to Fundação Getulio Vargas, Cr$218 thousand million for 1960. For 35 million peasants this means, at the free exchange rate of US$1/Cr$190 at that time, an annual *per capita* income of US$40.

[8] Before being sworn in, in September 1961, Goulart, in order to prevent an imminent civil war, accepted as a compromise a parliamentarian amendment to the Constitution which substantially reduced his power, a large part of which was redistributed to a cabinet and a prime minister chosen by the Congress. By combining all sorts of pressures, Goulart finally succeeded in submitting the new régime to a national plebiscite, in January 1963, which repealed the parliamentarian system by a 4 to 1 vote.

[9] Cf. Three Year Plan (1932), and speeches and lectures by San Tiago Dantas, in *Revista Brasileira de Politica Internacional*, VII, No. 27 (Set. Doz. 1964), pp. 375–652, and *Digesto Economico*, 174 (Nov. Doz. 1963), pp. 77–85.

[10] Unemployment, in the industrial area of São Paulo, after reaching more than 30 per cent in the first semester, stabilized at 15 per cent in 1965, according to research undertaken by the economist Dia Carneiro.

3

The Norm of Illegitimacy: Toward a General Theory of Latin American Political Development*

Contrary to academic mythology and sociological folklore, we are faced not with inadequate data in the area of Latin American studies, but rather conflicts between severely circumscribed and limited theories that work well enough for national units, and a collection of data about Latin American societies having little correlational significance at the hemispheric level. Macroanalysis has been especially weak in the area of Latin America for various reasons, primary of which is that almost every kind of theory about a developing nation has a contradictory outcome when applied to different nations within the hemisphere.

The dilemma of forging an adequate theory is not restricted to the practical side. There is also the broader confusion surrounding the concept of legitimacy. As in so many other areas, Weber turned Marx upside down. For Marx, the State represents a monopoly of illegitimate power because politics is merely the organized machinery of one class for oppressing the others. For Weber, on the other hand, the State is organized primarily as a service agency, not a power dispenser. The State is thus an administrative staff having a monopoly on the legitimate use of force in order to enforce order in society.[1] It is evident then that for Marx the essence of the State is power; while for Weber the core of the State is authority.

Without wishing to resolve such a pervasive dualism in the sociological literature by fiat, for the purpose of this study I consider it quite feasible that certain societies do operate in

* by Irving Louis Horowitz.

Weberian terms, while others operate in terms of the Marxian conception. More specifically, those societies which over a long period of time display norms sanctioned in law and made viable through mass participation can be considered legitimate; while those societies that rest visibly and demonstrably on unaccepted or barely tolerated power structures and relations can be considered illegitimate. One might declare that nations as different as Great Britain and the Soviet Union illustrate forms of legitimated authority; while most nations of Latin America illustrate forms of illegitimacy.

It is important to distinguish between illegitimacy and violence. Latin American societies operating in terms of the norm of illegitimacy, while often prone to greater outbursts of mass violence, just as often display an institutionalization of illegitimacy which drastically reduces the amount (and certainly the quality) of violence manifest in them. Illegitimacy may function as a Paretan device to circulate élites in the absence of either laws sanctioned at the top or recognized as valid guidelines at the bottom end of society. The definition herein used is that legitimacy is the perception of the State as a service agency rather than an oppressive mechanism, and that this perception is cemented by a common adhesion to either legality or mass mobilization. The norm of illegitimacy, to the contrary, is the perception of the State as primarily a power agency, which is cemented by a common reliance on illegal means to rotate either the holders of power or the rules under which power is exercised.

1. THE INTERNAL DYNAMICS OF ILLEGITIMACY

Consider the relationship of the middle classes and militarism. During the fifties the most popular theory advanced by scholars and policy-makers alike held that to the extent to which the size of the middle class is increased, there is a decrease in the extent of military involvement in political and social life. United States policy between 1957 and 1962 was largely based on the premise of this middle-class salvation theory of Latin America.

The data do show (as far as Uruguay and Costa Rica are concerned) that with an increase in the size of the middle class there has taken place a parallel decrease in the size of the military. Yet even this is dubious, given the election of a military leader as President of Uruguay and the increased participation of Costa Rica in Central American regional defense schemes. But in turning to countries like Argentina and Brazil, which also have large and growing middle classes – as a matter of fact the Argentine middle class is the largest of all Latin America – we find the reverse situation. Instead of showing an inverse correlation between middle-class growth and militarism, there are parallel growth lines of militarism and the middle class. The same is true for Brazil. And the steady promotion of "civic action" programs, with their direct appeals to middle-class military cooperation, only serves to stimulate such outcomes. In fact, a coalition between the urban bourgeoisie in Rio de Janeiro and São Paulo and the military served to oust the João Goulart régime in 1964. The middle sectors, far from weakening military dominion, had the reverse effect. The situation in Peru and Argentina, while showing national idiosyncracies, is analogous in that there too, military interaction with the middle classes provides stability with legitimacy. Clearly, *prima facie* theorizing is inadequate as a guide to the understanding of Latin American social structure. Unfortunately, when the myth of middle-class salvation broke down, it was replaced by an even less tenable myth, that of military salvation.

Old myths about the military die hard. There is a school of thought which attributes to the military a unique developmental orientation. We are told: if this generation wants to attain a rapid rate of development, social science must stop treating the military as pariahs. It is claimed that given the unique organizational efficiency of the military, the degree of their mobilization, the degree to which they have constant labor available for social purposes, and the degree to which they are a national force and symbol, they are not only a force for development, but may well turn out to be a unique force.[2] An empirical look at the data does not drive us to any such optimistic prospects for military rule. They fail to show that the military are especially good at promoting a developmental pattern, at least in Latin America.[3]

The military have simply failed to act as an autonomous or unified group. Oftentimes they act as agents of other social classes or powerful government alignments. The view of the military as leaders in civic action, with respect to Latin America, ignores one of the gravest difficulties of all, namely, the exorbitant cost factor in their maintenance. The military establishment is expensive and wasteful. When a country like Chile buys twenty subsonic jet fighters, that portion of the federal budget intended for agrarian reform or industrial modernization is seriously impaired. The developmental *ideology* of the military, even when present, is thus undermined by their feudalistic *organization*. The so-called modernizing military phenomenon does not stem from a sober appraisal of the complex social stratification system so much as from a profound search for the key to hemispheric stability.

It is not exclusively the contradictory aspects of Latin American development that makes a general theory an elusive goal, but the degrees of variation found in the social structure of the Hemisphere. Recently, for example, one writer has distinguished the following different types of working-class organizations that can be found and correlated with different nations. They are: (1) countries with little urban or industrial concentration and with a small middle class; (2) countries with isolated mass situations, without a large urban industrial concentration and with a small middle class; (3) countries with isolated mass situations, without large urban concentrations, and with a large middle class in their urban sector; (4) countries with little urban and industrial concentration, but with a large middle class; (5) countries with large urban-industrial concentrations, and a large middle class in their urban sectors; (6) countries with isolated mass situations, but without large urban-industrial concentrations and a large middle class.[4] While, formally speaking, such tabular compilations are useful, and can be transformed into elements of an operational appraisal, listing differences is no more a theory of Latin America than noting the existence of different regions can be said to comprise a theory of United States development. Nor will simplified attempts at correlational analysis take us very far, since the Bolivian working class exhibits political influence well beyond their economic level of existence, and likewise, the organizational strength of the Chilean working class exhibits a marked superiority with respect to that of Argentinian workers who, in turn, have a higher economic life style.

For many years, between 1945 and 1965, the nation-by-nation accounting system has served to overcome traditionalist obstructions placed in the path of intelligent theory construction by the *pensadores* and *historiadores*. But compensation has led to overcompensation – to the idealization of the nation as a unique unit of analysis. The limits of the nation-building model of analysis have not been accounted for. The needs of constructing a usable theory for the continental complex have not been explored. Although a significant start in overcoming a reliance on linear models has been made by Rodolfo Stavenhagen, the debris of nonsensical, but widely held, notions of Latin America persists.[5] It is now imperative to elaborate upon generalizations that help us to comprehend the level at which Latin America does exist as a unit.

We should first consider certain assumptions about the nature of Latin American politics that may appear outrageous at first glance. Above all, we must take a critical look at the doctrine that demands for survival require the stable maintenance of a democratic, libertarian, or parliamentarian order. The likelihood is that the reverse is more nearly the case. In order for a political system to "survive" in Latin America, it must perennially change its policies and generate instability as a survival pattern. This is not to say that instability must be attributed to a deliberate plan. Rather, that the political-military complex can respond to latent structural sources of instability, such as population explosion, crop failures, transportation and communication breakdowns, etc., in such a way as to manipulate these structural deformities for the purpose of maintaining political illegitimacy.

The maintenance of political illegitimacy has deep roots in the colonial history of Latin America. Under the Spanish legal and political organization the king held a position above the law. But this formula also involved an acceptance rather than an imposition upon the masses. The basic juridical formula of the crown being above the law had as its corresponding political formula the idea of acceptance rather than violence. The non-violent character of illegitimacy makes possible its continuance even at present. As one scholar recently noted, "the rule of the Spanish king was authoritarian in the sense that it was not bound by legal enactments and regulations. Under the Spanish conception of law, the king was acting within the system of *derecho* but without being subject, in practice, to the *ley*. The term *derecho* refers to the system of law in general, including its philosophical and idealistic aspects. The word *ley* applies to enacted legislation. Although it might sound redundant, the Spanish monarch was in possession of an 'authoritarian' authority."[6] This trans-legal status of rulers, combined as it was with incredibly detailed laws binding the ruled to the State, is therefore a longstanding condition.

Let us then start with what might be termed the norm of illegitimacy, or the norm of conflict, and consider those norms based on a consensualist apparatus to be largely inoperative. This kind of approach provides something valid and valuable in the study of Latin American society, namely, the comprehension of illegitimacy as a style of "doing business". Such an approach allows us to ask an entirely different set of questions than is generally asked by nation-building approaches to Latin America: in effect, how has the area engendered an "institutionalization of crisis" as a *normative* pattern of politics?

The methodological component in this dilemma is that we have sound treatises on each nation *in* Latin America, but correspondingly unsound doctrines *on* Latin America. The sociology of international stratification is roughly equivalent to where the formal study of social stratification was a quarter of a century ago. The units of measure are different, but the problems are roughly analogous. The work of the thirties convinced many that crude measures of social class needed refinement. This led to a series of doctrines that treated every sub-class as a unique entity that was qualitatively distinct from other sub-classes. Now, in the study of Latin America, and as a reaction to the totalistic approaches of the "big thinkers" of the classical tradition, the nation or even parts of nations have come to be defined as unique entities that are qualitatively distinct from other nations in the hemisphere. Mexico, Brazil, and Argentina have produced their "exceptionalist" theorists in good number. At a time when some researchers have given up the quest for a unified theory of the hemisphere, they have pointedly produced a sophisticated body of literature that is qualitatively superior to what previously existed. Yet, even in the results achieved, a certain parallelism with social stratification doctrines of yesteryear can be detected. While there are sophisticated studies available of every nation in Latin America – Casanova on Mexico,[7] Germani on Argentina,[8] Furtado on Brazil,[9] Fals Borda on Colombia,[10] to name but a few – there is no significant study of Latin America as a whole which can serve as an explanatory theory about the continent. The position can now be taken that available nation-by-nation accounts have a fragmentizing effect on theoretical generalizations of a hemispheric dimension, and hence result in the general acceptance of static models of Latin American social structure.

To accept the idea of nation-building as fundamental is no less unsatisfactory than to accept the idea that class uniqueness defines all aspects of stratification. To begin with, it is hard to prove that the idea of nationality is any more powerful than that of religion, ethnicity, urbanism, industrialism, or any other organizing principle of social life. Indeed, in many nations, the idea of nationhood is a referent only for the urban middle classes. But beyond the formalistic objections that might be raised by a pluralistic framework is the empirical objection to nation-building approaches that would deny the reality of Latin America.[11] There *are* commonalities: in social history, in class composition, in political organization, in language cluster, and above all, in the common subordinate positions the nations of Latin America occupy with respect to the United States.

In dealing with Latin America as a real entity we are no longer confined to nation-building concepts. It is the line, perhaps the chain, between the United States center and the Latin American peripheries that becomes the organizing link for understanding what constitutes Latin America. The relations between nearly every nation of Latin America and the United

States are more direct (at the technological, political, and military levels) than the relations between any two nations within Latin America. This is particularly plain in the military sphere, where the United States is the organizing element which fuses the various hemispheric Defense Pacts, and which unabashedly provides an ideological cement to such operations.[12] This is not to deny the relevance of civil or military arrangements among Latin American nations, but only to indicate that such relations are derivative rather than originative, secondary rather than primary.[13] Therefore, in explaining the absence of legitimation in both its political and military aspects we are compelled to introduce the external factor, the role of imperialism.

Latin American élites, while neither impotent or unified, are not legitimized by a pluralist ideology, nor are they formed primarily through social demands from the masses. Therefore, such élites often lack valued skills of public administration or civic expertise on one side, and the sure knowledge of popular support on the other. These States often acquire power by unstructured methods. They breed counter-élites with a similar dismissal of technical standards of competence and a like contempt for the popular classes. What evolves are neo-Falangist systems. There is no élite in Latin America which simply legitimizes itself by legal succession of its power. Rather there are class columns of particularistic power, each a pillar supporting a weak public government, and each cancelling the potential for total power of the other classes or sectors. Falangism is basically a system where multiple élites have a mutual cancellation effect in order to support a public government structure. But also each has the power to prevent any other class or group from ruling for any extensive length of time. What each lacks is the power to maintain, establish, and legitimize that rule for a long period of time. In this way, Falangism promotes the personalist style, the *caudillo* system. But since Falangism is a model for maintaining delicate balances between groups of equal weight by a strong central leader, any displacement of weight creates a crisis in the system as a whole. That is why the area has been run more by Machiavellian foxes than by Platonic lions.

Revolution, or the *coup d'état*, is often greeted with a sigh of relief by participating social sectors, no matter what the political coloration of the régime or the class involved in the *golpe*. The constancy of such revolutions remains a means to alleviate the tension of groups pulling with equal strength in all directions at once. The *golpe* is a *politically* distributive mechanism without being a *socially* disruptive mechanism. It is a means of changing established policy. No government is thereby ever able to fully legitimize itself by electoral procedures alone, thus producing what I call the "norm of illegitimacy". Long-range periods of constitutional, or at any rate tranquil, government rule become a heavy price to pay for many élite groups whose bases of power remain insecure – or never were secure. They must act quickly, decisively, since candidates who fill office for a legally prescribed period become a threat. If national office is legitimized in electoral procedures, many traditionalistic pillars of society would collapse. It is precisely to prevent their own collapse that such élite groupings of Latin America institute a norm of illegitimacy. This situation has been appreciated by Charles Anderson, when he noted that "with the possible exception of Peron, political intervention by the military in Latin America does not seem to have the effect of overhauling the power system of the society. Rather, under military governments in Latin America, holders of important power capabilities in the society are assured that their position in the society will not be endangered, and are permitted some participation in the political process."[14]

Why are élite groupings of Latin America unable to develop legitimizing models, and why are working classes unable to develop revolutionary models? In part it is because the management of their affairs is oftentimes not in their own hands. For example, although the working class of Brazil may be well organized into unions, and even constitute a "labor aristocracy", the fact is that the unions themselves are often dependent on the whims of the political organization of the State apparatus. This was particularly true from Vargas to Goulart. The State apparatus, for its part, is contingent for its support upon coffee growers and the profits that they bring in from Parana. In turn, the coffee growers in the South are dependent on the international monetary system which regulates the price of coffee, and even regulates the supply of, and demand for, coffee. In other words, élite formations lack a leadership base to press their members' claims and are not free to bargain, to negotiate a public policy. These élites have status without corresponding power. They have enough status to counteract the pressure of other groups, but not enough power to rule. Only the military can act freely to establish new balances and relieve the strain of equal pull in all directions. This it may do by permitting new élite groups to penetrate the political processes, but this mediating role only makes the army the backbone of illegitimacy. The military are too tied into foreign interests themselves, and too involved with commercial activities, to do anything more than underwrite the norm of illegitimacy throughout the Hemisphere.

The most sophisticated stage of the internal dynamics of illegitimacy is when military structures are overturned by other portions of the military élite. This serves to circulate élites without running even the small risks in civilianization of the nation. This sort of military rule is clearly indicated by the fact that not long after the Ecuadorian National Congress was dissolved by the Military Junta, it allowed a Constituent Assembly to be elected on 16 October 1966, to write a new Constitution. More realistically, the three man army junta was overthrown by an air force group, who in turn underwrote the Conservative Party rule and appointed Otto Arosemena Gomez as interim President.[15] This indicates how extensive the norm of illegitimacy is in Latin American politics – a form of politics that the military are largely responsible for, and yet a form of rule clearly unsuited to long-range mass political mobilization. For this reason, among others, civilian parties continue to prevail in the formal political infrastructure. Thus, the most advanced form of the norm of illegitimacy is when a ruling military junta so much as threatens to civilianize itself, i.e., liberalize its conditions of rule; other portions of the military rapidly move into the political arena to sustain the norm of illegitimacy.

Now are nation-building and revolution-making related to one another? How do such interconnections fit into any known facts about Latin America?

To establish such a connection we have to appreciate the role of the Latin American *Samurai* – the free floating nineteenth-century *caudillo* turned professional twentieth-century officer in a situation that demanded nationalism, but disallowed populism.

Since the armed forces of Latin America are interest armies, the analysis of military phenomena cannot be based on one structural type of armed force, such as the federal army sponsored by the national State, but must take into account those military groupings representing other élite (or would-be élite) interests: regional armies and gendarmeries sponsored by local sub-governmental units; feudal and private armies sponsored by the superordinate class, race, or ethnic groups. This classification illustrates not simply the divisions within the military, but how the norm of illegitimacy finds organizational representation and ideological expression in the military sector no less than the political sector.

Militarism is not simply a professional activity in Latin America. Because of its internal control character it seeps into the life styles of Latin American society in a way which is uncharacteristic of other regions of the world. The military ethic is far more extensive and more potent than the simple numerical count of the size of the armed forces and general staff would reveal. Precisely because the military underwrites the militarization of civil administration, it reinforces illegitimacy, and becomes the key source of right-wing nationalism. Given its domination by international powers, its nationalism is more rhetorical than real.

It might be objected that this view tends to consider the military a foreign body in the structure of social classes. In point of fact, the military are clearly integrated into most Latin American societies. However, it is important to recognize that the military are not a social class in themselves, but rather function as extensions of certain classes, *i.e.*, they are attached to the landed aristocracy or to the urban middle classes. They only rarely act as a class for themselves, even if they sometimes seem to act as a group in themselves. This marginal role in the social structure accentuates the instability of overt military rule. They are compelled to solicit support from one or another sector of the class network; this then creates the basis for further *golpes* and illicit politics.

This satellitic role of the military is particularly apparent in Latin America, while particularly well hidden in the Middle East, because of the well-defined and longstanding class network existing in Latin America. The "Nasserist option" does not really obtain. Nasserism depends for its strength on an ill-formed, mis-shapen "classlessness" which exists primarily in many parts of the Middle East. The role of the military as a force for national development, such as the monumental achievement made by Ataturk and the Kemalist forces in Turkey, simply cannot be replicated in Latin America because of the well-established sophistication of class organization in Latin America. Therefore, if the military are not a "foreign body" in Latin America, neither are they a unique force chosen by history to determine the destiny of Latin America.

2. THE IMPERIAL DYNAMICS OF ILLEGITIMACY

Take three terms like "modernization", "industrialization", and "development", which in the social science literature are used with such remarkable interchangeability that one begins to wonder why three words are required at all. From my perspec-tive, however, these words not only mean entirely different things, but are often at odds with one another.[16] Consequently, we have a linguistic barrier to a unified theory of Latin America. The indicators which we have of the Latin continent used in connection with modernization, when employed with any degree of precision, seem to refer to things extending from electrifica-tion, creature comforts, the construction of supermarkets and highways to the unfolding of innovative cultural forms.

Many indicators of modernization – life expectancy, literacy of the masses, sophisticated communication and transportation networks – seem to link up with the urban process. Indeed, modernization is oftentimes used as a surrogate for the urban process. On the other hand, the concept of development is often spoken of as a surrogate for industrialization. The measures used in defining economic development are intimately linked to industry – *per capita* national production, the consumption of energy, the population employed in business, commerce, and service industries. This distinction between modernization and industrialization is not simply academic. Even if we confine ourselves to the above measures, it is plain that the degree of modernization can diverge radically from that of industrialization. Argentina is as "modern" a society as West Germany, while both Brazil and Mexico are much closer to the big three of the United States, England, and Germany than they are to the Afro-Asian new nations. However, if we substitute measures of industrial potency, developmental levels reveal themselves to be radically different from modernization scales. At the industrial level, Argentina and Brazil come up as being more akin to the Congo and Haiti, rather than to the big three western powers.[17] Seen in this light, the ideology behind the "revolution in rising expectations" is anchored to the modernization process, while the ideology of "revolution from below" is clearly anchored to the industrialization process. Thus, development might be said to encompass a double interchange – the interaction of modernization and industrialization forming the core problems of developmental processes and strategies alike.

Economic theory has been adopted to clarify these differences between modernization and industrialization. However, it cannot go beyond its own limits as a science; it can ably *translate* into a more precise language the dilemmas of development, but it is no more in a position to *resolve* these dilemmas than phrenology was able to settle problems of mental disorder. Monetarism has been used, especially in present-day Brazil and Argentina, as a device for moving beyond the import-substitution bottleneck into the modern economic sector without revolution. Structuralism has been used, especially in Mexico in the thirties, Cuba in the sixties, and now to a lesser extent in Chile, to overcome import substitution bottlenecks by creating a more potent national heavy industrial and mining pattern. The link of structuralism is to industrialization what the link of monetarism is to modernization.[18]

Each strategy of economic growth has its own strains, and

each creates political spinoffs. The monetaristic solutions create internal colonial stress by sharpening the conflict between have and have-not sectors, between the largely urban sectors and the largely rural sectors. Thus modernization creates the seeds of social disequilibrium by sharpening the strain between sectors. The structuralistic solutions, in an effort to escape the control by foreign imperial economies of their national economy, face a different set of problems, but a set no less harsh in its implications. In order to lay the basis of an industrial society, a considerable amount of sacrifice is required of the lower classes, the rural classes, and even the middle classes. But what is sacrificed is precisely what monetarism can buy: creature comforts and high standards of personal living, nothing short of the most visible results of "modernization". Thus, structuralism too creates a strain toward disequilibrium within the underdeveloped societies of Latin America.

In short, monetarism and structuralism, which both start out with great expectations to alleviate the material conditions which create revolutions, seem to terminate as economic ideologies inadvertently inducing that which is most dreaded in the other – further dependence on the external economic sector.[19]

Modernization and developmental orientations do not exclude revolutionary alternatives and may parallel an increase rather than a decrease in revolutionary sentiment. The problem of this paradoxical convergence is this: Latin Americans perceive the most modern results of technology; but rarely do they acquire the industrial means for creating such results on an autonomous basis. Attempts to emulate and replicate specific national models oftentimes end in frustration and puzzlement. Frustration of mass goals, which is produced as much by the awareness of cases of advancement as by failure to reach it, makes for revolutionary types of people and for revolutionary types of situations. Revolutionary sentiments are not simply a consequence of underdevelopment, but more properly a result of polarization between developed and underdeveloped sectors. And these polarities confront each other in Latin America not exclusively as a class question, but as a question in international stratification. The large-scale foreign corporation, along with the large-scale penetration of foreign military-bureaucratic forces, produces the same effect in the "periphery" as it does at the "cosmopolitan center": it serves to absorb foreign wealth and soak up foreign labor power.

The factor of illegitimacy is enhanced by the simple device of removing basic strategy decisions from the Latin American orbit, and centering them in the imperial concentration points. To execute such control successfully, however, a portion of the Latin American decision-making élites, whether military or civilian in background or occupation, becomes intimately involved in the satisfactory conduct of the local groupings. Thus, instead of being linked to the developmental process, a portion of the local élites becomes tied to the security of foreign investments. Since this imperial dynamics has the deeper effect of placing the legitimating agencies in foreign control, the actions of the nation-State system in Latin America tend heavily to become repressive. The norm of illegitimacy is therefore guaranteed by an imperial system that sees the constant circulation of local élites as beneficial to its own interests.

The power of the imperial center to determine the forms of Latin American societies is perhaps best illustrated by the case of Bolivia. This country exhibited many tendencies present in Mexico and Cuba: an authentic popular revolution (of the MNR in 1952), a powerful trade union organization, and widespread political mobilization – conditions which are clearly necessary ingredients in any model based on legitimation from below. However, the economic fortunes of the nation, while emancipated from "internal colonialists", remained linked (more firmly than ever) to the foreign purchasers of Bolivian natural resources. The radical labor movement, which had the power to cancel national bourgeoisie, found itself overmatched in competition with the international bourgeoisie. Bolivia became the most heavily subsidized nation *per capita* in the entire world (including all the Near Eastern nations). The United States became the effective underwriter of what was supposedly the most radical political structure in South America. But if the Bolivian miner found his wages improved over pre-revolutionary times, the Bolivian political structure found itself even more dependent on foreign capital than in the pre-revolutionary era. Thus, far from guaranteeing legitimacy from below, such foreign imperial dominion only returned the situation to a *status-quo-ante*, in which the military sector performed its classic function of guaranteeing survival through illegitimacy.

Although it is readily admitted that United States policy, at both the diplomatic and defense levels, is a contributory factor to Latin American militarism, such an admission still perceives of such intervention as a response to, or a product of, local circumstances. I would advance the proposition that what has taken place in increasing degrees is the foreign management of internal conflicts in Latin America. This raises the possibility of a new United States imperialism based on political rather than economic considerations, and therefore tactically dedicated to indirect management of Latin American military establishments rather than direct interventionism. With the rise of overall strategies on a grand scale, with the assertion that the basic purpose of American national policy is to promote and secure a structure of hemispheric relationships compatible with the values of the United States, local control, idiosyncratic régimes, and classical Latin American strongmen must themselves be bridled – so that the local military no less than the local political administration are plugged into the norm of illegitimacy as a way of maintaining stability by virtue of the requirements of *Pax Americana*.

The new imperialism is conducted largely through political policy whose principal instrument is military assistance, with increasing emphasis on the preparation of the armed forces for counterinsurgency operations. As General Porter made perfectly plain in Congressional testimony, the aims of security must take priority over national development. "The Military has frequently proven to be the most cohesive force available to assure public order and support of resolute governments attempting to maintain internal security. Latin American armed forces, acting in conjunction with the police and other security forces, have helped to control disorders and riots, contained or eliminated terrorists and guerrillas, and discouraged those elements which are tempted to resort to violence to overthrow the government."[20] It will be observed that illegitimacy of rule is markedly different from the uses of violence as an agency of mass political mobilization. For what the imperial center requires is a continuation of illegitimacy, but not a continuation of violence. Hence, the classic function of the *coup d'état* is aborted. It becomes an instrument to prevent, rather than stimulate, rapid, unchallenged social change.

The norm of illegitimacy is underwritten by military assistance programs that transform disparate peripheral and regional military *caciques* representing indigenous factors, into a highly coordinated and unified grouping representing an international commitment against communist penetration of the Hemisphere. Joint military operations between the nations of Latin and North America, standardization of equipment, arranging central command structures, increasing conferences, and meetings at regional as well as continental levels – all of these serve to transform randomized types of illegitimate rule into a normative pattern of illegitimacy, or at the least a search for order in trans-national terms, *i.e.*, in terms of the interests of the cosmopolitan center.

Such programs, however, circumscribe the level and form of the political activity of Latin American military establishments. They are faced with the choice of supporting United States policy for developing counter-insurgency capabilities (and hence undermining any sort of legitimation that would be derived from mass participatory revolution), or supporting nationalistic factions and jeopardizing their foreign assistance pacts (and hence negating the military élite as a factor in policy-making in Latin America). Whatever the particular decisions taken now, United States policies of military globalism tend to make obsolete earlier efforts at a standard typology of Latin American military styles and forms based exclusively on internal political affairs.

There are severe limits placed upon any autonomous developmental pattern in Latin America. To be sure, these are old nations which have long histories. They are also far more developed than most Asian countries and most African countries in terms of the size of their respective modernized sectors. But the most important point is that Latin America shows the face of the future to other sectors of the third world. It reveals plainly that liberation from colonialism is radically different

from liberation from imperialism. Indeed, the positive termina-
tion of the colonial phase may, as a matter of fact, stimulate
imperial investment – both in terms of money and man-power.
Furtado has expressed the special characteristics of economic
instability which made possible the current imperial stage of
illegitimacy. "In Latin America, development induced by the
industrial revolution in Europe and the United States was enough
to transform part of the economic systems inherited from the
colonial epoch, but not enough to create autonomous systems
able to generate further growth. Hence, Latin America remained
on the 'periphery' of advanced industrial economies at a time
when markets for primary products were far from able to generate the dynamism required."[21]

The norm of illegitimacy can arise only in a context where
structural requisites for legitimate authority are absent. Legitimate authority can be institutionalized either through mechanisms of law or through mechanisms of class. But if mechanisms
of law are inadequate to meet the demands of the society, and
mechanisms of class are too underdeveloped to come to the fore,
and if both the legal machinery of the State and the class potency
of the State are blocked by imperial factors, then the whole
discussion of the nature of the legitimation process involves an
examination of imperialism.[22] Modernization and industrialization express the contradiction in developmental terms, just as
imperialism and nationalism express the contradiction in geopolitical terms. For this reason the connections between these
dual processes are necessary to understand if a theory of legitimation is to be forged.

It might be asked: Why doesn't a similar imperialism lead to
similar results the world over? If there is an imperialist factor,
should it not show up as roughly equivalent in its inputs and
consequences the world over? One response that presents itself
is that the United States has differential commitments the world
over; hence radically different consequences flow from its involvement. When one speaks of the "overextension of United
States commitment", it is hard to imagine that Africa can be
viewed in the same way as Latin America. Although a similar
set of "interests" may obtain, there are widely varying "obliga-

tions". The basic problem for the United States in the second half of the twentieth century is its "security". In determining this security, the place of Latin America is far more central than that of Africa. In Latin America, development induced by the industrial revolution was enough to transform part of the economic system inherited from the colonial epoch, but not enough to create an autonomous system capable of generating autonomous growth. In this, Latin America, precisely because of its profound *modernization*, is more directly linked to the cosmopolitan centers of industrialism than are the nations of Africa and Asia. The latter remain traditional, but also politically far more mobile and free-wheeling. Thus, the special relationship of Latin America for North America, and vice versa, creates a special set of results.

In the nineteenth century, imperialism was a less weighty phenomenon than now. However, if we take the relationship of the British Empire to the growth of Brazil, or if we examine the history of British colonial overseas relationships in Argentina in the nineteenth century, we will see everything from the organization of the cattle industry to the organization of the railroads directly related to the impact of the overseas factor. Whether we consider Spanish colonial rule in the eighteenth century, British colonial rule in the nineteenth century, or United States colonial rule in the twentieth century, one of the essential constants in Latin America – however shifting in form – has been the presence of an imperial factor. And it is the interpretation of traditional-istic classes with highly sophisticated international monetary élites that provides the material bases for the norm of illegitimacy.

What becomes clear is that the norm of illegitimacy is service-able both to the internal needs of the political-military order which gives visible direction to Latin American policies, and to the international needs of the economic order which limits the directions that the indigenous elements may chance upon. Thus, nationalism from within and imperialism from without, far from being at loggerheads over the management of Latin America, serve more often than not to complement each other. The touch-ing faith in nationalist solutions as a means for transcending imperial domination simply ignores the character of the national-isms manifested in Latin America. The nationalism of the Right, which has prevailed in nearly every country of the Southern Hemisphere, offers scant optimism for avoiding imperial control. Indeed, such "nationalist" leaders of the "whole people" as Juan Perón, Getulio Vargas, and Rojas Pinilla were compelled to abandon their optimal plans for a countervailing imperialism of the Southern Hemisphere and settle for a "partnership" with foreign corporate wealth. They were trapped in the supreme contradiction of satisfying the requirements of the neo-Falangist élite arrangement, and hence having to finance their nationalistic ambitions through outside sources, the much maligned foreign capital.

Given this set of circumstances, a theory of Latin America cannot avoid being incorporated into a larger framework of the interplay of nationalism and colonialism. The definition of Latin America is itself a consequence of this interplay. If this formu-lation strikes the observer as crude, lacking in sophistication, so be it! The objective situation is itself crude and lacking in sophistication. The norm of illegitimacy is informally sanctioned from the lowest petty official living off bribes in some remote customs house in Asuncion or São Paulo to the highest official living off the mineral produce of Latin America in some highly visible counting house in New York or London. To break the cycle of crisis and collapse, to eliminate the norm of illegitimacy as an operational code for Latin America, means to break the organizational impasse created by both local bureaucrats and imported businessmen.

APPENDIX: SOME QUALIFYING ASPECTS TO THE NORM OF ILLEGITIMACY

As I indicated at the outset, we do not have any adequate general social theory of Latin America. And although I would maintain that the kind of approach outlined in my paper, focusing on the interpenetration of national élites and imperial investors, is the main pivot in a system of survival through illegitimacy, this by no means explains the actual behavior of *all* Latin American nations. While it might be quite serviceable for sixteen of them, there are at least four cases where the norm of illegitimacy does not obtain – certainly not in "ideal-typical" form. They are Chile, Cuba, Mexico, and Uruguay (and perhaps Costa Rica). But rather than resort to a mobilization-integration model[23] which indeed was a first serviceable attempt at a general theory, I should rather like to explain why, at least in two cases – those of Mexico and Uruguay – the norm of illegitimacy does not presently obtain.[24]

The first fact to take into consideration about Uruguay is that from its inception there existed a relatively strong parallel dualism: a rural political party representing landholding economic interests; and an urban party representing middle class and organized working class interests. The stability of its political system was therefore more a result of the neatness in the division of power, in the stability of the equilibrium, than in any perfectly meshed network of mass mobilization and integration.[25]

The neatness of class and élite divisions is itself a consequence of the second major fact about Uruguay. It evolved as a buffer State separating the two titans of the Southern Hemisphere: Brazil and Argentina. Thus, it comes into existence without the myriad of sub-class pressure groups and shadow élites which pervade nearly every other nation in the Hemisphere. Uruguay has no need to call upon the military to expand or contract civil power, since the balancing act was achieved by administrative fiat at the start of its national independence period. At the same time, Uruguay is in a position to function in terms of legitimate authority, since such small-nation legitimacy itself provides essential security to the large nations with which it borders. Whatever the nature of Brazilian and Argentine politics, they nonetheless retain a shared interest in seeing to it that Uruguay is run on at least semi-democratic principles.

At the same time, the satellitic aspects of Uruguay are also reinforced by the fact that, like Denmark and Finland in Europe, Uruguay is a modernized nation and not a developmental nation. It has been moved to evolve satellitic economic relations without sacrificing its political autonomy. Indeed, Uruguay has engaged in an historic trade-off characteristic of a number of more advanced small nations: it performs a willing (or at least a know-ing) satellitic economic role in exchange for a guarantee of political sovereignty.

The exceptional circumstances in Uruguay's historical evolu-tion: its parity of class cleavage and absence of parasitic sectors, and its trade-off of economic independence for political sover-eignty, serve to explain why this small "Switzerland of the Western Hemisphere" is able to escape the hard fate of its more powerful neighbors. Yet it would not be quite accurate to say that Uruguay is a legitimate polity in the classical sense, since what one finds is a peculiar "withering away" of State power. The political system in Uruguay serves to allocate bureau-cratic functions and to adjudicate the claims of various social factions; however, it does not have real autonomous powers to act. This situation could thus be described as semi-legitimacy.

In a country like Mexico one might inquire: Does not legiti-mate authority obtain? Do you not have the orderly transfer of power? Have you had any revolutionary upheavals since the revolution of 1920? Is there any evidence of a military *coup d'état* coming? Surely, if the question of legitimacy is linked to the satisfactory management of succession crises, Mexico would be the direct opposite of Argentina or Peru. But is such a criterion of formalistic succession on much better footing than personal charisma? Several kinds of answers can be fashioned.

Mexico did have a twentieth-century national revolution which at the very least gives to it a degree of autonomy absent in most other countries in the Hemisphere. But Mexico is now undergoing a crisis of a very profound sort. Mexico is a single-party State. It has one major party which regularly receives between 85 and 90 per cent of the vote; two minor parties, one Left and one Right, share the remaining ballots. The choice of officialdom is increasingly becoming internal through the party mechanism. The party mechanism of PRI is becoming a political IBM system: balancing out the needs, requests, and demands of different sectors. The Mexican polity has been properly character-ized as "a complicated system of exchanges between interest groups and an oligarchy that provides decisive and sometimes rather ruthless leadership".[26] The pillars of power are becoming increasingly uneven, and the possibility of tumultuous change is pressing.

The crisis has not been made manifest in Mexico precisely because the public sector of the economy has become so powerful, bureaucratic, and entrenched that it is even hard for a class such as the private industrial class to exercise any autonomous power. The Mexican military budget has been considerably enlarged in the last three years. The widely reported growth of sporadic guerrilla insurgency, and the recent student riots at the National University of Mexico, have each indicated the growth of illegitimate forms of political behavior. The steady investment in domestic rather than foreign industry taking place in Mexico has exacted a great toll from the national working classes. The high growth rate of Mexico's economy prevents any outbreak of mass violence. But what would take place if there were a growth rate decline, or a weakening of Mexico's economy as a result of a concerted boycott by the Central American Trade Association, is difficult to ascertain.

In a country like Mexico the abortive character of the 1910–20 Revolution is beginning to have its effects. Nonetheless, it should be kept in mind that Mexico remains one of the most *stable* régimes in the Hemisphere. Yet even a background in revolution does not exempt Mexico from the legitimacy crisis. For although Mexico achieved its legitimacy through mass revolution, it was able to guarantee its polity only in the thirties, when it successfully carried through an oil nationalization plan that met with the hearty disapprobation of the United States. The Mexican problem is how to maintain this network of legitimacy in a period when its economic resources are now large enough to compete with the United States at least on a regional basis, but not powerful enough to cancel United States interests as a whole. How Mexico can manage the dynamics of imperialism will thus become a critical factor in evaluating its long run chances for legitimate rule to perpetuate itself much longer.

Therefore, as in the case of Uruguay, Mexico too reveals a peculiar deterioration of State power, or at least its inability to define its power in any context other than that provided by the ruling political party. The Mexican State does not have powers to act; the PRI does have such powers. In this situation, where the party rather than the polity is endowed with legitimacy, this condition could be described as *quasi-legitimacy*.

In the two negative cases introduced – Uruguay and Mexico – what one finds on inspection is not simply a generalized confrontation of legitimate versus illegitimate forms of polity, but rather some sophisticated shadings that reveal elements of both, and virtues (or vices) of neither.

NOTES

[1] Compare and contrast Karl Marx and Friedrich Engels, *Manifesto of the Communist Party* (New York: International Publishers, 1932), pp. 31–2, with Max Weber, *The Theory of Social and Economic Organization* (New York: Oxford University Press, 1947), p. 154.

[2] The best example of this kind of approach is in United States Department of Defense, "Civic Action: The Military Role in Nation-Building", in *Armed Forces Information and Education*, Vol. III, No. 14 (Jan. 15, 1964). For a more recent example along similar lines, see Willard F. Barber, "The American Concept of Counterinsurgency: Some Latin American Applications", presented at the American Association for the Advancement of Science, Washington, D.C., Dec. 26, 1966 (mimeographed).

[3] I have attempted to summarize the position of Latin American military in my study "The Military Élites", in Seymour Martin Lipset and Aldo Solari (eds.), *Elites in Latin America* (New York: Oxford University Press, 1967), pp. 146–89.

[4] Torcuato Di Tella has pointed out key differences related to these situations and provided a useful typology for examining working-class organization. See *El sistema político argentino y la clase obrera* (Buenos Aires: Editorial Universitaria de Buenos Aires, 1964); see also his paper "Populism and the Working Class in Latin America", in *Government and Politics in Latin America* (New York: Frederick A. Praeger, 1967).

[5] Rodolfo Stavenhagen, "Seven Erroneous Theses about Latin America", in *New University Thought*, Vol. 4, No. 4 (Winter 1966/67), pp. 25–37.

[6] Frank Jay Moreno, "The Spanish Colonial System: A Functional Approach", in *The Western Political Quarterly*, Vol. XX, No. 2, Part 1 (June 1967), pp. 308–20.

[7] Pablo González Casanova, *La democracia en México* (Mexico City: Ediciones Era, 1965).

[8] Gino Germani, *Estructura Social de la Argentina* (Buenos Aires: Editorial Raigal, 1955); and *Politica y Sociedad en una Epoca de Transición: De la sociedad tradicional a la sociedad de masas* (Buenos Aires: Editorial Paidos, 1962).

[9] Celso Furtado, *The Economic Growth of Brazil* (Berkeley and Los Angeles: University of California Press, 1963); and *Diagnosis of the Brazilian Crisis* (Berkeley and Los Angeles: University of California Press, 1965).

[10] Orlando Fals-Borda (with Herman Guzman Campos and Eduardo Umana Luna), *La violencia en Colombia: Estudio de un proceso social* (Bogata: Ediciones Tercer Mundo, 2nd edition 1963); *La subversion en Colombia: el cambio social en la historia* (Bogata: Ediciones Tercer Mundo, 1967).

[11] One scholar who has come to appreciate the reality of Latin America and to use it as an organizing principle in his work is Donald Marquand Dozer; see *Latin America: An Interpretative History* (New York: McGraw-Hill Book Co., 1962).

[12] See in particular the statement by General Robert W. Porter, Jr., U.S.A. Commander in Chief, United States Southern Command (Panama), before the House Foreign Affairs Committee on the FY 1968 Military Assistance Program (25 April, 1967).

[13] See on this Juan Saxe-Fernández, "El consejo de defensa Centroamericano y la *Pax Americana*", in *Cuadernos Americanos*, Vol. CLII, No. 3 (May–June 1967), pp. 39–57.

[14] Charles W. Anderson, "Toward a Theory of Latin American Politics", in Occasional Paper No. 2 in *The Graduate Center for Latin American Studies* (Nashville: Vanderbilt University, February 1964).

[15] Cf. Walter H. Mallory (ed.), *Political Handbook and Atlas of the World: 1967* (New York and Evanston: Harper & Row, 1967).

[16] I have tried to express the nature of such terminological differences in *Three Worlds of Development: The Theory and Practice of International Stratification* (New York and London: Oxford University Press, 1966).

[17] See on this G. Germani, *Politica y Sociedad* . . . (*op. cit*).

[18] See on this David Felix, "Monetarists, Structuralists, and Import-Substituting Industrialization", in *Studies in Comparative International Development*, Vol. I, No. 10 (1965), pp. 137–53.

[19] This dovetailing of outcomes between monetarism and structuralism is made painfully, if inadvertently, clear in the set of papers *Inflation and Growth in Latin America*, Werner Baer and Isaac

Kerstenetzky (eds.), a publication of the Economic Growth Center, Yale University (Illinois: Richard D. Irwin, Inc., 1964).

[20] Robert W. Porter, Jr., *op. cit.* For confirmation that Porter represents the dominant U.S. policy, and not simply an idiosyncratic viewpoint, see the testimony of Lincoln Gordon, "Foreign Assistance Act of 1966", in *Hearings Before the House Committee on Foreign Affairs* (Washington: USGPO, 1966), p. 372; and Richard R. Clark, "U.S. Military Assistance in Latin America", in *Army Digest* (Sept. 1966), pp. 18–19.

[21] Celso Furtado, "U.S. Hegemony and the Future of Latin America", in *The World Today: The Royal Institute of International Affairs*, Vol. 22, No. 9 (Sept. 1966), pp. 375–85.

[22] Whatever the evidential shortcomings, this response to the logic of the situation is well appreciated by Andre Gunder Frank in his work *Capitalism and Underdevelopment in Latin America: Historical Studies of Chile and Brazil* (New York and London: Monthly Review Press, 1967).

[23] G. Germani, "Social Change and Intergroup Conflicts", in I. L. Horowitz (ed.), *The New Sociology* (New York and London: Oxford University Press, 1964), pp. 391–408.

[24] My reasons for omitting Cuba and Chile from consideration here are that, in the case of Cuba, I have attempted to provide some sort of accounting elsewhere; see "The Stalinization of Castro", in *New Politics*, Vol. IV, No. 4 (1966), and "Cuban Communism" in *Trans-Action*, Vol. 4, No. 10 (Oct. 1966). In the case of Chile, my knowledge is far too limited to make an attempt at even an educated guess.

[25] See on this my study "La politica urbana en Latinoamérica", in *Revista Mexicana de Sociologia*, Vol. VIII, No. 1 (Jan. 1967). I might add in this connection that the discussion on Uruguay was omitted from the English language version of this paper.

[26] Bo Anderson and James D. Cockroft, "Cooptation in Mexican Politics", in *International Journal of Comparative Sociology*, Vol. 7, No. 1 (March 1966), pp. 11–28.

4

Violence, Revolution and Structural Change in Latin America*

A great deal is being written in America these days about Pax Americana and American hegemony in the underdeveloped world. No longer able to blot out the obvious, even calm, rational, conscientious academics are publicly lamenting America's increasingly bellicose policies from Vietnam to the Dominican Republic. Suddenly, as if awakened from a techni-colored dream, intellectuals are discovering such words as "imperialism" and "expansionism". And they are asking: Why? Who's to blame? What can be done to stop all this?

The questions are childish, the assumptions false, the implica-tions naïve. They reflect a liberal point of view, one that claims there is a qualitative difference between U.S. policies today and yesterday. In fact, American foreign policy has varied only in degree, not in kind. It has been cohesive, coherent and consistent. What has varied has been its strength – and its critics.

The basic difference between American imperialism today and American imperialism a century ago is that it is more violent, more far-reaching and more carefully planned today. But American foreign policy, at least since 1823, has always been assertive, always expansionist, always imperialist. Of course, it has rarely been pushed beyond America's capabilities. Thus, when the United States was weak, its interventions abroad were mild. When its strength grew, so did its daring. Today, as the most powerful nation on earth, with a technological advance over other countries of mammoth proportions, the United States can be imperialistic on all continents with relative security.

* by John Gerassi.

The main reason why we have not had the opportunity to discuss this imperialism frankly and openly within the United States, in its journals, in academia, and on platforms, is because Americans' interpretation of history has been dominated by liberal historians whose basic view of life is characterized by their inability or unwillingness to connect events. Thus, when viewing Latin America, where American policy has always been crystal clear, American historians will admit, indeed will detail, United States interventions in specific countries of Central America or the Caribbean, will sometimes even posit an imperialist explanation for a whole period of American history, but will never draw over-all conclusions, will never connect events, economics, and politics to arrive at a basic tradition or characteristic. To such historians, for example, there is little if any correlation between the events and policies of 1823 and those of 1845, between 1898 and 1961.

Most liberal historians will admit today that the United States has often been imperialistic in Latin America up to 1933. Yet, slaves of their own rhetoric, they will inevitably cite the rhetoric of Franklin Delano Roosevelt, the greatest liberal of them all, to insist that with the New Deal American imperialism came to an end. They can make this statement because they are committed to the proposition that it is the American State Department which makes foreign policy – simply because it is supposed to – and also because of their own fear of being identified with Marxist ideology, a fear that leads them to refuse to interpret imperialism as economic.

Rare is the liberal historian who first asks himself just what is imperialism or, if he does, rarer still is he who simply and succinctly admits that imperialism is a policy aimed at material gain. And this, in spite of the fact that he knows full well that there has never been a stronger or more consistent justification for intervening in the affairs of other countries than the expectation to derive material benefit therefrom. Imperialism has always operated in three specific, recognizable and analyzable stages: (1) to control the sources of raw material for the benefit of the imperializing country; (2) to control the markets in the imperialized country for the benefit of the imperializing country's producers; and (3) to control the imperialized country's internal development and economic structure so as to guarantee continuing expansion of stages (1) and (2).

That has been our policy in Latin America. It began in recognizable manner in 1823 with the declaration of President Monroe warning non-hemisphere nations to stay out of the American continent. Because of its rhetoric, America's liberal historians interpreted the Monroe Doctrine as a generous, even altruistic declaration on the part of the United States to protect its weaker neighbors to the south. To those neighbors, however, that doctrine asserted America's ambitions; it said, in effect, Europeans stay out of Latin America because it belongs to the United States. A liberal, but not an American, Salvador de Madariaga, once explained its hold on Americans:

> I only know two things about the Monroe Doctrine: one is that no American I have met knows what it is; the other is that no American I have met will consent to its being tampered with. That being so, I conclude that the Monroe Doctrine is not a doctrine but a dogma, for such are the two features by which you can tell a dogma. But when I look closer into it, I find that it is not one dogma, but two, to wit: the dogma of the infallibility of the American President and the dogma of the immaculate conception of American foreign policy.[1]

Indeed, in the year 1824, Secretary of State (later President) John Quincy Adams made the Monroe Doctrine unequivocally clear when he told Simon Bolivar, one of Latin America's great liberators, to stay out of – that is, not liberate – Cuba and Puerto Rico which were still under the Spanish yoke. The Monroe Doctrine, said Adams, "must not be interpreted as authorization for the weak to be insolent with the strong". Two years later, the United States refused to attend the first Pan American Conference called by Bolivar in Panama for the creation of a United States of Latin America. Further, the United States used its influence and its strength to torpedo that conference because a united Latin America would offer strong competition to American ambitions, on the continent as well as beyond.

The conference failed and Bolivar concluded, in 1829, that "the United States appear to be destined by Providence to plague America with misery in the name of liberty".

Nor was the United States yet ready to put the Monroe Doctrine into effect against European powers, at least not if they were strong. In 1833, for example, England invaded the Falkland Islands, belonging to Argentina, and instead of invoking the Monroe Doctrine to stop England, the United States supported it. England still owns those islands today. Two years later, the United States allowed England to occupy the northern coast of Honduras, which is still British Honduras. England then invaded Guatemala, tripled its Honduras territory and, in 1839, took over the island of Roatan. Instead of reacting, the United States moved against Mexico. Within a few years Mexico lost half of its territory, the richest half, to the United States.

In 1854, the United States settled a minor argument with Nicaragua by sending a warship to bombard San Juan Del Norte. Three years later, when one American citizen was wounded there and President Buchanan levied a fine of $20,000 which Nicaragua couldn't pay, the United States repeated the bombardment, following it with marines who proceeded to burn down anything that was still standing. The next year, the United States forced Nicaragua to sign the Cass-Irisarri treaty which gave the United States the right of free passage anywhere on Nicaraguan soil and the right to intervene in its affairs for whatever purpose the United States saw fit. If that doesn't make America's material interest obvious to a liberal, nothing will.

The liberal historian will insist, however, that during this period the State Department was often isolationist, indeed that it tried to enforce America's neutrality laws strictly. That is true, but that does not mean, once again, that America was not imperialistic, for policy was not – and is not – made by the State Department but by those who profit from it. This was quite clear during the filibuster era when American privateers raised armies and headed south to conquer areas for private American firms. In 1855, for example, William Walker, a Nashville-born doctor, lawyer and journalist, who practiced none of these professions, invaded Nicaragua, captured Granada and had himself "elected" President of Nicaragua. He then sent a message to President Franklin Pierce asking that Nicaragua be admitted to the Union as a slave state, even though Nicaragua had long out-lawed slavery. Walker was operating for private American corporations bent on exploiting Central America. The trouble was that these companies were the rivals of Cornelius Vander-bilt's Accessory Transit Company whose concessions Walker, as "President", canceled. Vanderbilt thereupon threw his weight, money, and power behind other forces and they defeated Walker at Santa Rosa. He was then handed over to the United States Navy, brought back to the United States and tried for violating neutrality laws. This had happened to him once before after failing to conquer lower California and he had then been acquit-ted. Now, he was again acquitted and, in fact, cheered by the sympathetic jury.

Was the jury corrupt? Was it imperialist itself? Or was it simply reflecting the teachings, the propaganda, the atmosphere of the United States?

When the first colonisers to the United States had successfully established viable societies in their new land, they launched themselves westward. Liberal historians tell us that this great pioneering spurt was truly a magnificent impulse, a golden asset in America's formation. In their expansionism to the west, the early Americans were ruthless, systematically wiping out the whole indigenous population. But they were successful and, by and large, that expansion was completed without sacrificing too many of the basic civil rights of the white settlers. Thus, early America began to take pride in its system.

Later, as American entrepreneurs launched the industrializa-tion of their country, they were equally successful. In the process, they exploited the new settlers, *i.e.* the working class, and their children, but they built a strong economy. So once again they showed themselves, and the world, that America was a great country, so great in fact that it could not – should not – stop at its own borders. As these entrepreneurs expanded beyond America's borders, mostly via the sea, and so developed America's naval power, they were again successful. Thus once again they proved that their country was great.

It did not matter that Jeffersonian democracy, which liberal historians praise as the moral backbone of America's current power, rested on the "haves" and excluded the "have nots" (to the point of not allowing the property-less to vote). Nor did it matter that Jacksonian democracy, which liberal historians praise even more, functioned in a ruthless totalitarian setting in which one sector of the economy attempted and, by and large, succeeded in crushing another. The rhetoric was pure, the results formidable, and therefore the system perfect. That system became known as "The American Way of Life", a way of life in which the successful were the good, the unsuccessful the bad. America was founded very early on the basic premise that he who is poor deserves to be poor; he who is rich is entitled to the fruit of his power.

Since America was big enough and rich enough to allow its entrepreneurs to become tycoons while also allowing the poor to demand a fair shake – civil rights and a certain mobility – the rhetoric justifying all the murders and all the exploitations became a theory. Out of the theory grew the conviction that America was the greatest country in the world precisely because it allowed self-determination. From there it was only a step to the conclusion that any country which could do the same would be equally great. The corollary, of course, was that those who did not would not be great. Finally, it became clear to all Americans that he who is great is good. The American Way of Life became the personification of morality.

From America's pride in its way of life followed its right to impose that way of life on non-Americans. Americans became superior, self-righteous and pure. The net result was that a new Jesuit company was formed. It too carried the sword and the cross. America's sword was its marines, its cross was "American democracy". Under that cross, as under the cross brandished about by the conquistadors of colonial Spain, the United States rationalized its colonialism. Naval Captain Alfred Thayer Mahan even developed a theory based on social Darwinism to prove that history is a struggle of the strongest and fittest to survive.[2] The Protestant clergy also joined in to ennoble American imperialism.[3]

The jury that tried Walker for violating America's neutrality laws, which he had clearly violated, expressed that imperialist duty and colonialist spirit when it cheered Walker out of the court. It was simply reflecting its deep-rooted conviction that Nicaragua would be better off as a slave state in the Union than as a free country outside of it. To that jury, as to the American people today, there can be only one democratic system worthy of the name – the American. There can be only one definition of freedom – American free enterprise. Thus, there is no need for the State Department to proclaim an imperialist policy; the Vanderbilts or the Rockefellers or the Guggenheims, the United Fruit Company or the Hanna Mining Company or the Anaconda Company can do what they please. After all, they represent democracy, they are the embodiment of freedom. What's more, they know that when the chips are down, America might will stand behind them – or in front.

Within the last century, America's colonial expansionism, based on and strengthened by the American Way of Life, has become consistently bolder. In 1860, the United States intervened in Honduras. In 1871 it occupied Samana Bay in Santo Domingo. In 1881 it joined Peru in its war against Chile in exchange for the port Chimbote (as a United States naval base), nearby coal mines and a railroad from the mines to the port. In 1885 it again torpedoed the Central American Federation because such an organization might jeopardize an Atlantic–Pacific canal owned by the United States.

Meanwhile, in 1884, official United States Government commercial missions were launched throughout Latin America for one purpose only and, as one such mission reported, that purpose was successfully carried out: "Our countrymen easily lead in nearly every major town. In every republic will be found businessmen with wide circles of influence. Moreover, resident merchants offer the best means to introduce and increase the use of our goods." (Nothing, of course, has changed in this respect. Notice, for example, a report in *Newsweek* magazine of 19 April 1965: "American diplomats can be expected to intensify their help to United States businessmen overseas. Directives now awaiting Dean Rusk's signature will remind United States embassies that their efficiency will be rated not only by diplomatic and political prowess but by how well they foster American commercial interests abroad. Moreover, prominent businessmen will be recruited as inspectors of the foreign service.")

In 1895, President Cleveland intervened in Venezuela. In 1897, and again in 1898, the United States stopped further Federation attempts in Central America. In 1898, after fabricating a phony war with Spain, the United States annexed Puerto Rico, the Philippines and Guam, and set up Cuba as a "republic" controlled by the United States through the Platt Amendment (1901). This Amendment gave the United States the right to intervene in matters of "life, property, individual liberty, and Cuban independence". That is, in everything.

> The near-absence of significant public outcry in the United States against this policy of open imperialism in both the Caribbean and Pacific shows once again that the people of the United States were convinced that it was her destiny to expand, and that her superiority demanded it.[4]

After 1900, even liberal historians lament America's foreign policy. Theodore Roosevelt, who is nevertheless admired as one of America's greatest presidents, intervened by force of arms in almost every Caribbean and Central American country. Naturally, the real beneficiaries always remained American businessmen. It is worth repeating an often quoted statement to this respect:

> I helped make Mexico, and especially Tampico, safe for American oil interests. I helped make Haiti and Cuba a decent place for the National City Bank boys to collect revenue in. I helped pacify Nicaragua for the international banking house of Brown Brothers. I brought light to the Dominican Republic for American sugar interests. I helped make Honduras "right" for American fruit companies. . .[5]

That harsh but accurate indictment was supplied by a much

decorated United States patriot, Major-General Smedley D. Butler of the United States Marine Corps.

Against such interventions, some local patriots fought back. In Haiti, where United States marines landed in 1915 and stayed until 1934, 2,000 rebels called *Cacos* had to be killed before the United States pacified the Island. And there were other rebellions everywhere. In Nicaragua, one such rebel had to be tricked to be eliminated. Augusto César Sandino fought American marines from 1926 until 1934 without being defeated, though the marines razed to the ground various towns in Nicaragua and, by accident, some in Honduras to boot. In 1934 he was offered "negotiations", was foolish enough to believe them, came to the American Embassy to confer with Ambassador Arthur Bliss Lane and was assassinated. (Such incidents are so common in American foreign policy that no intelligent rebel who has popular support can ever again trust negotiation offers by the United States, unless the setting and the terms of these negotiations can be controlled by him. It seems as if Ho Chi Minh *is* just that intelligent.)

On 4 March 1933, the United States officially changed its policy. Beginning with his inauguration address, Franklin D. Roosevelt told the world that American imperialism was at an end and that from now on the United States would be a good neighbor. He voted in favor of a non-intervention pledge at the 1933 Montevideo Inter-American Conference, promised Latin American countries tariff reductions and exchange trade agreements, and a year later abrogated the Platt Amendment. His top diplomat, Sumner Welles, even said in 1935: "It is my belief that American capital invested abroad, in fact as well as in theory, should be subordinated to the authority of the people of the country where it is located."

But, in fact, only the form of America's interventionism changed. Franklin D. Roosevelt was the most intelligent imperialist the United States has had in modern times. As a liberal, he knew the value of rhetoric; as a capitalist, he knew that he who dominates the economy dominates the politics. As long as American interventionism for economic gain had to be defended by American marines, rebellions and revolutions would always be inevitable. When a country is occupied by American marines, the enemy is always clearly identifiable. He wears the marine uniform. But if there are no marines, if the oppressors are the local militia, police, or military forces, if these forces' loyalty to American commercial interests can be guaranteed by their economic ties to American commercial interests, it will be difficult, even impossible, for local patriots to finger the enemy. That, FDR understood. Thus, he launched a brilliant series of policies meant to tie Latin American countries to the United States.

In 1938, Roosevelt set up the Interdepartmental Committee of Cooperation with American Republics, which was, in effect, the precursor of today's technical aid program of the Organization of American States (OAS). (The OAS itself had grown out of the Pan American Union which had been set up by Secretary of State James G. Blaine as "an ideal economic complement to the United States".)[6]

FDR's Interdepartmental Committee assured Latin America's dependency on the United States for technical progress. During the war, the United States Department of Agriculture sent Latin America soil conservation research teams who helped increase Latin America's dependency on one-crop economies. In 1940, FDR said that the United States Government and United States private business should invest heavily in Latin America in order "to develop sources of raw materials needed in the United States". On 26 September 1940, he increased the limitations of the Export Import Bank, which is an arm of the American Treasury, from $100 million to $700 million, and by Pearl Harbor Day most Latin American countries had received "development loans" from which they have yet to disengage themselves. Latin America's economic dependency was further secured during the war through the United States Lend Lease program which poured $262,762,000-worth of United States equipment into eighteen Latin American nations (the two excluded were Panama, which was virtually an American property, and Argentina which was rebellious).

Roosevelt's policies were so successful that his successors, liberals all whether Republican or Democrat, continued and strengthened them. By 1950, the United States controlled 70 per cent of Latin America's sources of raw materials and 50 per cent of its gross national product. Theoretically at least, there was no more need for military intervention.

Latin American reformers did not realize to what extent the economic stranglehold by the United States ensured pro-American-business governments. They kept thinking that if they could only present their case to their people they could alter the pattern of life and indeed the structure itself. Because the United States advocated, in rhetoric at least, free speech and free institutions, they hoped that it would help them come to power. What they failed to realize was that in any underdeveloped country the vast majority of the population is either illiterate and therefore cannot vote or else lives in address-less slums and therefore still cannot vote. What's more, there is no surplus of funds available from the poor. Thus, to create a party and be materially strong enough to wage a campaign with radio and newspaper announcements for the sake of the poor is impossible. The poor cannot finance such a campaign. That is why the United States often tried to convince its puppets to allow freedom of the press and freedom of elections; after all, the rich will always be the only ones capable of owning newspapers and financing elections.

Now and then, of course, through some fluke, a reformist president has been elected in Latin America. If he then tried to carry out his reforms, he was always overthrown. This is what happened in Guatemala where Juan José Arevalo and then Jacobo Arbenz were elected on reformist platforms. Before Arevalo's inauguration in 1945, Guatemala was one of the most backward countries in Latin America. The rights of labor, whether in factories or in fields, including United Fruit Company plantations, had never been recognized; unions, civil liberties, freedom of speech and press had been outlawed. Foreign interests had been sacred and monopolistic, and their tax concessions beyond all considerations of fairness. Counting each foreign corporation as a person, 98 per cent of Guatemala's cultivated land was owned by exactly 142 people (out of a population of 3 million). Only ten per cent of the population attended school.

Arevalo and Arbenz tried to change these conditions. As long as they pressed for educational reforms, no one grumbled too much. Free speech and press were established, then unions were recognized and legalized, and finally, on 17 June 1952, Arbenz proclaimed Decree 900, a land reform which called for the expropriation and redistribution of uncultivated lands above a basic average. But Decree 900 specifically exempted all intensively cultivated lands, which amounted to only 5 per cent of over-1,000-hectare farms then under cultivation. The decree ordered all absentee-owned property to be redistributed but offered compensation in 20-year bonds at 3 per cent interest, assessed according to declared tax value.

America's agronomists applauded Decree 900. On page 179 of *Latin American Issues* published by the 20th Century Fund, one can read: "For all the furore it produced, Decree 900, which had its roots in the constitution of 1945, is a remarkably mild and fairly sound piece of legislation." But, since much of Guatemalan plantation land, including 400,000 acres not under cultivation, belonged to the United Fruit Company, the United States became concerned, and when Arbenz gave out that fallow land to 180,000 peasants, the United States condemned his régime as Communist. The U.S. convened the OAS in Caracas to make that condemnation official and found a right-wing Colonel named Castillo Armas, a graduate of the U.S. Command and General Staff School at Fort Leavenworth, Kansas, to do its dirty work. It fed him arms and dollars to set up a rebel force in Honduras and Nicaragua and helped him overthrow Arbenz. No matter how good a neighbor the United States wanted to appear, it was perfectly willing to dump such neighborliness and resort to old-fashioned military intervention when the commercial interests of its corporations were threatened.

Since then, of course, the United States has intervened again repeatedly, most visibly in the Dominican Republic in 1965. Today, there can no longer be more than two positions in Latin America. As a result of the Dominican intervention, in which 23,000 American troops were used to put down a nationalist rebellion of 4,000 armed men, the United States has made it clear that it will never allow any Latin government to break America's rigid economic control.

And what is that control? Today, 85 per cent of the sources of raw material are controlled by the United States. One American company (United Fruit) controls over 50 per cent of the foreign earnings, therefore of the whole economic structure, of six Latin American countries. In Venezuela, Standard Oil Company of New Jersey (Rockefeller), through its subsidiary the Creole Oil Corporation, controls all the bases of the industrialization processes. Venezuela is potentially the second richest country in the world. Its $500,000,000-plus net annual revenue from oil could guarantee every family, counting it at 6½, an annual income of almost $3,000. Instead, 40 per cent of its population lives outside the money economy; 22 per cent are unemployed, and the country must use over $100 million a year of its revenue to import foodstuffs, whereas the country has enough land, under a proper agrarian reform, to be an exporter of food.

Chile, with enough minerals to raise a modern industrial state, flounders in inflation (21 per cent in 1966) while, despite all the talk of "Revolution in Freedom", there is only freedom for at most one-fifth[7] of the population – and revolution for no one. So far, the best that Frei has been able to do is to launch sewing classes in the slums. The Right accuses him of demagogy, the Left of paternalism; both are correct while, as the *Christian Science Monitor* (19 September 1966) says, "Many of the poor are apathetic, saying that they are just being used, as they have in the past."

The continent as a whole must use from 30 to 40 per cent of its foreign earnings to pay off interest and service charges, *not the principal*, on loans to the industrialized world, mostly the United States. The Alliance for Progress claims that it is helping Latin America industrialize on a social progress basis. Now more than six years old, it has chalked up remarkable successes:[8] right-wing coups in Argentina, Brazil, Honduras, Guatemala, Ecuador, the Dominican Republic and Salvador. In exchange, U.S. businessmen have remitted to the U.S. $5 billion of profits while investing less than $2 billion. And the Alliance itself, which is supposed to lend money for strictly social progress projects, has kept 86 per cent of its outlay to credits for U.S.-made goods, credits which are guaranteed by Latin American governments and are repayable in dollars.

But then, under Johnson, the Alliance no longer maintained its social pretenses. In fact, no United States policy does, as President Johnson himself made clear when he told American GIs at Camp Stanley, Korea (and as recorded and broadcast by Pacifica radio stations): "Don't forget, there are only two hundred million of us in a world of three billion. They want what we've got and we're not going to give it to them."

Interventionist and imperialist policies of the United States in Latin America are now successfully in the third stage. Not only does the United States control Latin America's sources of raw material, not only does it control its markets for American manufactured goods, but it also controls the internal money economy altogether. Karl Marx had once warned that the first revolutionary wave in an imperialized country will come about as the result of frustration by the national bourgeoisie, which will have reached a development stage where it will have accumulated enough capital to want to become competitive to the industrializing corporations. This was not allowed to happen in Latin America.

As American corporations became acutely plagued by surplus goods, they realized that they must expand their markets in underdeveloped countries. To do so, however, they would have to help develop a national bourgeoisie which could purchase these goods. This "national" bourgeoisie, as all such classes in colonialized countries, had to be created by the service industries, yet somehow limited so that it did not become economically independent. The solution was simple. The American corporations, having set up assembly plants in São Paulo or Buenos Aires, which they called Brazilian or Argentinian corporations, decided to actually help create the subsidiary industries – with local money – themselves. Take General Motors, for example. First, it brought down its cars in various pieces called parts (thus eliminating import duties). Then it assembled them in São Paulo and called them Brazil-made. Next it shopped around for local entrepreneurs to launch the subsidiary industries – seat covers, spark plugs, etc. Normally, the landed oligarchy, and entrepreneurs in the area, would do their own investing in those subsidiary industries and, having successfully amassed large amounts of capital, would bind together to create their own car industry. It was this step that had to be avoided. Thus General Motors first offered these local entrepreneurs contracts by which it helped finance the servicing industries. Then it brought the entrepreneurs' capital into huge holding corporations which, in turn, it rigidly controlled. The holding corporations became very successful, making the entrepreneurs happy, and everyone forgot about a local, competitive car industry, making General Motors happy.

This procedure is best employed by IBEC, Rockefeller's mammoth investing corporation in Latin America. IBEC claims to be locally-owned by Latin Americans since it does not hold controlling interest. But the 25 to 45 per cent held by Standard Oil (it varies from Colombia to Venezuela to Peru) is not offset by the thousands of individual Latin investors who, to set policy, would all have to agree among themselves and then vote in a block. When one corporation owns 45 per cent while thousands of individual investors split the other 55 per cent, the corporation sets policy – in the United States as well as abroad. Besides, IBEC is so successful that the local entrepreneurs "think American" even before IBEC does. In any case, the result of these holding corporations is that the national bourgeoisie in Latin America has been eliminated. It is an American bourgeoisie.

IBEC and other holding corporations use their combined local-U.S. capital to invest in all sorts of profitable ventures, from supermarkets to assembly plants. Naturally, these new corporations are set up where they can bring the most return. IBEC is not going to build a supermarket in the Venezuelan province of Falcón, where the population lives outside the money economy altogether and hence could not buy goods at the supermarket anyway. Nor would IBEC build a supermarket in Falcón, because there are no roads leading there. Thus, the creation of IBEC subsidiaries in no way helps develop the infrastructure of the country. What's more, since such holding corporations have their tentacles in every region of the economy, they control the money market as well (which is why U.S. corporations backed, indeed pushed, the formation of a Latin American common market at the 1967 Punta del Este Conference. Such a common market would eliminate duties on American goods assembled in Latin America and being exported from one Latin American country to another). Hence no new American investment needs to be brought down even for the 45 per cent of the holding corporations. A new American investment in Latin America today is a paper investment. The new corporation is set up with local funds which only drains the local capital reserves. And the result is an industry benefiting only those sectors which purchase American surplus goods.

Having so tied up the local economic élites, the United States rarely needs to intervene with marines to guarantee friendly governments. The local military, bought by the American-national interests, guarantees friendly régimes – with the approval of the local press, the local legal political parties, the local cultural centers, all of which the local money controls. And the local money is now tightly linked to American interests.

Latin American reformers have finally realized all this. They now know that the only way to break that structure is to *break* it – which means a violent revolution. Hence there are no reformers in Latin America anymore. They have become either pro-Americans, whatever they call themselves, who will do America's bidding, or else they are revolutionaries.

American liberal historians, social scientists and politicians insist that there is still a third way: a non-violent revolution which will be basically pro-democracy, i.e., pro-American. They tell us that such a revolutionary process has already started and that it will inevitably lead to equality between America and its Latin neighbors. Liberal politicians also like to tell Americans that they should be on the side of that process, help it along, give it periodic boosts. In May 1966, Robert Kennedy put it this way in a Senate speech: "A revolution is coming – a revolution which will be peaceful if we are wise enough; compassionate if we care enough; successful if we are fortunate enough – but a revolution which is coming whether we will it or not. We can affect its character, we cannot alter its inevitability."

What Kennedy seems incapable of understanding, however, is

that if the revolution is peaceful and compassionate, if Americans *can* affect its character, then, it will be no revolution at all. There have been plenty of such misbred revolutions already. Let's look at a couple.

In Uruguay, at the beginning of this century, a great man carried out the modern world's first social revolution, and he was very peaceful, very compassionate, and very successful. José Battle y Ordoñez gave his people the eight-hour day, a day of rest for every five of work, mandatory severance pay, minimum wages, unemployment compensation, old-age pensions, paid vacations. He legalized divorce, abolished capital punishment, set up a state mortgage bank. He made education free through university, levied taxes on capital, real estate, profits, horse racing and luxury sales (but not on income, which would curtail incentive, he thought). He nationalized public utilities, insurance, alcohol, oil, cement, meat-packing, fish-processing, the principal banks. He outlawed arbitrary arrests, searches and seizures, and separated the state from the church, which was forbidden to own property. He made it possible for peons to come to the city and get good jobs if they didn't like working for the landed oligarchy. All of this he did before the Russian Revolution – without one murder, without one phony election.

But what happened? A thriving middle class became more and more used to government subsidy. When the price of meat and wool fell on the world market, the subsidies began to evaporate. The middle class was discontented. Used to government support, it demanded more. The government was forced to put more and more workers, mostly white collar, on its payroll. The whole structure became a hand-me-down because the people had never participated in Battle's great revolution. Nobody had fought for it. It had come on a silver platter, and now that the platter was being chipped away, those who had most profited from the so-called revolution became unhappy.

Today, in Uruguay, more than one-third of the working force is employed by the government – but does not share in the decision-making apparatus. And the government, of course, is bankrupt. It needs help, and so it begs. And the United States, as usual, is very generous. It is rescuing Uruguay – but Uruguay is paying for it. It has too much of a nationalistic tradition to be as servile as the banana republics, but on matters crucial to the United States, Uruguay now toes the line. It either abstains or votes yes whenever the U.S. wants the Organization of American States to justify or rationalize U.S. aggression. And, of course, free enterprise is once again primary.

The oligarchy still owns the land, still lives in Europe from its fat earnings. There are fewer poor in Uruguay than elsewhere in Latin America, but those who *are* poor *stay* poor. The middle class, self-centered and self-serving, takes pride in being *vivo*, shrewd and sharp at being able to swindle the government and each other. Uruguay is politically one of the freest countries in the world and Montevideo is one of the most pleasant places to live in, but only if one has money, only if one has abandoned all hope of achieving national pride – or of a truly equitable society.

In 1910, while Uruguay's peaceful revolution was still unfolding, Mexico unleashed its own – neither peacefully nor compassionately. For the next seven years, blood was shed throughout the land, and the Indian peasants took a very active part in the upheaval. But Mexico's revolution was not truly a people's war, in so far as it was basically controlled by the bourgeoisie. Francisco I. Madero, who led the first revolutionary wave, was certainly honest, but he was also a wealthy landowner who could never feel the burning thirst for change that Mexican peasants fought for. He did understand it somewhat and perhaps for that reason was assassinated with the complicity of the U.S. Ambassador, Henry Lane Wilson.[9] But he was incapable of englobing into his program the unverbalized but nonetheless real plans that such peasant leaders as Pancho Villa and Emiliano Zapata embodied in their violent reaction to the long torment suffered by their people.

As Gunder Frank has written, the bourgeoisie and the peasants "faced a common enemy, the feudal order and its supporting pillars of Church, army, and foreign capital. But their goals differed – freedom from domestic and foreign bonds and loosening of the economic structure for the bourgeoisie; land for the peasants. Although Zapata continued to press the interests of the peasants until his murder in 1919, the real leadership of the

Revolution was never out of the hands of the bourgeoisie, except insofar as it was challenged by the Huerta reaction and American intervention. The elimination of feudal social relations was of course in the interests of the emerging bourgeoisie as well as of the peasants. Education became secularized, Church and state more widely separated. But accession to power by the peasantry was never really on the cards."[10]

Thus kept out of power, the peasants never genuinely bene-fited from their revolution. They did receive land periodically, but it was rarely fertile or irrigated, and the *ejidos*, communal lands, soon became the poorest sections of Mexico. The bourgeois-revolutionary élite grew into Mexico's new oligarchy, and while some of its members did have darker skins than the old Spanish colonialists, the peasants were never integrated into the new Institutional Party power structure.

Today, not only do they rarely vote (in the 1958 presidential elections, for example, only 23 per cent of the population voted officially, and that only after frauds upped the count), but they barely profit from the social laws instituted by the Revolution. As Vincett Padgett, who is no revolutionary, has written: "To the marginal Mexican, the law and the courts are of little use. The formal institutions are not expected to provide justice. There is only acceptance and supplication. In the most unusual of circumstances there is for the marginal man the resort to vio-lence, but the most significant point is that there exists no middle ground."[11]

In Mexico today, peasants still die of starvation. Illiteracy is about 50 per cent, and 46 per cent of school-age children do not attend schools at all. Most of the cotton is controlled by one U.S. outlet, Anderson-Clayton, and 55 per cent of Mexican banks' capital is dominated by the United States. Yet Mexico's Revolu-tion was both anti-American and violent. What went wrong?

What went wrong is that the Revolution failed to sustain its impulses. It is not enough to win militarily; a revolutionary must continue to fight long after he defeats his enemy. He must keep his people armed, as a constant check against himself and as a form of forcing the people's participation in his revolutionary government. Yet he must also be careful not to guide this popular participation into a traditional form of party or state democracy, lest the intra-mural conflicts devour the revolution itself, as they did in Bolivia.[12] He must make the transition from a generalized concept of anti-Americanism to a series of particular manifestations – that is, he must nationalize all the properties belonging to Americans (or Britons or Turks or whatever is the dominating imperialist power). Like all of us who can never find ourselves, psychologically, until we face death, until we sink to such an abyss that we can touch death, smell it, eat it, and then, and only then, rise slowly to express our true selves, so too for the revolution and the revolutionary. Both must completely destroy in order to rebuild, both must sink to chaos in order to find the bases for building the true expression of the people's will. Only then can there be a total integration of the population into the new nation.

I am not trying here to define a psychological rationalization for violent revolution. What I am maintaining is that if one wants an overhaul of society, if one wants to establish an equitable society, if one wants to install *economic* democracy without which all the *political* democracy in heaven and Washington is meaningless, then one must be ready to go all the way. There are no short cuts to either truth or justice.

Besides, violence already exists in the Latin American continent today, but it is a negative violence, a counter-revolutionary violence. Such violence takes the form of dying of old age at twenty-eight in Brazil's Northeast. Or it is the Bolivian woman who feeds only three of her four children because the fourth, as one told me, "is sickly and will probably die anyway and I have not enough food for all four".

Liberals, of course, will argue that one can always approximate, compromise, defend the rule of law while working for better living conditions piece by piece. But the facts shatter such illusions. Latin America is poorer today than thirty years ago. Less people drink potable water now than then. One third of the population lives in slums. Half never see a doctor. Besides, every compromise measure has either failed or been corrupted. Vargas gave Brazilian working-men a class consciousness and launched a petroleum agency; his heirs filled their own pockets but tried to push Brazil along on the road to progress. They were smashed by the country's economic master, the United States. Peron, whatever his personal motivation, gave Argentinians new hopes and new slogans; his successors, pretending to despise him, bowed to U.S. pressure, kept their country under their boot and sold out its riches to American companies.[13] In Guatemala, as we saw, Arevalo and then Arbenz tried to bring about social and agrarian reforms without arming the people, without violence. The United States destroyed them by force and, when the right-wing semi-dictatorship of Ydigoras Fuentes decided to allow free elections in which Arevalo might make a comeback, America's great liberal rhetoretician, President Kennedy, ordered Ydigoras's removal, as the *Miami Herald* reported.[14] In the Dominican Republic, a people's spontaneous revulsion for new forms of dictatorships after thirty-two years of Trujillo was met by U.S. Marines. And so on, the list is endless.

Latin America's revolutionaries know from the experience of the Dominican Republic, of Guatemala, and of Vietnam that to break the structure is to invite American retaliation. They also realize that American retaliation will be so formidable that it may well succeed, at least under normal conditions. In Peru, in 1965, Apra Rebelde went into the mountains to launch guerrilla warfare against the American puppet régime of Belaunde. Gaining wide popular support from the disenfranchised masses, it believed that it could go from phase 1 (hit-and-run tactics) to phase 2 (open confrontation with the local military). It made a grievous mistake because the United States had also learned from its experience in Vietnam. It knew that it could not allow the local military to collapse or else it would have to send half a million men, as in so small a country as Vietnam. The United States cannot afford half a million men for all the countries that rebel. Thus, as soon as Apra Rebelde gathered on a mountain peak of the Andes for that phase 2 confrontation, the United States hit it with napalm. Apra Rebelde was effectively, if only temporarily, destroyed; its leaders, including Luis de la Puente Uceda and Lobaton, were killed.

But the guerrillas have also learned from that mistake. Today, in Guatemala, Venezuela, Colombia, and Bolivia, strong guerrilla forces are keeping mobile and are creating such havoc that the United States is forced to make the same mistake it did in Vietnam: it is sending Rangers and Special Forces into combat. In Guatemala, as of 1 January 1967, twenty-eight Rangers have been killed. The United States through its partners in Venezuela and Bolivia have again used napalm, but this time with no success. In Colombia, the United States is using Vietnam weapons as well as helicopters to combat the guerrillas, but again without noticeable success. New guerrilla uprisings are taking place, as of May 1967, in Brazil, Peru, and Ecuador.

But, more important than that, a new attitude has developed, an attitude clearly enunciated by Che Guevara when he was in Latin America organizing these rebellions. That attitude recognizes the fact that the United States cannot be militarily defeated in one isolated country at a time. The U.S. cannot, on the other hand, sustain two, three, five Vietnams simultaneously. If it tried to do so, its internal economy would crumble. Also, its necessarily increasing repressive measures at home, needed to quell rising internal dissent, would have to become so strong that the whole structure of the United States would be endangered from within.

The attitude further exclaims with unhesitating logic that imperialism never stops by itself. Like the man who has $100 and wants $200, the corporation that gets $1 million lusts for $2 million and the country that owns one continent seeks to control two. The only way to defeat it is to hit each of its imperialist tentacles simultaneously. Thus was Caesar defeated. Thus, also, was Alexander crushed. Thus, too, was the imperialism of France, of England, of Spain, of Germany eventually stopped. And thus will the United States be stopped.

Che Guevara had no illusions about what this will mean in Latin America. "The present moment may or may not be the proper one for starting the struggle, but we cannot harbor any illusions, we have no right to do so, that freedom can be obtained without fighting. And these battles shall not be mere street fights with stones against tear gas bombs, nor of pacific general strikes; neither shall it be the battle of a furious people destroying in two or three days the repressive scaffolds of the ruling oligarchies; the struggle shall be long, harsh, and its front shall be in the guer-rilla's refuge, in the cities, in the homes of the fighters – where the repressive forces shall go seeking easy victims among their families – in the massacred rural populations, in the villages or in cities destroyed by the bombardments of the enemy."[15]

Nor shall it be a gentleman's war, writes Che. "We must carry the war into every corner the enemy happens to carry it: to his home, to his centers of entertainment; a total war. It is necessary to prevent him from having a moment of peace, a quiet moment outside his barracks, or even inside; we must attack him wherever he may be; make him feel like a cornered beast wherever he may move. Then his moral fiber shall begin to decline. He will even become more beastly and we shall notice how the signs of decadence appear to begin."

Che concludes candidly: "Our soldiers must hate; a people without hatred cannot vanquish a brutal enemy."

This analysis is the inevitable and necessary conclusion of anyone who faces squarely the history of American imperialism and its effect on the imperialized people. Latin America today is poorer and more suffering than it was ten years ago, ten years before that, and so on back through the ages. American capital has not only taken away the Latin American people's hope for a better material future but their sense of dignity as well.

This analysis will shock the liberals and they will reject it. But then they are responsible for it, for American foreign policy has long been the studious creation of American liberals. That is why an honest man today must consider the liberal as the true enemy of mankind. That is why he must become a revolutionary. That is why he must agree with Che Guevara that the only hope the peoples of the world have is to crush American imperialism by defeating it on the battlefield, and the only way to do that is to coordinate their attacks and launch them wherever men are exploited, wherever men are suffering as the result of American interests. The only answer, unless structural reforms can be achieved in the United States which will put an end to the greed of American corporations, is that, as Che Guevara has said, the poor and the honest of the world must arise to launch simul-taneous Vietnams.

NOTES

[1] Salvador de Madariaga, *Latin America Between the Eagle and the Bear* (1962).

[2] Alfred Thayer Mahan, *The Influence of Seapower Upon History* (1890).

[3] Kenneth M. MacKenzie, *The Robe and the Sword: The Methodist Church and the Rise of American Imperialism* (1961).

[4] Brady Tyson, *The Roots and Causes of U.S. Policy Towards Latin America* (unpublished manuscript, 1966).

[5] Maj.-Gen. S. D. Butler in *Common Sense* (19 Nov. 1933), quoted in C. Wright Mills, *Listen Yankee*.

[6] Lloyd Mecham, *A Survey of United States–Latin American Relations* (1965).

[7] Federico G. Gil, *The Political Systems of Chile* (1966). See also his "Chile: 'Revolution in Liberty'", in *Current History*, Vol. 51, No. 303 (Nov. 1966).

[8] Jorge Graciarena, "Desarrollo y política", in Torcuato Di Tella, G. Germani and J. Graciarena (eds.), *Argentina, Sociedad de masas* (1965). See also Henri Edme, "Révolution en Amérique Latine?", in *Les Temps Modernes*, XXI, No. 240 (May 1966).

[9] Jesus Silva Herzog, *Breve historia de la revolución Mexicana* (1960).

[10] Andre Gunder Frank, "Mexico: the Janus Faces of Twentieth Century Bourgeois Revolution", in *Monthly Review*, Vol. 14, No. 7 (Nov. 1962).

[11] L. Vincett Padgett, *The Mexican Political System* (1966).

[12] J. Gerassi, *The Great Fear in Latin America* (revised 1965). See also Richard W. Patch, "United States Assistance in a Revolutionary Setting", in Robert D. Tomasek (ed.), *Latin American Politics: Studies of the Contemporary Scene* (1966).

[13] Torcuato S. Di Tella, "Populism and Reform in Latin America", in Claudio Véliz (ed.), *Obstacles to Change in Latin America* (1965).

[14] 24 December, 1966.

[15] *Message to the Tricontinental* (1967).

5

Latin America: Capitalist Underdevelopment or Socialist Revolution?*

Latin America and other parts of the world which became underdeveloped were long ago incorporated into the expanding world mercantile capitalist and then imperialist system as political and/or economic colonies. Any adequate comprehension of the economic, social, political and cultural characteristics of Latin America and other underdeveloped areas therefore requires the scientific examination not only of their societies in and of themselves but also of the colonial and class structure of this world system as a whole. This study, both in its historical and contemporary aspects, must be undertaken in part by historians and social scientists from these underdeveloped countries themselves if they wish to understand their own societies. This is all the more so necessary because the analysis of the productive capacity and relations of capitalism and imperialism, even by most Marxists, has so far been pursued from a metropolitan perspective in which the colonial countries are viewed more as supplementary annexes than as integral parts of the structure and development of this capitalist system. The resulting distortion of the picture and analysis of capitalism must be corrected, especially by social scientists from the capitalist system's underdeveloped part, through its scientific examination from a worldwide perspective which corresponds to capitalism's world-wide reality.

Latin American reality and underdevelopment derives from its integration in this world mercantile capitalist and imperialist

* by Andre Gunder Frank.

system. The understanding of this reality and the analysis of the causes of this underdevelopment must be derived from the scientific examination of Latin American participation in the historical and still ongoing process of world capitalist development. This is most evidently the case for those parts of Latin America which comprise the majority of its population and land area, notably the Caribbean, Brazil, and the southern cone countries, where this historical process painted contemporary society on what was virtually a tabula rasa with no or immediately replaced population when the Europeans arrived. Nonetheless, the contemporary society of Indoamerica, in which lived nearly fifty million descendants of the pre-Hispanic population, was no less shaped by this same historical process: the Indians, involuntarily, gave their land and labor to the development of the national and overseas metropolises in the colonial, national, and still contemporary period. To hold that these Indians have been left essentially untouched by this historical process or that they are substantially isolated from Latin American and world capitalist society today is contrary to all historical and contemporary fact.

The class structure of Latin America has throughout this process been the product essentially of the colonial structure which the Iberian and later the British and North American metropolis imposed and impressed on Latin America in their successful drive to make the latter's people into the producers and suppliers of raw materials *and capital* for the world productive process that led to metropolitan economic development. Thus, and this is true not only on the national level but also on the local one, Latin America came to have and still has the class structure of a colonial or neo-colonial export economy.

Ferrer notes:

Mining, tropical agriculture, fishing, hunting, and lumbering (all of which are basically connected with export trade) were the developing industries in the colonial economies and, as such, attracted available capital and labour resources. . . . The groups with interests in exporting activities were merchants and property owners with high incomes and high crown and church officials. These sectors of the population . . . constituted both the internal colonial market and the source of capital accumulation. . . . The greater the concentration of wealth in the hands of a small group of property owners, merchants and influential politicians, the greater the propensity to obtain durable and manufactured consumer goods from abroad. . . . Thus, the export sector by its very nature would not allow the transformation of the system as a whole . . . [and was] the basic obstacle to the diversification of the internal productive structure and, therefore, to the consequent elevation of the technical and cultural levels of the population, the development of social groups connected with the evolution of internal markets and the search for new lines of exportation free from the metropolitan authority.[1]

Of the remaining potentially investible capital, the structure of underdevelopment directed a large part into mining, agricultural, transport, and commercial enterprises for *export* to the metropolis, much of the rest to luxury *import* from the metropolis, and only very little into manufacturing and consumption related to the internal market. Thanks to foreign trade and finance the economic and political interests of the mining, agricultural, and commercial bourgeoisie did not lie with internal development.[2]

The productive relations and class structure of the latifundium, the mine, and their economic and social hinterland grew up in response to the colonialist exploitative needs of the overseas and Latin American metropolises. They were not, as is so widely but falsely claimed, the result of the transfer of Iberian feudal institutions during the sixteenth century. The development of this class structure and its contemporary economic and political consequences still demands additional research.

Nonetheless, even on the basis of the facts that are already universally known today, it is possible to affirm with confidence that the class structure and productive relations associated with the nineteenth- and twentieth-century latifundium in Cuba, Argentina, coastal Peru, coffee-growing São Paulo, and contemporary post-agrarian reform northern Mexico can have absolutely nothing to do with the supposed importation of feudal institutions from the Iberian peninsula during colonial times (nor can, of course, the quite similar institutions in the

British West Indies). As I have argued elsewhere,[3] the same thing, exactly, is shown by the historical evidence from eighteenth-century Chile, seventeenth-century Mexico, and elsewhere. In reality, though this requires further study, it is the productive and mercantile requirements of the colonial mercantile capitalist and imperialist system which have shaped the essentially capitalist class structure of the agricultural and mining export regions. The consequences of introducing modern industry into this colonial and class structure will be touched on below.

Until imperialism, the only exception to this pattern had been the weakening of the ties of foreign trade and finance during metropolitan wars or depressions, such as that of the seventeenth century, and the initial absence of such effective ties between the metropolis and isolated non-overseas export oriented regions, which permitted a temporary or incipient autonomous capital accumulation and industrial development for the internal market, such as that of the eighteenth century in São Paulo in Brazil, Tucuman and others in Argentina, Asuncion in Paraguay, Queretaro and Puebla in Mexico, and others.[4]

In the colonial era of capitalist development, then, foreign finance was primarily a stimulatory adjunct to the pillage of resources, the exploitation of labour, and the colonial trade which initiated the development of the European metropolis and simultaneously the underdevelopment of the Latin American satellites.

The economic and political ascendancy of Great Britain and the political independence of Latin America after the Napoleonic Wars left three major interest groups to decide the future of Latin America through their tripartite struggle: (1) The Latin American agricultural, mining, and commercial interests who sought to maintain the underdevelopment-generating export economy structure – and only wanted to replace their Iberian rivals from their privileged positions in it: (2) the industrial and other interest groups from the afore-mentioned and other interior regions, who sought to defend their budding but still weak development-generating economies from more free trade and foreign finance, which was threatening to force them out of existence: and (3) the victorious and industrializing British, whose Prime Minister Lord Canning noted in 1822: "Spanish America is free; and if we do not mismanage our affairs, she is English." The battlelines were drawn with the traditional Latin American import-export and metropolitan industrial-merchant bourgeoisies in natural alliance against the weak Latin American provincial and industrial nationalists. The outcome was practically predetermined by the past historical process of capitalist development, which had stacked the cards this way.

During the period of the mid-twenties to the mid-forties or fifties, the nationalist interests from the interior were still able to force their governments to impose protective tariffs in many countries. Industry, national flag shipping, and other development-generating activities showed spurts of life. At the same time, Latin Americans themselves rehabilitated old and opened new mines, and began to develop their agricultural and other primary goods export sectors. To permit and promote internal economic development as well as to respond to increasing external demand for raw materials, the liberals pressed for land and other reforms as well as immigration that would increase the domestic labor force and expand the internal market.

The export-import metropolitan oriented Latin American bourgeoisies and their national mining and agricultural allies opposed this autonomous capitalist development because, with tariff protection, it took place at the cost of their export-import interests; and they fought and defeated the provincial and industrial nationalists, who claimed the protection of federal states' rights, in the federalist-unitarist civil wars of the thirties and forties. The metropolitan powers aided their Latin American junior trade partners with arms, naval blockades, and where necessary direct military intervention and instigation of new wars, such as that of the Triple Alliance against Paraguay, which cost six-sevenths of its male population in the defense of its nationally financed railroad and genuinely independent autonomous development effort.

Trade and the sword were readying Latin America for metropolitan free trade; and to do so the competition of Latin American industrial development had to be eliminated; and, with the victory of the outward oriented economic interest groups over the inward oriented ones, ever more of the Latin American economy and state as well had to be subordinated to the metropolis. Only then would trade become free and foreign finance again come into its own. A contemporary Argentinian nationalist noted: "After 1810 . . . the country's balance of trade had been consistently unfavourable, and at the same time native merchants had suffered irreparable losses. Both wholesale export trade and retail import commerce had passed into foreign hands. The conclusion seems inescapable, therefore, that the opening of the country to foreigners proved harmful on balance. Foreigners displaced natives not only in commerce but in industry and agriculture as well." Another added: "It is not possible that Buenos Aires should have sacrificed blood and wealth solely for the purpose of becoming a consumer of the products and manufacture of foreign countries, for such is degrading and does not correspond to the great potentialities which nature has bestowed upon the country. . . . It is erroneous to assume that protection breeds monopoly. The fact is that Argentina which has been under a régime of free trade for over twenty years is now controlled by a handful of foreigners. If protection was going to dislodge foreign merchants from their positions of economic preeminence, the country would have occasion to congratulate itself on making the first step toward regaining its economic independence. . . . The nation cannot continue without restricting foreign trade, since restriction alone would make industrial expansion possible; it must no longer endure the weight of foreign monopoly which strangles every attempt at industrialization."[5] But it did.

As Burgin correctly analyzes in his study of Argentine federalism: "The economic development of post-revolutionary Argentina was characterized by a shift of the economic center of gravity from the Interior towards the seacoast, brought about by the rapid expansion of the latter and the simultaneous retrogression of the former. The uneven character of economic development resulted in what was to some extent a self-perpetuating inequality. The country became divided into poor and rich provinces. The Interior provinces were forced to relinquish ever larger portions of the national income to Buenos Aires and other provinces of the East.["6] In Brazil, Chile, Mexico, throughout Latin America, industrialists, patriots, and farsighted economists similarly denounced this same inevitable process of capitalist underdevelopment. But in vain: world capitalist development and the sword had made free trade the order of the day. And with it came foreign capital.

Free trade, as the German nationalist Friedrich List aptly noted, became Great Britain's principal export good. It was not for nothing that Manchester Liberalism was born in Cottonopolis. But it was embraced with enthusiasm, as Claudio Veliz has pointed out, by the three legs of the Latin American economic and political table, which had survived since colonial times, had defeated their national developmentist domestic rivals and captured the Latin American state, and were now naturally allied and subservient to the foreign metropolitan interests through free foreign trade to secure their and the foreigners' closed national monopoly.

Not surprisingly, but in terms both of historical reality and present-day political and ideological needs regrettably, we owe most existing interpretations of these and other events in Latin America to interested liberal contemporaries and historians, who have shaped our image of the events in terms of their interests. Unfortunately, Marxists who have drawn primarily on metropolitan theory have also drawn primarily on liberal researched fact for their analysis. In consequence, they have also all too often bottled a liberal admixture of wine and water under a Marxist label. Revolutionary political policy today could well benefit from truly scientific Marxist re-interpretation of such historical figures as Rosas and Rivadavia in Argentina, Dr. Francia and Lopez father and son in Paraguay, Rengifo and Balmaceda in Chile, Maua and Nabuco in Brazil, Mora or Lucas Alaman and Juarez in Mexico, and their respective economic and political policies or epochs. Some of these appear to have attempted, and others to have opposed or co-opted, already in the early nineteenth century, the bourgeois democratic revolution and nationalist industrialization program for which certain political interests are not trying to rally popular support in the late twentieth century in Latin America.

The previous period paved the way for the emergence of imperialism and its new forms of foreign investment both in the metropolis and in Latin America, where free trade and liberal land and other reforms had concentrated land into fewer hands, had thus created a larger agricultural and unemployed labor force, and had brought forth governments dependent on the metropolis, who now opened the door not only to more metropolitan trade but to the new imperialist investment finance which were quick to take advantage of these developments.

The new metropolitan demand for and Latin American profitability of raw materials production and export attracted both private and public Latin American capital into expanding the infrastructure necessary for this export production. In Brazil, Argentina, Paraguay, Chile, Guatemala, and Mexico (to the author's knowledge, but probably in other countries as well), domestic or national capital built the first railroad in each of these countries. In Chile, it opened up the nitrate and copper mines that were to become the world's principal supplier of commercial fertilizer and red metal, in Brazil the coffee plantations that supplied nearly all the world's tables, and similarly elsewhere. Only after this proved to be a booming business – as after Britain had to find outlets for its steel – did foreign capital enter into these sectors and take over the ownership and management of these initially Latin American enterprises by buying out – often with Latin American capital – the concessions of these natives.

In Latin America, this same imperialist trade and finance did more than increase the amount of production, trade, and profit by accumulating about U.S. $10,000 million of investment capital there. The imperialist metropolis used its foreign trade and finance to penetrate the Latin American economy far more completely and to use the latter's productive potential far more efficiently and exhaustively for metropolitan development than the colonial metropolis had ever been able to do. As Rosa Luxemburg noted of a similar process elsewhere, "stripped of all obscuring connecting links, these relations consist in the simple fact that European capital has largely swallowed up the Egyptian peasant economy. Enormous tracts of land, labour, and labour products without number, accruing to the state as taxes, have ultimately been converted into European capital and have been accumulated."[7]

Indeed, in Latin America imperialism went further. It not only availed itself of the state to invade agriculture; it took over nearly all economic and political institutions to incorporate the entire economy into the imperialist system. The latifundia grew at a pace and to proportions unknown in all previous history, especially in Argentina, Uruguay, Brazil, Cuba, Mexico, and Central America. With the aid of the Latin American governments, foreigners came to own – usually for next to nothing – immense tracts of land. And where they did not get the land, they got its products anyway; because the metropolis also took over and monopolized the merchandizing of agricultural and most other products. The metropolis took over Latin American mines and expanded their output, sometimes exhausting irreplaceable resources, such as the Chilean nitrates, in a few years. To get these raw materials out of Latin American and to get its equipment and goods in, the metropolis stimulated the construction of ports, of railroads, and, to service all this, of public utilities. The railroad network and electric grid, far from being net- or grid-like, was ray-like and connected the hinterland of each country and sometimes of several countries with the port of entry and exit, which was in turn connected to the metropolis. Today, four score years later, much of this export-import pattern still remains, in part because the railroad right-of-way is still laid out that way, and more importantly because the metropolitan oriented urban, economic, and political development which nineteenth-century imperialism generated in Latin America gave rise to vested class interests who tried and with metropolitan support managed to maintain and expand this development of Latin American underdevelopment during the twentieth century.

Implanted in colonial and deepened in the free trade eras, the colonial and class structure of underdevelopment was consolidated in Latin America by nineteenth-century imperialist trade and finance. Latin America was converted into a primary monoproduct export economy with its latifundium and expropriated rural proletariat or even lumpen-proletariat exploited by a satellized bourgeoisie acting through the corrupt state of a non-country: "Barbarous Mexico" (Turner);[8] the "Banana Republics" of Central America, which are not company stores but "company countries"; "The Inexorable Evolution of the Latifundium: Overproduction, Economic Dependence, and Growing Poverty in Cuba" (Guerra y Sanchez);[9] "British Argentina"; and "Pathological Chile" of which the historian Francisco Encina wrote in 1912, under the title, *Our Economic Inferiority: Its Causes and Consequences*:[10] "Our economic development of recent years exhibits symptoms which characterize a real pathological state. Until the middle of the nineteenth century, the foreign trade of Chile was almost exclusively in the hands of Chileans. In less than fifty years, foreign trade has choked off our nacent commercial initiative abroad; and in our own home it eliminated us from international trade and replaced us, in large part, in retail trade. . . . The merchant marine . . . has fallen into sad straits and continues to cede ground to foreign shipping even in the coastwide trade. The majority of the insurance companies that operate among us have their head office abroad. The national banks have ceded and keep ceding ground to the branches of foreign banks. An ever growing share of the bonds of the savings institutions are passing into the hands of foreigners who live abroad."

With the development of nineteenth-century imperialism, foreign investment came to play an almost co-equal part with foreign trade in harnessing Latin America to capitalist development and in transforming its economy, society, and policy until the structure of Latin American underdevelopment was firmly consolidated.

Bourgeois Nationalism
In Latin America, the First World War had given the satellite economies a respite from foreign trade and finance as well as other ties with the metropolis. Accordingly, as had happened before and would again, Latin Americans generated their own industrial development, mostly for the internal consumer goods market. No sooner did the war end, than did metropolitan, now

increasingly United States based, industry expand into precisely those regions and sectors, especially consumer goods manufacture in Buenos Aires and São Paulo, which Latin Americans had just opened up industrially and shown to be profitable. Here, then, supported by their financial, technological, and political power, the giant American and British corporations displaced and even replaced – that is, depatriated – Latin American industry. The naturally following balance of payments crises were met by foreign loans to cover the Latin American deficits and to extract governmental concessions for increased metropolitan penetration of the Latin American economies.

The 1929 Crash, contrary to international trade theory but true to historical precedent, sharply reduced foreign finance along with foreign trade and prices, and therewith the transfer of satellite investible resources to the metropolis. This weakening of economic ties with and reduction of metropolitan political interference in Latin America was begun by the Depression of 1930, maintained by the recession of 1937, and continued by the Second World War and its reconstruction aftermath until the early 1950s. It created economic conditions and permitted political changes in Latin America which resulted in the beginning of its strongest nationalist policy and biggest independent industrialization drive since the post-independence 1830s and 1840s, and possibly ever.

It is essential to understand that the recent changes in the class structure of Brazil, Argentina, Chile, Venezuela, Mexico and other parts of Latin America have occurred both within their external and internal colonial structure and substantially in response to metropolitan generated changes in their colonial relations. And it is important to interpret these changes of class structure in terms of the colonial structure that underlies them. This also must be done primarily by Latin American social scientists and other intellectuals who have been able to free themselves from the ideological and political commitment to the bourgeois order created by these developments.

The economic shock of drastic reduction of Latin American import capacity and the decline of metropolitan manufacturing exports and of foreign investment and loans, which were caused by the Great Depression in the metropolis, had far-reaching economic and political consequences in many parts of Latin America. It is essential to understand both the extent *and the limitations* of these consequences before we can adequately comprehend the resulting economic and political problems of today. The onset of the Depression changed national income and its distribution so much in Latin America that the existing institutional framework was unable to cope with the necessary adjustments: revolutions occurred in 1930 or soon thereafter in Brazil, Argentina, Chile, Cuba; and the Mexican Revolution of 1910, which had nearly come to a halt, was given a new impulse. Revolutionary activity agitated other parts of the continent. The metropolitan allied export interests were obliged to form a coalition with the still weak industrial interests and (at least in Brazil) with new regional interests, who forced themselves into the government. Counter-revolutions representing some of the traditional interests were attempted within two or three years; and they were partially successful in Cuba and Chile, though not in the three major Latin American countries. Throughout, the relaxation of the economic colonial ties with the metropolis and in general (though not in Cuba) the relative paralyzation of imperialist political intervention, which the metropolitan depression produced in Latin America, also laid the economic and political basis for new class alignments and industrialization policies. So long as the national governments continued to protect the export interests (as the Brazilian government did through coffee price supports), these interests were now willing and in some cases anxious to permit the promotion of domestic manufacturing – at a time that the Depression had ruined the export business anyway.

Some Latin American countries began to produce at home the consumer goods they had imported before. But this process of "import substitution" had two major limitations built in, both of which derived from the existing class structure. First, they had to begin with the existing income distribution and demand structure. This meant that they had to concentrate on consumer goods, particularly for the high income market. Without a major change in the class structure and in income distribution, the internal market could not expand fast enough to sustain the import substitution process indefinitely. For the same reason, they did not produce enough industrial equipment or producers' goods (Sector I in Marxist terms); so that they were increasingly obliged to import these from abroad, in order even to keep the import substitution process going. That is, they ended up only substituting some imports for others. This renewed their dependence on the metropolis and led to the renewal of foreign investment. To have avoided these two limitations, these Latin American countries would have had to follow the Soviet industrialization model in which the state, rather than consumer demand, determined the goods – capital goods – to be produced first. But for that they would have had to have a Soviet state, that is a socialist class structure. The domestic political arrangements of the thirties were able to survive the depression for some time, because the Second World War, though it improved the export picture, still did not permit the renewal of imports from the metropolis. But the end of the Korean War finally terminated this Latin American honeymoon in which the colonial export interests had maintained an uneasy marriage with national bourgeois industrial interests and a growing industrial proletariat, producing as offspring an ill-formed national industry, and all with imperialism's grudging blessings.

It is particularly important to understand not only the successes but the limitations of this period, because two principal political problems of our day arise out of the survival of its deformed offspring and out of some people's attempts to breathe new life into it or to produce another such child today. This period saw the flowering of the political and ideological movements of Vargas, Peron, Cárdenas, Haya de la Torre, Aguirre Cerda, Betancourt, Figueres, Arevalo-Arbenz (and, one might note, of Ghandi and Nehru in another colonial part of the same world-wide system). And it was the time of economic nationalism, national, and in some cases industrial, development, growth of urban industrial workers and middle sectors (*capas*), democratic reformism, welfarism, and populism, associated with these names (except for Haya, who never got the reins of government, and Betancourt, of whom, notably, this holds only for his first presidential period). These developments require further study, particularly to account for the differences in their scope and timing. Why, for instance, is Peronism and Arevalo-Arbenzism so late in this period, compared to developments in Brazil, Chile, Mexico?

We may be tempted to call this the work of the national bourgeoisie in Latin America, who perhaps attempted a colonial version of the "bourgeois democratic revolution" or of a "marriage of rye and iron" on the German Bismarckian or Japanese Mejii Restoration model, all while the colonial ties were temporarily weakened by depression and war in the imperialist metropolis. But perhaps, if we must look for any at all, it may be historically more accurate to look for the bourgeois democratic revolution a hundred years earlier when the generations of Francia, Lopez, Rosas (before he, like Betancourt after him, changed colours), Juarez, and later Nabuco and Balmaceda had symbolized essentially similar attempts at nationalist and national development.

Irrespective of our answer to this question, it is imperative to understand that this industrial development, this bourgeois nationalism, this alliance of the working class with national bourgeois elements against imperialism abroad and the export interests at home, and the whole ideological superstructure that goes with them, all were the product of particular historical circumstances, which have definitely come to an end with the recovery of the metropolis after the Second World War and with the important changes that the metropolis and the remainder of the world have undergone since then, particularly the technological revolution and the militarization of the United States and the socialist revolution and development in some of the metropolis's ex-colonies. These events, these changes in the colonial structure of the world capitalist system, render the continuation of such bourgeois nationalist development in Latin America impossible and make all dreams of its re-initiation in the future entirely Utopian – that is, Utopian for the bourgeoisie, but politically suicidal for the people. And this is so not only in Latin America, but as the evidence from the neo-colonies of Africa, Asia, and particularly Indonesia shows, it is true for the colonial part of the imperialist system generally.

Neo-Imperialism
Imperialism is certainly the principal enemy of mankind today.
But how does this enmity express itself in the heart of contemporary Latin American society? What expression does this
enemy take there, and how must we fight him? To find answers
to these questions it is well to inquire further into the complex
and still changing relationship between colonial and class structure in Latin America. We may begin with some questions posed
by recent changes in the colonial structure.

The classical colonial relationship between the metropolis and
Latin America, in which the former's exploitation of the latter
was principally arranged through the productive division of
labor and monopolistic exchange of manufactured commodities
and raw materials, is being replaced or at least supplemented by
a new form of exploitation through foreign investment and
so-called aid. As the metropolis achieves increasingly more
capital intensive, and particularly more technologically complex,
forms of production at home, it increasingly replaces simple
foreign trade by foreign investment in manufacturing subsidiaries
facilities abroad, which now produce the formerly imported consumer and some producer goods locally – but with equipment
and technology imported from the home office (*matriz*) in the
imperialist metropolis. The Latin American and other colonies'
loss of capital on account of the terms of trade (not only the
deterioration of the terms of trade of which CEPAL and
UNCTAD complain, but also the monopoly exploitation that
these terms of trade represent at their least unfavourable level,
such as that of the Korean War period) is thus increasingly
supplemented by an additional flow of capital from the colonies
to the metropolis on account of profit remittance, debt service,
royalties, etc. Thus, in 1961–3 Latin America's payment for
these "invisible" financial "services" amounted to 40 per cent
of Latin America's foreign exchange earnings; and payment for
foreign-provided transportation and other services amounted to
another 21.5 per cent, for a total of 61.5 per cent of its foreign
exchange earnings that Latin America was obliged to spend for
services, without the importation of a single penny's worth of

goods. This meant an annual expenditure of U.S. $6,000 million, or 7 per cent of Latin America's gross national product (GNP) for these years.[11] By comparison, the deterioration of the terms of trade since the early 1950s, which is CEPAL's principal complaint, represented 3 per cent (additional) loss of Latin American GNP;[12] and total Latin American expenditures for education, from kindergarten through to university, public and private, were 2.6 per cent of its GNP.[13] Since that time the debt service component of this capital drain has risen from 15 per cent to 19 per cent (in 1966) of foreign exchange earnings, probably raising the total of service payments to over 65 per cent of foreign exchange earnings or nearly 8 per cent of the GNP – plus the 3 per cent or more represented by the deterioration of the terms of trade and an incalculable amount of loss through the monopoly exploitation in these terms of trade. Yet even this calculable capital drain out of Latin America is three or four times as great as that mentioned in the Second Declaration of Havana and in estimates by Fidel Castro. No wonder that this colonial relationship turns Latin America's balance of trade surplus into a chronic and growing balance of payments deficit, which, in a vicious spiral, makes the Latin American bourgeoisie ever more dependent on imperialism. This growing problem is worthy of much more study than it has so far received.

Nonetheless, worse than the drain of capital is the structure of underdevelopment and the brake and mischanneling to which it subjects national development, which imperialism deepens in Latin America through increasing foreign investment. The institutional mechanisms through which this flow of capital from the poor to the rich is effected also pose a number of questions. What is the source of this capital in Latin America, and most particularly how is foreign, principally U.S., investment in Latin America financed? The evidence suggests that an increasingly small share of "North American" investment capital is brought to Latin America from North America, and that an ever greater part of it is raised in Latin America itself.

Thus, according to the United States Department of Commerce, of the total capital obtained and employed from all sources by United States operations in Brazil in 1957, 26 per cent came from the United States and the remainder was raised in Brazil, including 36 per cent from Brazilian sources outside the American firms.[14] That same year, of the capital in American direct investment in Canada, 26 per cent came from the United States while the remainder was also raised in Canada.[15] By 1964, however, the part of American investment in Canada that entered from the United States had declined to 5 per cent, making the average American contribution to the total capital used by American firms in Canada during the period 1957–64 only 15 per cent. All the remainder of the "foreign investment" was raised in Canada through retained earnings (42 per cent), depreciation charges (31 per cent), and funds raised by American firms on the Canadian capital market (12 per cent). According to a survey of American direct investment firms operating in Canada in the period 1950–9, 79 per cent of the firms raised over 25 per cent of the capital for their Canadian operations in Canada, 65 per cent of the firms raised over 50 per cent in Canada, and 47 per cent of the American firms with investments in Canada raised all of the capital for their Canadian operations in Canada and none in the United States. There is reason to believe that this American reliance on foreign capital to finance American "foreign investment" is still greater in the poor underdeveloped countries, which are weaker and more defenseless than Canada. This, then, is the source of the flow of capital on investment account from the poor underdeveloped countries to the rich developed ones.

No wonder that between 1950 and 1965 the flow of capital on private investment account registered by the U.S. Department of Commerce was U.S. $9,000 million from the United States to the world other than Europe and Canada, and U.S. $25,600 million from these same countries in Asia, Africa and Latin America to the United States – of which U.S. $3,800 million was from the U.S.A. to Latin America and U.S. $11,300 million from Latin America to the U.S.A.[16] It is therefore necessary to inquire with greater care into the Latin American banking system (government banks, nationally owned private banks, and foreign owned private banks), stock markets and other financial institutions, and foreign and nationally owned and especially mixed ownership industrial and commercial enterprises, which make this capital flow possible.

Especially important, both on economic and political grounds, is the growing association of foreign and national capital in these mixed enterprises; and most important – and least studied – is the recent emergence of mixed enterprises which associate private foreign capital with Latin American national governments, as in the "Chilenization" of copper. Who provides the bulk of the capital (the Latin Americans, presumably); who has or achieves effective control of the enterprises, and therefore decides what goods to produce, what industrial equipment and processes to use, when to expand and contract, etc. (the Americans, presumably); and who reaps the bulk of the profits (the Americans, presumably); and who is left with the losses when business is unfavorable (the Latin Americans, presumably)? What are the *political* consequences of this association – no, incorporation – not only of Latin American export interests but now also of the Latin American industrial bourgeoisie, the erstwhile "national" bourgeoisie, with/by the imperialist monopoly? Some Latin American countries passed laws requiring 49 per cent or 51 per cent "national" participation in certain enterprises, supposedly to "protect" the national interest. It is now clear that these measures only served to submerge surviving elements of the "national" bourgeoisie in the imperialist one. Then some Latin American bourgeois governments proposed to "protect" or even "further" the "national" interest by themselves entering such mixed partnerships. The result can only be that these colonial governments lose even what little political bargaining power they have left in their already all too junior partnership with imperialism. This matter also demands greater scientific and political clarification.

The other arm of the contemporary economic and political offensive of American imperialism in Latin America is "foreign aid" and particularly its institutional expression in the "Alliance for Progress" and "economic integration". These have been denounced by the left in Latin America, though the latter hardly even that; but they have by no means been adequately analyzed. Exactly who is allied to whom, and who is aided by whom?

There is evidence, which bears further investigation, that much of the aid does not even go to the Latin American bourgeoisie, and of course much less to the Latin American people, but rather to the U.S. firms operating in Latin America. If the Latin American bourgeoisie is to benefit from this part of the "aid", it must do so through its association with these imperialist monopolies. What then, precisely, is the relation of this aid to foreign investment? Most denounced are the monetary, fiscal, exchange, and wage policy strings attached to the foreign loans of U.S. and U.N. agencies, especially the International Monetary Fund. Yet these policies do not benefit only the imperialist bourgeoisie but also most sectors of the Latin American grand bourgeoisie, and the latter accept and execute them – like devaluation – eagerly. Why? With what political implications?

The Alliance for Progress began with substantial propaganda about land, fiscal, and other reforms, which had earlier been promoted by the more progressive and nationalist sectors of the Latin American bourgeoisie, and which more recently had been recommended by their ideological mouthpiece, the United Nations Economic Commission for Latin America (CEPAL). But these reform proposals were soon archived along with their associated economic "plans" (for reasons to be inquired into below); and their pride of place has since been taken, as was confirmed by the last "Inter" American Presidents' meeting in Punta del Este in 1967, by proposals to accelerate the formation of a "Latin American" common market. This latter proposal enjoys very much more economic realism and political backing from the point of view of the United States, the grand bourgeoisie in the major Latin American countries, and the governments, including that of the "nationalist" Frei, which serve them. Evidently, it is much more realistic to try to expand industry by realigning the colonial structure abroad than by reforming the class structure at home in these Latin American countries – especially if in the process the degree of monopolization and the amount of monopoly profit can be increased at the expense of the already weak medium bourgeoisie and the popular classes at home, that is, through what will amount to a counter-reform of the class structure at home. It is worthy of note that this "economic integration" proposal also enjoys the blessings of that defender of supposedly "national" bourgeois interests, CEPAL. Yet there are scarcely half a dozen articles and not a single serious study of the economic basis or consequences and the political implications of this move toward economic – and with it political and military – integration by the imperialist and Latin American bourgeoisie. Who is to make la patria América, and on what basis, imperialism or revolution?

Class Structure

What then is the class structure in Latin America and how is the anti-colonial and class struggle to proceed to socialism? We may inquire into the national, urban, and rural class structure in turn. The "national" governments are mostly more colonial even than the bourgeoisies they represent. It seems legitimate to ask – and in the case of contemporary Africa there can be little question – to what extent national states in the classical sense have existed in Latin America since Independence, and to what extent the state machinery has been at most times since then an instrument of a coalition between the metropolitan bourgeoisie and the major sectors of the Latin American bourgeoisies, who have always been the junior partners or even only the executors of imperialism. Military governments have been installed to manage state affairs for these interests when civilian governments were unable to do so. (The new military governments of Brazil and Argentina, which represent an important new departure, will be discussed below.)

The agricultural and mining export bourgeoisie owes its existence and survival to the colonial structure, and it is loyal to its colonial patron. This is true both of its productive sector and its commercial one, in the countryside and in the city. The latifundia "oligarchy" has no independent existence and – as we shall ask below – we must in fact question the extent to which it is even identifiable separately from the commercial and now also industrial bourgeoisie. This latter sector of the bourgeoisie, as appears from the examination of foreign investment, has now been also solidly integrated into the coalition between imperialism and its Latin American comprador and bureaucratic bourgeois partners and executors. The combination of imperialist penetration, the decline in the terms of trade, devaluation, the consequent reduction in capacity to import industrial equipment, decline in growth and profit rates, and in some cases inflation, since the mid-1950s has all but forced the medium industrial "national" manufacturer and his distributor out of business or into the business empire of a foreign "investor" who bought him out. The foreign enterprise then sometimes converts him, literally, into a bureaucratic employee of the imperialist enterprise in which he is allowed to continue on as "manager" of or "consultant" to his old firm, with a salary or some stock in the imperialist enterprise for himself. What part of the national bourgeoisie, which developed under particular conditions during the thirties and forties, has been able to survive this process in the fifties and sixties? What political power do those who survive, if any, retain for use in any anti-imperialist struggle, when as in Brazil the imperialist squeeze obliges them to react by squeezing their workers, thereby undermining their erstwhile political alliance with the unionized industrial proletariat, which used to provide the national bourgeoisie with one of its major sources of political power?

Industrial development produced an industrial proletariat of consequence in some Latin American countries. So did the mining and petroleum industries, though the latter never accounts for a large part of the labor force. This industrial proletariat, especially in large industry, has been unionized in part under the aegis of the national bourgeoisie, which wanted to guarantee itself both political support from and control over this labour movement, and by Communist parties, who have been by and large allied to this national bourgeoisie. The unionized industrial workers, though exploited, were often rewarded by wage incomes that were high relative to the bulk of the population and by social security coverage that was hardly available to most others.

Since the metropolis pre-empts an increasing share of the most profitable Latin American business and forces the remainder into growing economic difficulties, the Latin American bourgeoisie that lives off this less profitable business is left no choice but to fight – even if vainly – for its survival by increasing the degree of wage and price exploitation of its petty bourgeoisie, workers, and peasants, in order to squeeze some additional blood out of that stone; and at times, the Latin American bourgeoisie must resort to direct military force to do so. For this reason – no doubt more than for idealistic or even ideological reasons – almost the entire Latin American bourgeoisie is thus thrown into political alliance with – that is into the arms of – the metropolitan bourgeoisie: they have more than a common longterm interest in defending the system of capitalist exploitation; even in the short run, the Latin American bourgeoisie cannot be national or defend nationalist interests by opposing foreign encroachment in alliance with Latin American workers and peasants – as the Popular Front rule book would have them do – because the same neo-imperialist encroachment is forcing the Latin American bourgeoisie to exploit its supposed worker and peasant allies ever more and is thus forcing the bourgeoisie to forego this remaining source of political support. While the Latin American bourgeoisie is pursuing wage, price, and political policies that exploit its workers and that repress their legitimate demands for relief from this growing exploitation, the Latin American bourgeoisie cannot rally their support against the metropolitan bourgeoisie; while the economic inefficiency of this exploitation interferes with domestic saving for investment and obliges the bourgeoisie to turn abroad for immediate foreign finance.

The Brazilian bourgeoisie has been trying to find an additional way out, first through the "independent" foreign policy of Presidents Quadros and Goulart (who sought new markets in Africa, Latin America, and the socialist countries) and, after that proved impossible in an already imperialized world, through the "inter-dependent" sub-imperialist foreign policy, begun by the present military government as a junior partner to the United States. Brazilian sub-imperialism also requires low wages in Brazil, so that the Brazilian bourgeoisie can enter the Latin American market on a low cost basis, which with obsolete but still modern American equipment is the only one it has. In the sub-imperialized countries of Latin America, the Brazilian invasion also leads to depressing wages, since doing so is the local bourgeoisie's only possible defensive reaction. Thus, sub-imperialism also aggravates the contradictions between the bourgeoisie and labor in each of these countries.

Therefore, neo-imperialism and monopoly capitalist development in Latin America are drawing and driving the entire Latin American bourgeoisie class – including its comprador, bureaucratic, and national segments – into ever closer economic and political alliance with and dependence on the imperialist metropolis. The road of national or state capitalism to economic development is already foreclosed to them by neo-imperialist development today. The political task of reversing the development of Latin American underdevelopment therefore falls to the people themselves.

Under these circumstances, what is the economic and political future of this industrial proletariat and its political organizations? The recent economic stagnation of much of Latin America has been translated, among other things, into declining real wages for these workers. This, and the declining fortunes of the national bourgeoisie, seems to have seriously undermined this worker-bourgeoisie alliance. The 1964 and 1966 military coups in Brazil and Argentina, which were not simple palace revolts in the "traditional" Latin American style, have substantially undone the remainder of the uneasy marriage between the colonial and national bourgeois interests of the Vargas and Peron eras and have effectively cemented the imperialist-export-foreign association industry and commerce-bourgeois marriage. (Internationally these coups correspond to the world-wide imperialist counter-offensive that also includes the African and Indonesian coups.) Will this new bourgeois régime continue to repress the economic and democratic political demands of the industrial workers, as it did in Brazil, or will it try and succeed to co-opt the labor movement as did the national bourgeoisie, perhaps on the Mexican model? And how will labor and its movement fare in the other Latin American countries? Have the Communist parties, whose principal political power rests on this labor union base, been substantially and bureaucratically integrated into the bourgeois establishment? What part will the industrial workers and the Communist parties play in the present stage of the revolutionary process?

Two other urban "sectors" remain, the petit bourgeois middle "class(es)" and the "marginal" "floating" population, some but by no means all of them recent migrants from rural areas, who live in the *favelas, villas miserias, callampas, barriadas, ranchos,* etc. and in the *conventillos* of the inner city (though part of these are also industrial workers or ex-workers). These comprise the vast and still growing bulk of the urban population. It is no accident that these population groups are generally defined by their placement in the middle of the other classes and/or by their residence. This is because their relation to the means of production or even to the productive process is uncertain at best, and their political behavior is extremely volatile at worst. That is, both are characterized by extremely complex and changing patterns of economic and social relations and political behavior, which require considerable scientific aclaration. Are the middle sectors, or particular parts of them, politically progressive because, except for the upper middle class, their income is compressed and their economic and social horizon is restricted by the polarization of the economy and the stagnation of many of its sectors? Or does reduction of their income and threat of proletarianization make them pursue reactionary political policies in alliance with the grand bourgeoisie and its military régime? Large sectors of the middle class enthusiastically supported the Brazilian and other military coups, only to become disillusioned with the new régime's economic policies. Why does this middle "class" generate the progressive petit bourgeois and especially student movements, which so far, however, do not represent the majority of their social base? Is it really correct to dampen the class struggle in order to maintain or attract these social groups into an "anti-imperialist" electoral struggle, or must larger sectors of the petit bourgeoisie be led into political opposition against the Latin American grand bourgeoisie, and thereby against imperialism?

Is the "floating" or "marginal" population, which may well account for half of the Latin American urban population (which in turn approaches half the total population) a "lumpen-proletariat"? Are these people really ideologically untouchable and politically irresponsive and unorganizable? Imperialism and the bourgeoisie do not think so and are, so far all too success-fully, harnessing them to their political purposes, which is only partially manifested by electoral support from these groups for Odria, Frei, Adehmar de Barros, etc. Yet in Caracas the left was able to mobilize part of this population, and in Santo Domingo they ended up mobilizing Coronel Camaño.

Perhaps the first and most important question to ask about the rural class structure is to what extent, if at all, it is separate and different from the national and urban class structure in Latin America. The importance of this question derives from the near universal answer by both bourgeois and Marxist scholars and political leaders that much of rural Latin America is in another "semi-feudal" world apart from the urban, national, and inter-national capitalist system – and from the political policy asso-ciated with this view. Does Latin America really have a "dual" economy and society, in one part of which "survives" a pattern of feudal or semi-feudal productive relations and even a non-capitalist class structure? Does this "survival" really call for a bourgeois democratic revolution or even a national democratic revolution to extend capitalism into the countryside? Or is this one of the series of supposedly scientific and revolutionary "Marxist" models number 12, 13, 14 which Fidel Castro de-nounced as a reactionary cathecism in his OLAS speech?

The historical record and contemporary reality, whose scien-tific examination was recommended above, suggest that it has for over four centuries been the world and national capitalist colonial structure which has shaped the productive relations and class structure of rural Latin America. This part of society, therefore, has never been separate from the capitalist world and national metropolises; and if it has been different, this is because the bourgeois interests of the latter have required rural Latin America to become and remain so. Rural Latin America has been colonially exploited by the world capitalist metropolis both directly and indirectly through the Latin American national metropolises. These latter subject their rural (and urban) hinter-land to the same kind of "internal" colonial exploitation and capital drain as they suffer at the hands of imperialism. The bourgeoisie in the national metropolis collaborates with imperialism in the class and colonial exploitation of its own people. And the parts of the bourgeoisie which own the latifundia and which exercise monopoly control over internal trade, of course, form an integral part of this capitalist colonial and class system. Far from asking how isolated and "feudal" this rural "oligarchy" is, we must inquire how commercially the latifundista bourgeoisie (if it is rural at all) is tied to the major urban commercial and industrial monopolies; to what extent in fact landed monopoly is owned by the same persons, families, or corporations as commercial and industrial monopoly; to what extent latifundistas derive their income from agricultural production on their land and to what extent their monopoly ownership of the land simply renders possible the commercial, financial, and political exploitation of those who work the latifundium and neighboring land. But this again leads to asking how colonial capitalist exploitation creates and maintains the productive relations on the latifundium and the class structure in rural Latin America, which may superficially appear "feudal" but which make this capitalist exploitation possible. Finally, we must ask who wants to change these productive relations – certainly not the Latin American grand bourgeoisie – and how – certainly not by an "anti-feudal" or "anti-imperialist" bourgeois democratic revolution.

What, then, is the essential relationship between the large landowner-merchants and those who work the land in Latin America? Do the latter constitute a peasantry, serf-like or free? It is suggested that more careful inquiry will show that, irrespective of the multitude of *forms* of payment between those who own and those who work the land, for both the essential relation between them – no less than in industry – is the exploitation of the latter, who lack the means of production to support themselves, by the former who own them. Far too little is known about the variety of forms, and particularly about the vast areas of Brazil (as in the Northeast), Argentina, the Caribbean, but also Indian populated countries like Peru and Guatemala, in which large parts of the rural population are essentially agricultural workers – a rural proletariat – who work for what is essentially a wage, though a low and unsteady one, as they migrate from farm to farm, from region to region, and even to other countries (as do Mexican *braceros*) when economic and climatic conditions demand. Nor do they work only for large landowners. They work wherever and however they can, in and out of agriculture. And they are hired also by medium-scale owners, small owners, and even by tenants, who sometimes use them to fulfil their labor quota obligation to their own landlords. What is this complex pattern of exploitation? To what extent is this rural proletariat interested in land, and to what extent in higher wages or greater employment security? And to what extent are small owners and tenants, who are themselves exploited but who hire wage labor, interested in keeping wages from rising, and minimum wage laws from being passed or enforced in rural areas, lest their competitive position be worsened in the face of the larger landed monopolies who can better afford such wage increases? To what extent are these small owners and tenants themselves wage workers – and interested in higher wages – and/or merchants – and interested in higher or lower prices – because the land they own or rent or share-crop is insufficient to support their family? To what extent are owners of medium-sized farms not farmers at all, but rural and urban petit bourgeois merchants, employees, or professional people, who want to squeeze the maximum out of those who work their land? Some claim that small owners and tenants can be politically mobilized before the rural proletarians, and revolutionary experience seems to agree with them. But others maintain the opposite. Where then must political work be begun, with what slogans, and with what allies?

Latin American Indians are said to live in a world apart. It is true that, wherever they can, they try to preserve their culture and where possible a corporate community which presents a common front against the outsider. This has been their best – and at best inadequate – protection against the exploitation they suffer as a result of having been forced to the very bottom of both the internal colonial and domestic class structures. Far from being outside the colonial and class structure, they are its most integrally exploited members. As such, they have just suspicions, based on 400 years of experience, of all proposals to eliminate their exploitation by reforms from above. Does this mean that they will not incorporate themselves into revolutionary struggle from below, if they once come to perceive it as that – and if it once becomes revolutionary enough to permit and justify such perception? Historical evidence shows that the Indian can be politically mobilized, as in Guatemala; in fact, that his mass movement at the base can mobilize the revolutionary leadership into greater militancy, as in Bolivia in 1952. The question is not so much whether the Indian will participate in the struggle as it is whether the revolutionary leadership will be capable of channeling this participation into revolution or back into reform and reaction.

This raises questions about revolutionary and reformist organization in the countryside as a whole – and its relation to political organization for revolution in the city, the nation, the continent, and the world.

The weakest links in the world capitalist chain have so far proved to be not in the metropolitan class structure but in the imperialist colonial structure. It is here that the Soviet, Chinese, Cuban and other revolutions took place. Where, then, in the colonial structure of the world and Latin America, are the weakest links now? What is the imperialist and Latin American bourgeoisie doing in attempts to cement these links through community development, health, education, "land reform", and other programs which, at the Alliance for Progress conference at Punta del Este, Che Guevara called the "latrinization" of Latin America? How far can these programs be carried – the latest effort, for instance, is to have the Latin American military occupation forces improve their reputation in the countryside by undertaking Latin American versions of the imperialist "pacifi- cation" program in Vietnam – and what effect will they have, if not for the acceleration of economic development, in the deceleration of political development in the countryside?

If we can find the weakest links in the colonial and class structure, how do we break them? Certainly not by exhortation to fight an invisible imperialist enemy by nationalization for the benefit of "all the people"; nor by abstruse explanations to make

Wall Street or perhaps even the Presidential Palace visible in the peasant or agricultural worker hut. These will make *themselves* all too visible if the Latin American rural masses, or even a small part of them, move to struggle against their immediately visible oppressors of long standing, who are the local economic and political agents of the imperialist and national capitalist colonial and class structure. What allies will these popular forces have – what alliances can they previously form and on what basis – with those elsewhere in the country, in Latin America, in the world, who are in a position to support them when the Latin American and then the imperialist bourgeoisie move in to try to save their local agents and therewith the whole exploitative colonial and class structure of capitalism?

Revolutionary political organization and mobilization could benefit from Marxist analysis of the class and colonial structure of particular regions or local areas. This study cannot, of course, be undertaken abroad and in terms of general pre-conceived schema. It must be pursued by revolutionary Marxists on the spot, who participate in the political movement the study is intended to serve. But the same principle also applies to theoretical work on broader political problems. Real Marxist theory can only be produced through revolutionary political practice. And for the intellectual from Latin America and other underdeveloped countries, this also means ideological struggle.

Ideology and Marxism

The colonial and class structures generate counterparts to justify themselves, and these also reflect themselves in the social "science" used to "study" them. For revolutionaries, therefore, the battleground includes the field of ideology, as Fidel suggests. For revolutionary social scientists, the ideological battle extends to the field of social science. The preponderant ideology, including its social "scientific" component, was developed by the bourgeoisie in the metropolis for use at home and for export to the colonies. The latter, at least in Latin America, have always had some awareness of the colonialist elements of this ideology and science. Particularly during and after times of nationalist upsurge, the nationalist sectors in Latin America have attempted to resist these colonialist elements and to develop nationalist ones in their stead. The nationalist alternatives are presented as a direct challenge to the colonial order, and as such are supposedly substantially different from the imperialist ideology and science. But since this nationalist alternative comes from the national bourgeoisie in Latin America, it reaffirms rather than challenges the class order at home. Revolutionaries must inquire how different this Latin ideology and science really is. Perhaps in the ideological part of the battleground, as well as in the political and military one, we must also – or first – combat the class enemy's ideology, in order thereby to combat this principal enemy, that is imperialism.

During the last century the principal imperialist bourgeois ideological exports have been liberalism, positivism, and now a sort of technological pragmatism or pragmatic technologism. Part of the Latin American bourgeoisie has eagerly accepted each of these, sometimes becoming more Catholic than the Pope, as the Latin American export interests did in the matter of the free trade doctrine. Some bourgeois and petit bourgeois sectors resisted the most flagrantly colonialist aspects of these doctrines, but they nonetheless accepted their essentials when they served their class interests with respect to the popular classes.

The latest ideological invasion proposes that North American "know how" and technology can solve all their problems for the people of the world, if they would only allow the North Americans to apply it without interference. In industry this means foreign investment and a higher degree of monopolization – and unemployment. In agriculture it means North American farming methods, seeds, fertilizers, farm machinery, etc. – and fertilizer and machinery production by Standard Oil and Ford. For the population this means birth control pills and drugs – and drug companies. For culture it means the "American Way of Life" through and with "mass" media, "popular" education, computerized statistical "science", etc. – all without, or rather against, any political and social revolution. The grand Latin American bourgeoisie accepts all this on a junior partner basis. The "nationalist" elements of the bourgeois and part of the petit bourgeoisie reject the "North American" part but accept the technological part: they say they will do it themselves – and better!

The imperialist ideological offensive in the social sciences may in recent times be said to have taken two major forms, structuralism and then its degeneration into institutionalism, culturalism, or behaviorism. Structuralism long dominated economics and sociology, which claimed to analyze the market structure and the social structure. But this was – and is – either the abstract study of idealized modes of a competitive market or of a consensual society, which may refer to any possible imaginary social system ranging from a family to the whole world, but which do not explain any particular real social system. Or structuralists deal with some particular social systems, which are always local, regional, or national units that are not the determinant social whole. This abstract or concrete, but limited, "structuralism" diverts the investigator's attention away from the real world wide capitalist system, its class and colonial structure, and the history of its development, which have determined social reality in both the metropolitan and colonial parts of the imperialist system.

Recent developments in metropolitan social science, and their export to the underdeveloped countries, divert the investigator's attention still further from fundamental social and political problems and solutions. Institutionalism describes the supposed social and political institutions of bourgeois society and "democracy", as they superficially appear. Culturalism focuses on cultural manifestations of the underlying economic and social structure, and more recently even on psycho- (that is individual) cultural characteristics. Behaviorism, now rampant in political "science" and increasingly in other social sciences, advances ever more computerized techniques of rigorous statistical analysis of all sorts of social variables, without ever coming to terms with the structure and development of the social system – lest we get the idea that it requires structural change. In addition to the limitations (advantages from the point of view of the bourgeoisie) of structuralism, these degenerations permit the differentiation of the same thing and the comparison of different things: the fact that the metropolis and its colonies are part of the same capitalist system is masked by discovering the supposedly independent existence in them of the very cultural and institutional differences that this colonial relationship creates. At the same time the discovery of superficial institutional and behavioristic similarities between capitalist and socialist countries permits the bourgeoisie statistically (that is, in apparent ideological "neutrality") to "prove" to the class it exploits that the class structure is really irrelevant – and need not be changed.

This ideology in the guise of science is today being propagated throughout the capitalist world – and even into the socialist camp – through countless channels. The enlightened elements of Latin American colonial bourgeoisie eagerly cooperate in this process today as they did in the past, while some national bourgeois elements have been attempting an ideological social scientific offensive of their own. After the bourgeois nationalist upsurge of the thirties and forties, but apparently with a cultural lag of a decade or more, these Latin American bourgeois interests established several institutions whose express purpose is the development of a nationalist scientific ideology. First and foremost among these is the United Nations Economic Commission for Latin America (CEPAL) and its more recent offspring, the Instituto Latinoamericano de Planificación Económica y Social (ILPES), both in Santiago, Chile. In Brazil it was the Instituto Superior de Estudios Brasileiros (ISEB), in Argentina the Instituto Torcuato di Tella, in Mexico the Escuela Nacional de Ciencias Políticas y Sociales of the National University (UNAM). The names of their founders, directors, and principal collaborators have become universally known in Latin American social science and even broader intellectual circles: Raul Prebisch, Anibal Pinto, Oswaldo Sunkel, Celso Furtado, Helio Jaguaribe, Gino Germani, Pablo Gonzales Casanova, etc.

Their major theses are well known: The metropolis exploits Latin America, but primarily through declining terms of trade. Thus, they complain of a colonial relationship, but they do not go on to analyze the monopolistic colonial structure and the increasing role within it of foreign investment and foreign aid, which they generally welcome, subject only to certain "safeguards". They attribute Latin American underdevelopment to the mistaken choice of "underdevelopment towards the outside" when Latin America was finally awoken from its feudal slumber in the mid-nineteenth century. Had Latin America then "chosen development toward the inside" it would not have suffered from declining terms of trade and would have been able to industrialize. Therefore, they argue, Latin America should choose national capitalist development toward the inside now.

The obstacle to this is a small internal market, they say. Domestically, then, they advance virtually the same interpretation of Latin America as that embodied in the Alliance for Progress and enlightened structuralism: Latin America is divided into a "dual" economy and society, part capitalist and progressive and part feudal and retrograde. Land reform, tax reform, etc., and economic "planning" initiated by the progressive industrialists and middle classes would remove "feudal" obstacles and integrate the vast rural population, and especially the Indians, into the national market and society. These "scientific" ideologists argue that the rural poor are poor because they are outside the market or money economy, and that is why industrial and economic development does not proceed. They call themselves "structuralists", and they employ what they find useful in Marxist analysis and terminology – to propose *reform* for the structure.

But these "structuralists", who complain of metropolitan exploitation, do not observe or analyze the internal colonial structure of Latin America, through which the national metropolis sucks out of the "feudal" countryside most of the capital for its own limited industrial investment and development. Nor do these ideologists for the national bourgeoisie analyze the domestic class structure of Latin America. Instead they import the latest North American techniques for the study of "élites" and "social stratification", and their students increasingly fall prey to the new metropolitan offer to substitute objective statistical for scientific political analysis and solution of Latin American problems.

In other words, in the first place the Latin American "progressive nationalist" version of this bourgeois social science is only superficially but not fundamentally different from the imperialist model. In the second place, the nationalist ideological offensive in the social sciences did not really begin until the economic, social, and political movement from which it came had passed its peak and had already begun to recede into history. Finally, imperialism has in the sixties begun a counter-offensive in this field as well, with the result that its behavioral "science" is increasingly neutralizing elements of the Latin American petit bourgeoisie who a few years ago were still politically progressive. In this connection it is noteworthy that imperialism is now using invitations to conference, scholarships, "joint" U.S.–Latin American "research" projects, etc., both in the United States and in its Latin American affiliates, to court precisely the left Latin American (and other) intellectuals whom it had previously shunned and persecuted.

What is the Latin American revolutionary left's response to this ideological offensive in the field of social science?

Many thousands of Latin American students and workers – among them perhaps another Fidel, Che, Camilo – are searching for scientific and political guidance beyond that offered them by the metropolitan bourgeoisie, by their Latin American followers or revisers, or by certain Marxist revisionists. Are they to be instructed and guided by the metropolitan derived "Marxist" models 14, 13, or 12 (as Fidel Castro derided them at OLAS) according to which all humanity necessarily passes successively through stages from communal communism, through slavery, feudalism, capitalism, socialism, to communism? Will these students, as well as industrial and agricultural workers, be united by theorists who tell them – no less than the national bourgeois ideologists – that Latin America is now divided in two parts, one still in the feudal stage and the other already in the capitalist stage; that a feudal oligarchy and imperialism but not the bourgeoisie are the obstacles to national development? *Latin Americans will never be led to revolution* by the principal political thesis derived from this "Marxist" pseudo-science, which at OLAS Fidel called "the famous thesis about the role of the national bourgeoisies, for example . . . how much paper, how many phrases, how much empty talk have been wasted waiting for a liberal, progressive, anti-imperialist bourgeoisie. . . . And many people are told this is Marxism . . . and in what way is it different from catechism, and in what way is it different from a litany, from a rosary?"

This means that political necessity confronts us with an ideological task to fulfil, both to assure the firmness of the revolutionary militants, and to recruit more and more Latin Americans, especially young ones, to their ranks. We also have important theoretical work to do to complement revolutionary practice with the necessary revolutionary theory. And we need to analyze Latin American society, especially its rural regions, in order to help the popular forces in their revolutionary struggle. For that, Marxists will have to create the leading and revolutionary ideas which, as Fidel says, the Latin American Revolution needs. Ideological clarity about these problems becomes especially essential when the revolutionary movement is temporarily slowed down, because it is at that time that ideological firmness is necessary in order to resist the temptations – which the bourgeoisie always offers – to recede towards a reformist policy, suggesting for example the supposed possibility and necessity of a "democratic peace", as the PCV is doing at this time. To reach this ideological and theoretical clarity, Marxists will have to work intellectually, but not only intellectually, inspired by the example of Che, who is revolutionary first and then intellectual.

To pursue this ideological and revolutionary objective, which is the real responsibility of the Latin American intellectual, and of the Marxists especially, will mean – as Che Guevara also found – leaving the institutional bounds of the Latin American and imperialist to bourgeoisie. The Latin American intellectual – and this is true as well for the artist or writer as for the social scientist – will have to become conscious of the fact that he has been working for the bourgeoisie. He will have to realize also that, the acuter the contradictions become and the more the revolutionary process advances, the less will the bourgeoisie permit the Latin American intellectual to take advantage of its bourgeois institutions – universities, publishing houses, press, etc. – for the development of a really revolutionary Marxist theory and practice. In some parts of the continent, the hour at which the doors of the bourgeoisie institutions close to the Marxist has already come; in the remaining parts that time will come soon. The Latin American intellectual and Marxist will have to decide if he will remain inside pursuing reformism, or outside with the people making the revolution.

NOTES

[1] Aldo Ferrer, *The Argentine Economy* (Berkeley: University of California Press, 1967); quotation from Spanish edition, pp. 31–2.

[2] For more detailed analysis, see Andre Gunder Frank, *Capitalism and Underdevelopment in Latin America – Historical Studies of Chile and Brazil* (New York: Monthly Review Press, 1967).

[3] See A. G. Frank, "The Development of Underdevelopment", in *Monthly Review*, Vol. 18, No. 4 (New York: September 1966).

[4] See Frank, *ibid*.

[5] Miron Burgin, *The Economic Aspects of Argentine Federalism 1820–1852* (Cambridge: Harvard University Press, 1946), p. 234.

[6] Burgin, *op. cit.*, p. 81.

[7] Rosa Luxemburg, *The Accumulation of Capital* (New York: Monthly Review Press, 1964), p. 438.

[8] John Kenneth Turner, *Mexico Barbaro* (Mexico: Ediciones del Instituto Nacional de la Juventud Mexicana, 1964; originally published in English, 1908).

[9] Ramiro Guerra y Sanchez, *Sugar and Society in the Caribbean: An Economic History of Cuban Agriculture* (New Haven and London: Yale University Press, 1964); translated from *Azucar y Poblacion en las Antillas* (La Habana).

[10] Francisco Encina, *Nuestra Inferioridad Economica: Sus Causas y Consecuencias* (Santiago, 1912).

[11] See Frank, "Services Rendered", in *Monthly Review*, Vol. 17, No. 2 (June 1966). See also "Servicos Extranjeros o Desarrollo Nacional?", in *Commercio Exterior*, Tomo XVI, No. 2 (Mexico, Febrero 1966).

[12] Computed from United Nations, ECLA, *El Financiamiento Externo de America Latina* (New York: E/CN. 12/649/Rev. 1, Diciembre 1964).

[13] See Lyons, p. 63.

[14] See Claude McMillan, *International Enterprise in a Developing Economy: A Study of U.S. Business in Brazil*, M.S.U. Business Studies (East Lansing: Michigan State University Press, 1964), p. 205.

[15] See A. E. Safarian, *Foreign Ownership of Canadian Industry* (Toronto: McGraw-Hill Company of Canada, 1966), pp. 235, 241 for all data on Canada.

[16] See Harry Magdoff, "Economic Aspects of U.S. Imperialism", in *Monthly Review*, Vol. 18, No. 6 (November 1966), p. 39.

6

Gradual Change or Violent Revolution in Latin America?*

Violence belongs to the world of feeling just as the experience of peace does. Gradualness indicates the speed at which structures change. A mood and a speed are not commensurate, nor can they be substituted and interchanged. But gradual change of structure can go hand in hand with a violent expression of the experience of newness. Both creation and destruction are explosive when they are rooted deeply in life and must overcome a barrier. Spring, too, can "break out"!

Can gradual change be an alternative to violent revolution? Those who ask this question are convinced that change is necessary, unavoidable. They want to understand violence so that they may propose alternatives to it. My task here is to highlight how difficult this understanding is. The other man's violence always threatens. My violence soothes me. This ambiguity makes it difficult to understand the other man's anger in the other man's terms. I know no more peaceful men than Dom Helder Cámara (Archbishop of Recife, Brazil) or Francisco Julião (exiled Brazilian labor leader), but since they speak with strong feelings, they are both called violent men.

When interests are involved, objectivity is actually more difficult for the doctor than it is for the priest. So let us act, for the time being, neither as patient nor as doctor in international affairs, but as students. We know that a patient's primary feelings might contain a far better diagnosis than a doctor's reasoned conclusion. We want to prepare ourselves to register the signals on which such feelings are transmitted.

* by Ivan Illich.

Which Way Violence?

On the one hand, the disciplined and purposeful planning of a counter-insurgency school in Panama might be an initial symptom of a mortal disease: of a Vietnam to the South, an incubating demon of a "Viet Lat" in the seventies. On the other hand, outbreaks by undisciplined guerrillas in the Peruvian Andes might be an advanced symptom of incipient health, an outcry of budding awareness. Which way lies violence?

It is obviously far more pleasant to consider and advocate "gradual change" and its sister notion, "constructive alternatives to violence", than it is to develop discriminating empathy with a foreign, changing texture of life. Let us make this "academic" effort. This empathy with social process beyond the barrier of culture should be a major goal for education, especially in the political sciences.

As students of change, it is important and significant for us to feel what urbanization means – deep down – to the man who arrives in industrial São Paulo after a month's trip from Belem at the mouth of the Amazon. We must consider how urbanization affects his character, his self-image. Our co-living with him seems more important than the development of new instruments to plot the directions of his surface responses or economic behavior. We are committed to share in our guts the anxiety and bewilderment of a man from the fields suddenly taken into a factory. Only slowly, and with tenderness, may we sense the pain of another when his old world dims, when new stars bewilder him; when words lose their traditional meaning, and new words that he does not grasp sparkle, seduce, and betray. I believe that only the man who knows himself as being constantly subject to this experience can share in this experience of others.

Everyone knows that some words upset and others soothe. But not everyone remembers that there are some words which may have either effect, depending on the social context, the semantic ghetto in which they rally a group. "Violence" is one of these, and on this I guess we agree. I also believe that, since 1965, in the United States and Latin America, "gradual methods" has been another such expression. I want to call your attention to this especially.

I remember well a night with a group of students at the central university in a Latin American country. Their commitment to the word "violencia" was so strong that those who did not feel swept away by it were considered unreal, outsiders. Earlier that same day, I had spent an hour with a key man in the country's industrial renewal, one of the great men in the Council for Latin America. As I listened to him, I sensed his fear of violence, his reasoned and intelligent commitment to gradual methods of societal change. More than that: I had heard him detail the need for arming private goon squads, composed preferably of reliable Catholics, who would insure the time needed for this gradual change. Again, which way lies violence?

On the same day, then, I had shared in both poles of the same social mood. It is obvious that violence and gradual change meant very different things for the patient and the doctor on the same day in the same city.

Semantic Ghettoes Coexist

Within one semantic ghetto – one conception universe – reasonable discourse is possible. Supposed agreement *can* be questioned, and one's opponents *can* make their points. But what happens *between* two semantic ghettoes? Between distinct semantic ghettoes, only diplomatic notes can be exchanged, or shouts can clash. Finally, narcissistic coexistence of two sick units can be imagined. Let us study how men can be trained so that in their hearts the words from two ghettoes can meet.

Peru, for example, is an infinite distance from the ghetto of meaning which is a U.S. university. The latter is a strange ghetto and utterly removed from that of Peru. It is a ghetto where the problem of "unbalanced diet" and "death from over-nutrition" has been substituted for the world problem of hunger. But in the Andes of Peru, thousands still *die* of plain hunger.

The United States is a land so rich that it can consider with some comfort the proposal to tax the rich so as to guarantee an annual $4,000 income to all those who do not produce. Off there, is the rest of the world: the world of those destined, at best, merely to survive.

With a guaranteed income, we could push Watts beyond our borders and surround the North Atlantic with a "World Harlem". Would this cure the basic sickness of our society? At this moment we are becoming aware of the common roots of slums and underdevelopment. The events of 1966 made public opinion aware that, for reasons much deeper than had been assumed, Harlem and Fifth Avenue cannot mingle. First of all, words in the two ghettoes *cannot* mean the same things. Now we learn to see further implications: *gradualness* of change just cannot be experienced the same way in the *first* year of settlement in a neo-colony as it can in the *twentieth* year of a bull market in megapolis. And yet we must relate them. We cannot afford to coexist, we must *live* together. The bridge of words is not sufficient if it is not paralleled by a bridge of feeling.

It takes time to acquire empathy with the growing pains of a foreign society, to train oneself to academic contemplation as opposed to operation research, to commit oneself to real observation which does not exclude the heart. Such growth is difficult because it takes much time and peace for the student, and because it is frowned upon as innocent dreaming by most people. The high concentration on operation-oriented research in foreign relations is certainly not a result of the CIA, but it is a sad indicator of the decline of institutional commitment to deep insight in our universities. Our task should be assistance to men preparing themselves for disinterested awareness across cultural lines, service to men seeking to become capable of non-condescending *respect* for the alternatives actually open to growing societies.

Contrasting Views of Violence

Violence, or the social expression of nonrational aggression, has a different meaning for the holdup man, the cashier in the bank, and the bystander. What does gradualness or violence mean for different men in Bogota? For Camilo Torres, violence is one thing. For the clergy of Bogota, it is another. And finally, violence means something else again for a planner in the Colombian

Ministry of Education. Camilo believes himself an educator and tries to teach that gradual improvement, even if it were possible under the present structure, could not bring any meaningful change. The Cardinal of Bogota believes that he is charged with, and is a guardian of, peace. Of course, the Cardinal believes in change – as long as it fits into the established order. (For the man in power, violent protest cannot mean "education".) The third man, the bureaucrat who is trying to multiply little red schoolhouses, feels threatened by the clash of the first two men, because it calls his attention to something which does not fit into his professional schemes. He thinks to himself: "Could it be that Camilo's type of *adult* education – adult education through testimony – must come first? Must it come before *our* kind of schooling in little red schoolhouses can be of any value at all?" Must perhaps Camilo precede the bureaucrat and the multiplication of little red schoolhouses?

It makes little sense to build schools in Latin America before we have really begun to engage in adult education. And this, I believe, we cannot do without uncorking violence.

Let me illustrate what I mean. It was in a shed in Aracaju, in Northeast Brazil, December 1964. Twenty men were assembled around a slide projector. A picture of a man with a pick and a pile of stones was projected onto a sheet of brown paper. With it were four syllables: "*ter-ra*", "*ho-mem*". Then, another word was added: "*nossa*". "Land", "man", and finally, "ours". The men around the projector had the skin of hunger, the ashen quality almost unknown in the United States. They were undernourished by custom and heredity, unable to know what a healthy appetite means. You could sense their lacks which had not yet developed into needs. You could see how unaware they were of crying injustice. These laborers were learning to recognize some written words – words which they themselves had picked as the most meaningful to them that year in that village: *terra, homem*. Suddenly one man got up. Trembling, he stammered: "Last night I could not sleep, because yesterday I wrote my name. I saw my name written on paper. *Entendí que eu sou eu* – I understood that I am I." Surely, this is anguish – the anguish of birth. There is nothing gradual about that awakening.

He said, "*Eu sou eu, e por isso somos responsáveis*" (I am I, and therefore, we are responsible).

Certainly, this is what we want to happen in development, and I hope that we want it to happen at all cost. The cost of such awakening is high. Awakening of this kind does not fit men into the slots available. Education of this kind is more than instruction. It is silly to propose some training for gradual change to people who have seen such dramatic instances of awakening awareness.

The above case occurred in 1964. The first thing the Brazilian military government did in 1965 was to suppress this type of education, or at least to control it. No government at present can afford indiscriminate and free *concientização para a politização* (mobilization of consciousness for political purposes). Not Cuba. Not Acción Popular in Peru.

Even in the United States, discussions about the nonpermissible forms of slum education within the poverty program during the past year have made us humbler. The poverty program has opened the eyes of politicians to the ambiguities that Latin American *políticos* face in grass-roots movements. It is easier now to speak about this delicate subject in the United States.

Social Structures or Creativity?

No government wants to educate, unless it is moderately certain that its system will be accepted by those educated. We all prefer to trust our social structures rather than bubbling creativity.

In Latin America, relatively small capital investment would be needed to create widespread expansion of truly adult education: education which transforms unconscious lack into conscious needs; education which mobilizes creative imagination. At present we may advocate such education but we cannot obtain the funds for it. We are faced with a continental political commitment to gradual change. We are faced with paternal governments who want to prepare the structures before people become aware that they need them. Within the context of gradual change, the type of education I described cannot but be called "subversion". Within the political context to which our nations are subject, you may not awaken creative needs *you* cannot satisfy.

If *gradualness* in change, at all cost, is the main criterion for development, then the very first thing a government must do is this: impose strict controls on *adult* education. You may put any amount into little red schoolhouses, into trade schools and universities. *Socialization* through schooling will be called a most significant and productive investment. But beware of truly adult education! Beware of the power you unleash! Commitment to gradualness, at least in education, means a lack of confidence in our generation of living men. Gradualness, at least in education, means the decision of those in power today to make their children *feel* as our system requires them to.

Perhaps this provides a first reason why today it is difficult in Latin America to understand U.S. public concern for "gradualness" in change. The inhabitants of U.S. slums, perhaps, find gradualness just as hard to swallow.

Uncle Sam and Social Change

Another peculiar phenomenon makes it difficult to discuss change in Latin America without emotion: namely, continued implication of the United States when change *is* discussed. At the Center of Intercultural Documentation in Cuernavaca, we have under study some twenty public controversies which took place in Latin America in the last few years. They were chosen at random. On each controversy we collected hundreds of editorials and analyzed their "ideological" content. We set out to understand what arguments are used, what symbols manipulated, what feelings triggered, when people take sides on public issues. We wanted to see how people explain their options, how they justify their preferences, and how they extrapolate the consequences of decisions they hope, or they fear, will be taken. Now we have found that whenever structural change is the issue of a controversy, "Tio Sam" is always dragged in. It matters not whether the subject is Petrobras, a new university, educational reform, a new press law, or a violent death. This is a fact. I do not intend to explain it. I simply indicate this insistent reference to the United States as one factor which complicates any study of change in Latin America. All reference to change, to its speed or its meaning today in Latin America, implies a statement on foreign policy. This reference to the United States is, of course, ever present when one discusses Latin American events in English. Recently, it has assumed a new dimension, because the U.S. intellectual community is discovering the parallels between hurdles the poverty program meets and those implicit in foreign assistance. Both are upsetting.

Underdevelopment and the Poverty Program

In December 1966 we at Cuernavaca had a striking example of the deep meaning this parallel has for North Americans today. Some sixty people involved in poverty programs in U.S. slums met for consultation at our Center. The theme was an analysis of poverty as alienation and experience. We asked the participants to formulate the true aims of their programs. Our staff studied the sixty responses. They compared the attitudes the poverty workers held toward the *poor*, with the clichés well known from foreign assistance programs of AID, CARE, and mission societies. They found many coincidences. Poverty workers, just like missioners, seemed obsessed with the desire to "share" their blessings. The desire to incorporate the slum poor into an "achieving society" parallels the U.S. manifest destiny to extend the benefits of the "great society" beyond its borders.

"Expand and protect the great society" seems to be the almost religious banner which gives respectability to any decision made in the United States affecting investments, services (many of them gratuitous and social), establishments (not a few, para-military), and sales in Latin America. A decision-making process affecting Latin America which is dispersed through thousands of centers in the United States is given some kind of rationale by means of this consenting rationalization. For many observers in Latin America, the U.S. desire to share the "great society" lingers behind any discussion of change. Expansion and/or defense of the "great society" lies behind any discussion on the proper speed of social change in Latin America. The almost compulsive repetition that change in Latin America must happen "gradually though rapidly" is interpreted in Latin America as a fear of any form of development that might lead the southern continent out of U.S. hands and outside the U.S. market.

There cannot be any doubt that the gradual, orderly, and controlled increase of the gross national product is a major criterion for policy. How primary this criterion is, I do not want to say. Many critics, from François Peroux to Eduardo Frei, insist that this particular measuring stick is given too much importance.

Making the growth rate of per capita income the most significant indicator for growth can lead to a planned division of our societies into two sectors. In one sector you find the growing minority whose income increases at a rate superior to the gross national product. But the majority are aggregated in the other sector. And they are on the way to relative impoverishment, even though their purchasing power – in absolute terms – might increase.

Politicians argue that this arrangement insures stability. Indeed it does insure the established system. All those who "fit" and grow into the new society are also favored by it and are, therefore, purchased for its maintenance: they can only lose by revolution.

Perhaps this argument puts the cart before the horse: it measures social goals in terms of a method chosen *a priori*. The argument is also indicative of an emotional attitude which must be taken seriously. And today, this is our task: to elicit respect for emotions – even if they do not fit our scheme.

Gradualism Reinterpreted

All over Latin America one can now hear a new type of interpretation of U.S. concern for gradualism. It is an attitude more difficult to put into a few words without repeating expressions which smack of demagoguery. This interpretation focuses on the increase of U.S. federal agencies – especially dependencies of the Department of Defense – in Latin America. The question raised by this increasing apparatus is whether, consciously or unconsciously, the United States is preparing the groundwork for a "Viet Lat". The impression given is that a continent-wide system of counter-insurgency is growing. The inter-American police force to control guerrillas is seen in the same perspective as that in which the increase of state police is seen by the southern Negro. Those people in South America who use this argument see orderly and gradual change as a strategic attempt designed to gain time to establish an airtight network of repression.

In this war-focused context, resistance to U.S.-induced development is advocated as an improved alternative to the preparation for war in the seventies. The argument runs along the following lines: it would be a better thing to *prevent* lethal establishments of U.S. para-military agencies than to have to abort them later; but given that it is too late now for that kind of contraception, it is better that violence abort any further development of them than to collaborate in the incubation of the "demons of Viet Lat".

These feelings might shock, they might stem from bad dreams, but they are real. And they are now beginning to be understood in the United States. I attended a recent meeting of a group of graduate students and professors at an Ivy League college – serious men who have organized to systematically document U.S. activities in Latin America. It is their particular aim to ferret out blatant abuses of confidence, to unmask the establishments which pretend to serve development but in reality are instruments to draw Latin America into a global military strategy corresponding to somebody's view of the U.S. national interest. I was deeply touched when I saw that these men seemed willing to organize a U.S. citizens' group for nonviolent protest to U.S. exploitation in Latin America. The ghost of "Viet Lat" is uglier, but nowhere less real, than the equally ghostly Alliance for Progress.

Qualitative Changes in Life Experience

We have had to go into some detail to establish how touchy it is, given the screens of a semantic ghetto, to discuss the desirable speed of change. I repeat: If we were interested only in plotting and planning economic rates, abstracting from human experience, all this effort could be foregone. But we believe that qualitative changes in life experience are much more important for development than economic indicators and cement. Let me illustrate one scheme which we can follow to analyze this experience. It is a scheme which the members of our continuing faculty seminar in Cuernavaca have adopted, and we are indebted for its development to men like Fromm, Maccoby, Erikson, Helio la Suaribe, and many others. We have set out to understand social change as an interrelated transformation of (1) institutional structure, (2) formulated values or ideologies, and (3) social character. Our principal concern is that of understanding how the human heart reacts to this three-pronged change.

We try to focus on institutional structure and ask: By what law or assumptions or persuasions are these held in place? By what appeals to abstract value systems can the Mexican revolution promote private schools for the rich or the Brazilian revolution its new press laws?

But we will not be content to analyze this relationship between structure and rationale, we will not just seek to understand what persuasion a given functional mechanism exudes. We will try to understand what personality characteristics it favors. With concern we will watch the survival and renewal of that authentic mass outbreak of joy which is the carnival in Rio.

Finally, we want to know something about the relationship between character and ideology. What kind of personality finds most strength and support and consolation in a given type of faith? Who are those drawn to the Macumba, to the sects, to the guerrillas, or to achievement in well-organized business? Who are those people in Chile who can – and want to – recognize themselves in the ads in LIFE *en Español*? Who can be motivated by the picture of a portly middle-aged executive from Minnesota to change his way of life by foregoing immediate gratification to save for later, more conspicuous consumption?

Violence, A Response to Experience

This is an ambitious program, we admit. We want to try the impossible in order to come closer to grasping the mysterious workings of drastic social change. Of course, if we engage in this type of analysis, gradualness and violence assume a new meaning. Violence is not the measure of the speed with which one of these three variables changes. Violence is not a measure of structural reorganization. It is not a measure of change in persuasion. And it is not the measure of a new social type. Violence is rather a response of experience, of feeling, to the tensions created among these three.

It would be fascinating for me to heap example upon example. But for the time being, we want only to understand the impact which the U.S. presence in Latin America has on the quality of change there. I only want to indicate a model for analysis which may make the mode of U.S. impact on Latin American change a bit more amenable to discussion. Let me exemplify, separately, the impact of U.S. technical assistance on each of the three factors mentioned: institution, persuasion, personality. In other words: structure, ideology, and character; mechanisms, conceptual systems, and the character of those who fit them. Allow me to play with oversimplification and caricature to make my point and elicit needed discussion.

U.S. College Board Exams for Latin America

First, an example: an attempt is now being made to persuade Latin American universities to adopt the U.S. College Board Entrance Examinations. Considerable amounts of U.S. money have been spent on their development, particularly in Puerto Rico, and they are now available in Spanish. These tests are generally, though perhaps grudgingly, accepted in Puerto Rico. At first sight, their export – free of charge, since a foundation picks up the tab – may be seen as the simple concession of a benefit of our college machinery to others who are in need of it. Looking more carefully, we see that their adoption in other countries will ultimately have an important impact on those universities which do accept this testing tool. The acceptance of an admission test alters the social function of a university system. To be more explicit: This test is a filter designed to eliminate from further study those whose character or ability does not favor their academic achievement in a U.S. university. Those screened out are not considered proper material for U.S. higher education, because achievement at a university is interpreted as a forecast of achievement or leadership in later life. But leadership or achievement *where?* Success as it is defined and made necessary by an achievement-oriented society as we now know it in the United States. The adoption of this test, therefore, represents a decisive, profound, and covert long-range manipulation of the quality of life in a whole country. The adoption of the U.S. College Board examinations by a Latin American university contributes to making that university a far more important tool for the expansion of the basic mood of the "great society" than any direct changes in curriculum schedule, teaching method, or faculty training. The transfer of a small device from one culture to another can ultimately affect the *face* of a whole society: with the adoption of this device one type of character is preferred over others, and what is perhaps more significant, a certain type of self-image, copied from that of the United States, is subtly made into the standard of success in São Paulo.

To elaborate further – not on a fact, but on a certain danger. The U.S. college entrance exam is one small but effective contribution to the development of an overseas "white America" (to use the U.S. jargon of 1966). *Gradually* and *without violence* those who fit and aspire to a new societal pattern proposed to them from the outside are selected to manage it. The protests from Harlem are now getting a hearing. It is time to attune our ears to the same protest reaching us in foreign idioms.

Implications of Exporting Ideas
Discussion in depth is needed on this question: May we export the *motivational structure* which corresponds to our *cherished persuasions* (in other words, to the American way of life) if this implies also the reverse – the export of Watts and Harlem and Selma on a gigantic scale? This question, if properly understood, is so disturbing and discouraging to me that I formulate it with fear – particularly the fear that it be understood as an expression of despair, while in truth it is meant as an enormous challenge. We must not be lazy. Thomas Aquinas says that laziness is the worst of sins: the deadly inactivity of a man who has given up living because he has become aware of how hard it is to live.

The highly ambiguous assistance of the United States in Latin America represents an inevitable involvement. The involvement is inevitable because it meets the objective demands of international political and economic fact, and because it satisfies deep-rooted needs which stem from the prevalent U.S. self-image: the U.S. tenet of "secular religion" (to speak with Bellah) that every American at any moment can, must, and may share the blessings of his country with those less fortunate than he. The radical's demand that the United States "drop out of international relations because it cannot but do damage" is on the opposite pole from the new isolationist's aggressiveness; but both attitudes are marginal and but a frame which highlights the commitment of the majority here to the utopia of a worldwide "great society".

Concern with the world beyond national borders is a deep-rooted part of U.S. ethics. There is no other country in which the ethos of international help has marked with equal depth the basic creed of a nation. There is no other people which could produce as a trademark – alongside Uncle Sam and the big stick – the image of the Quaker missioner. There has never been another government which has set up the like of its world-spanning institutional network for assistance: social, economic, military, and religious.

The U.S. enveloping involvement in Latin America, therefore, is both socio-politically and psychologically inevitable. Discussion of this involvement has afforded me the opportunity to demonstrate the difficulties which threaten misunderstanding of the relationship, as well as to point to the challenge that these same difficulties present – the striving toward an understanding that will lead us to greater human depths.

The obstacle on which I have focused is operational and concerns those in the United States who want to deal with Latin America. This obstacle is the tendency to underestimate how difficult it is even for the highly educated North American to reach a deep, a realistic, a humble awareness of the ambiguity implicit in his participation in the development process outside the "great society". This difficulty will increase for every North American in Latin America. The ability to let himself be adopted into the feeling of authentically rooted Latin American groups or crowds is not acquired in libraries. Neither is it achieved simply by participating in action programs. This ability is rather a measure of the personal maturity and the personal commitment of the individual North American to utter simplicity and openness of heart – two phrases not too current in our academic circles. Therefore, this ability is restricted to exceptional men and women, and will remain so. It should be our stated task to seek them out and to encourage them to commit themselves generously and without reserve to voluntary immigration into Latin America.

After the obstacle, I focused on a value – a value which I consider the critical element in development, the element which will decide if economic growth and technological abundance will meet real needs or only create new awareness of deficiencies. This element, this value – if present – will condition human freedom. Its absence will result in deadly coexistence of men and groups without a future. Drastic change, as we have seen, can leave in its wake either violently bewildered wrecks or men who experience new dimensions of personal freedom and creativity bursting open. Will drastic change rest in men who experience their awareness and feelings, or will it make men less poets, make men into just more effective and productive manpower?

The ability to experience change seems to be the decisive indicator of the value of change. Change which cannot be lived is deadly. Change which diminishes the ability of a man to feel related and a participant cannot be going in the right direction.

At a recent course in our Center in Cuernavaca, a participant (a cattle breeder bent for the altiplano) told me: "I get it! You don't grow people. If they are men, they each grow. And each better know that he himself is responsible for this growth. You don't develop people and societies. They do."

The ultimate criterion for the planner of social change cannot be the mode of its production or the technical structure to which it leads, but rather the quality of leisure, of creativity, of celebration it makes possible.

7

Identity and the Nature of Revolution*

What are the beliefs or assumptions about human nature and psychological process which should or should not guide the practitioners of foreign policy in dealing with the politics and revolutions of other people? Of course, in discussing this, one almost inevitably must observe that some events in the history of our own recent foreign policy suggest that the beliefs about human nature held by some of the practitioners on our side seem to be a little primitive. Someone once said that war is diplomacy carried on by other means. But there are politics and politics, and in the context of this discussion, it is necessary to distinguish between two main types of political revolution, distinguished on the basis of the motivations of the people who are conducting the revolutions. First, there are revolutions based on and deriving from what we can call politics of the appetites. These are efforts to seize political power in essentially intact social systems. The effort is not to destroy the system, but to seize positions of power and influence within it. The motives behind this have to do with the gratification of individual human appetites which lead men to want power in order to acquire wealth, to loot and plunder, to gain personal advancement in an existing system, to achieve success in career, perhaps to change particular policies, but to leave the system itself alone. And here one thinks of *coups d'état* and palace revolutions and treasonable conspiracies and changes in the ruling families and that type of thing. The other kind of revolution, the kind which is of concern here, is the revolution based on what can be called politics of identity. Here, the effort is to seize political power and thereby be able to

* by Anthony F. C. Wallace.

change radically the nature of the social and cultural system of the society in order to realize a new and better identity – in other words, to achieve salvation. The people who are organized to prosecute the second kind of revolution are motivated by the politics of identity.

These identity revolutions are members of a class of organizations which I call revitalization movements, exemplified by European and American millenial movements, New Guinea Cargo cults, and American Indian nativistic movements. The important thing about revitalization movements and the revolutions which sometimes grow out of them is that the followers of the leader in the movement and in the revolution are fundamentally searching for salvation. They are not primarily interested in economic goals, and an ordinary hedonistic calculus does not explain their behavior. They seek salvation in a true religious sense, and this is the case whether or not the movement itself is primarily religious in a ritual or ceremonial way, with supernatural beliefs lying behind it, or whether it appears to be a rational political movement, as may be the case with a communist revolution. The main theme, then, of these remarks will be that the motivational force behind those revolutions which grow out of revitalization movements is the attempt to acquire a new and better identity. Involved here, too, are the assumptions with regard to these motivations that policy makers can make and the effect they will have on the course of a revitalization movement or an identity revolution.

One can illustrate the conscious awareness of identity in the members of revitalization movements from their own remarks. This is usually not an inference which has to be made cautiously and very guardedly about revitalization leaders at least. These people are consciously aware and speak easily and readily about the nature of their own identity problems. Here, for instance, is a description by K. O. L. Burridge of the feelings of the Tangu, a Melanesian people who had been involved in a Cargo cult:

> The fact is that when Tangu face a European, eye to blazing eye, within arm's length, the sap runs dry, the Tangu submit, and they know that they do so. They

would like it to be otherwise. "Are we dogs?" they cry, in impassioned fury, "are we not men as they are?"

Margaret Mead, describing a similar movement among the Manus, quotes the Manus as saying: "All men are brothers, black, white, green, red, all are brothers." President Nasser, in his autobiographical account of the Egyptian revolution, says that his revolution "demands that we restore our lost dignity to our moral values", and C. Wright Mills, in his presentation of the Castro case, expresses the position of the Castro revolution as follows (as if quoting from the Cuban side):

> Because we have been poor, you must not believe that we have lost our pride. You must not believe that we have no dignity, no honor, no fight. Now we are assuring you as calmly as we are able that we do have these qualities. In future we will continue to reveal them to you – by our actions as well as our words. Either you will see this, or you won't see it. If you do, perhaps we can be friends again. If you don't, it will be a very bad time of troubles for us all.

And finally, in regard to American Negro revitalization movements, C. Eric Lincoln in his book on the Black Muslims describes a sign carried by a follower of Marcus Garvey, simply labeled, "We are men and brothers." Throughout these instances and others, the theme being asserted by the people concerned with revitalization is that they feel an uncertainty about their personal worth, their worth as human beings, their worth as men, their worth in regard to intellectual qualities. They feel inferior, either with regard to their ancestors or with regard to some other people who are politically dominant over them, and they demand that the circumstances change in such a way that this sense of inferiority and inadequacy in identity can be removed.

One should probe a bit into the nature of those aspects of personality dynamics which refer to identity and then see how they are applicable to the phenomena which occur in revitalization movements. And then it may be possible to make a few very simple deductions about appropriate psychological assumptions in regard to foreign policy.

My own interest in identity dynamics grew out of clinical experience in a psychiatric setting, observing the work of a therapeutic team dealing with the families of schizophrenic patients, and in that connection reviewing the literature on identity and personality. It seemed that what we saw there was a classic example of a struggle between people each of whom was asserting a claim to a kind of identity, having this claim batted down, and in response attacking the identity of others. These identity struggles seem to be painful, protracted, and peculiarly characteristic of those stressful and pathological family situations in which schizophrenic people are apt to be involved. The identity struggle, in which two or more people assert an identity of their own and attack someone else's identity, is best illustrated in the phenomenon of brainwashing. Anyone who has read anything about brainwashing – efforts to change identity in a political context – will realize that the major reliance in the techniques is not upon physical torture or physical stress. What is set up is a systematic and prolonged identity struggle between an organized group of inquisitors and a victim who may have to attempt to withstand the pressures of this struggle over a period of months. The art of the inquisitor in a brainwashing situation is to learn enough about the victim to be able to identify those aspects of the victim's identity with which he is personally least satisfied, the things about which he feels uncomfortable, inadequate, or guilty. He does this by interviewing the victim, by requiring him to write autobiographies, by demanding that he introspect and think about himself and his problems. The inquisitor takes on the role of a kind of therapist, psychiatrist, friend, guide. He denies that he is the warden and captor, and over a period of time he is able to convince the victim that indeed the inquisitor's identity is really that of a friendly therapist and, furthermore, that the victim's personal qualities and characteristics are, in some area of life that is important to him, extremely inadequate, and that he must either substitute a new ego-ideal, a new goal for personal aspiration, or at least recognize that he has fallen far, far short of success in certain important areas of his life. If this is continued long enough, a real personality change can be accomplished and a "new man", as the Chinese put it, can be produced.

Now, this kind of identity struggle in which one person says, "I am like this and you are like that," and his partner says, "No, you're not the way you say you are, you're something else, and I'm not the way you say I am, I'm something else," is apt to occur not only between individuals but also between groups. One can look at the dialogue between American Negro and anti-Negro white groups in this country as an identity struggle of precisely this kind, in which the Negro says, "Well, I am such-and-such a kind of a person, not at all the way you say I am," and the white person says, "I am not bigoted at all the way you say I am, I'm really a very friendly type of person." This kind of dialogue can continue indefinitely, with extremely intense emotion, and can contribute to the development of an explosive kind of inter-group situation. The possible outcomes of a situation of prolonged and intense identity struggle between groups would seem to be four. First, a disruption of the relationship by violence; second, some sort of accommodation in which the two parties finally agree about what to call themselves and each other, so that they both feel good about it; third, simply separation, physically moving apart and no longer communicating; and fourth, the suffering by one party or the other of real identity destruction and subsequent change.

Behind these observations about the dynamics of identity struggles lies, implicit in the literature on identity, a general theory about a kind of personality dynamics that is different from the dynamics of appetites as it is described in classical psychoanalytic theory from which most clinical personality theories are derived. In the theory of personality based on the concept of identity, one must not think of a total identity as one big wad of interlocking characteristics, but as a series of dimensions. Within each dimension of identity, each aspect with regard to which a person may evaluate himself, one can distinguish three separate features: there is an ideal identity, the person as he would like himself to be; a feared identity, with regard to the same dimension – that characteristic or that state which he would dread to accept as characterizing him; and finally, more or less in between these two, what can be called real identity in the sense that here is where the person thinks he is. Let's say, in an academic situation, the student would like to think that he is able to get good grades without much trouble. The nightmarish possibility exists that he is the kind of person who would be unable to make good grades no matter how much sweat and blood he put into it. But usually he thinks, well, he's not really making out that easily, but on the other hand, he isn't doing that badly and wasting that much time at it either. Now, with respect to any such dimension, one postulates that there is a motive to minimize the distance between the real identity and the ideal identity and to maximize the distance between the real and feared identity. Furthermore, these aspects vary in salience or importance to the individual, partly depending on situation and partly depending on prevailing personal characteristics. Some things are crucially important and the person will fight desperately to maintain a good sense of self-esteem in these areas. In others he would be willing to make compromises or simply just let the matter slide. A complete identity, then, is the sum total, and the structure of a number of separate dimensions, in each of which the person is constantly monitoring his own adequacy, based partly on experience of success in his own efforts and partly on the evaluations of him which are communicated by others. Now, circumstances can exist where an important, salient aspect of identity is involved, where any appetite will be sacrificed in order to maintain the adequate level of self-esteem. Thus there are circumstances which will lead people to stop behaving according to motivations based on the satisfaction of such appetites as hunger, sex, the desire for physical comfort, or the preservation of life, and to commit themselves completely to the protection or advancement of their identity in some salient area.

Now, in the case of revitalization movements, it would appear that the prime motive force is not the satisfaction of appetites but the enhancement of identity in important areas where the person or persons involved feel seriously threatened. We can define a revitalization movement as a conscious, organized effort by some members of a society to construct a more satisfying culture. The persons who want such movements are apt to have experienced an intense religious experience, a moment of revelation, after some prolonged period of personal dissatisfaction and disillusionment, and see as a combined task the salvation of their own souls and the salvation of the world around them. Typically, a revitalization movement can be considered as pursuing some six distinguishable stages. The first is the moment of revelation, in which a leader or prophet experiences, often in a visionary and hallucinatory way, both a diagnosis of his own identity problems and a diagnosis of what is wrong with the world. He is instructed, furthermore, in what to do in order to save himself and to save the world around him. He, in the second stage, communicates this to potential followers. This is an important experience in himself and it also applies to the society as a whole. He preaches – he becomes an evangelist. His preaching manages to attract some followers who in turn carry the word, and a systematic missionary effort is conducted to make converts. Now, in this stage the converts are preaching in effect a code which asserts three things. First, it asserts a diagnosis of what's wrong with the world right now, what's wrong with society. It describes the present state of society as evil and specifies in what ways it is evil. Second, it describes an ideal society, the way things ought to be, different in important respects from the way things are now. Third, it defines a transfer culture, a set of procedures which if followed will make over the evil present society into the Utopian society of the future. The communist doctrine fits this code neatly, first giving a diagnosis of the inadequacies of the capitalist system, then describing an ideal communist stateless society as the goal, and finally describing a situation of class war and the dictatorship of the proletariat as the transfer culture by which one can get from one condition to another. As the prophet and his first immediate disciples begin to gain converts, a process of organization has to occur in which there is a division of labor. The prophet is often relieved of some of his executive responsibilities by a lieutenant who takes over, handling the routine details of the movement while the prophet remains in charge of reformulations of the code; and there will be a division between an inner circle of disciples and a group of mass followers. As the organization goes on in the process of attempting to make converts and to communicate with people outside the movement, it will usually be necessary to make some adaptation. Often movements of this kind, while they demand radical changes in the society, are not fundamentally hostile to the personnel of the Establishment. They view the rest of the world as a field to be won over by words, a group to be converted. If, however, the Establishment is adamant, the revitalization movement is faced with the alternative of either modifying its code or taking up arms. Modification of the code is possible only insofar as it does not threaten the personnel of the movement with an abandonment of their identity claims. Therefore an adamant refusal is likely to precipitate what started as a reasonably friendly group into a violent and hostile conspiratorial group. If the movement is successful in achieving political power, either peacefully or by violence, there will be an effort to produce the cultural transformations necessary to realize the Utopian society; and finally, the movement will shrink as the need for a charismatic leadership in positions of executive power diminishes. And at such point the movement is apt to become something like a church, separate from the political bureaucracy: it monitors the success of government and checks up on the conduct of people, but is no longer personally demanding political power.

In order to distinguish between a group which is involved in a revolution of the first (appetite-motivated) kind mentioned and of the second (identity-motivated) kind, the nature of the code itself is obviously crucial. If the code envisages a radical transformation of the society rather than a change in personnel, if one can distinguish a charismatic, prophetic leadership, the phenomenon is a revitalization movement. This should also serve to distinguish a revitalization movement simply from situations of widespread alienation or dissatisfaction or complaint, or vague beliefs, prevalent in a society, in such things as the coming of the Messiah, or the belief that the Cargo will some day arrive. Such widely held beliefs often lie behind and rationalize a particular revitalization movement, but their presence in itself is not evidence of a movement.

Because of the claim in the code that people are going to be transformed and become virtuous and admirable and possess new identities, one can infer that a necessary condition for the development of a revitalization movement is a widespread feeling of inadequacy among the members of the society with respect to some major and important aspects of identity. Such a situation can be produced in the course of an identity struggle with another society, and this is the typical situation in which anthropologists observe phenomena like this in the field. Usually the primitive society being studied is under the political domination of a European power. Anthropologists have spent most of their professional lives over the last three generations studying those societies in the world which are politically dominated by Europeans, and this in fact is almost an operational definition of the word "primitive society". Another possible situation in which this kind of identity conflict can develop without problems of foreign domination would be simply a decline within the society in the efficacy of the means to achieve conventional goals. This could come about through such circumstances as natural disaster or overpopulation, or perhaps various economic processes which could cause many people to feel that they cannot become the kind of successful persons which they have learned to believe they should be. A third circumstance which could generate this type of tension between real identity and ideal identity is the introduction of new goals without introduction of means by which they can be achieved, and here one is reminded of the familiar observation that the point at which a colonial society is most likely to enter a period of active revolution is not at the point of most serious realistic economic and political deprivation, but at some point on a rising curve. When things begin to get better and levels of aspiration are raised, expectations are apt to run ahead of actual accomplishment and at that point the tension between ideal identity and real identity is most apt to be severe. The main point about this, however, is that one cannot attribute this sort of identity conflict to absolute levels of poverty or deprivation. The absolute discomforts, measured on some universal scale, suffered by a population are not predictors of how much identity discomfort they will feel, nor are the actual circumstances of subjugation predictors. If a subjugated population has long been willing to accept an inferior status, it will not feel personally threatened because of the development of appropriate ideal identities. Again, the mere fact of social inferiority will not justify predicting a revitalization movement or a revolution.

How do these identity processes work in actual instances? Two particular cases provide pertinent examples: first, some features in the life history of the leader of a Chinese revolution, the Taiping rebellion; and second, the American Indian revitalization movement led by Handsome Lake. The leader of the Taiping rebellion was the son of a village leader. He became a schoolteacher and was a member of a minority group in the region in which he lived. He failed three times to pass civil service examinations, and at the end of the third try had a nervous breakdown, was carried back home, and experienced a series of hallucinatory episodes in which he felt that some sort of religious revelation was being communicated to him. He worked as a schoolteacher for some time, and on a visit to Canton several years later picked up some Christian missionary tracts, read them, and suddenly realized that they explained to him what the visions meant. He then attempted to formulate a new code for China involving various reforms, including especially a reform in the civil service examination system, and sought to get support from the Europeans along the coast for this quasi-Christian reform movement which he was starting. The Europeans, however, did not see any particular advantage to themselves in this. He was proposing in effect to make changes in Chinese society which the Manchu dynasty presumably would not be able to accept, and he was turned down. The Manchus did not look with favor on this prophet's proposals. The movement was forced into a military posture, rapidly gained converts, and before long fomented civil war which lasted for several years and is said to have produced more casualties than any other war in human history up to that date (about the middle of the nineteenth century). Here one sees obviously the role of identity and dynamics in the case of the prophet himself, a person who was dramatically rejected in his repeated attempts to pass the civil service examinations; who, as a member of a minority group, was rejected by the next group with whom he tried to identify, namely the European Christians; and who was then finally attacked and rejected by the Establishment of the society. His efforts at reform, reasonable or not, were denied, along with his own self-esteem, and the movement became a revolution.

A happier outcome occurs in the case of a Seneca Indian in New York State, who, in 1799, had a vision of what was wrong with the American Indians living on reservations and who prescribed a new way of life for his people. Handsome Lake was a chief in a confederacy which during his lifetime had experienced a tremendous decline in public respect and power, a confederacy which in fact was treated with a studied and planned contempt by American negotiators who neglected no opportunity to publicly insult the chiefs and the confederacy that they represented. Handsome Lake was a drunkard, sick in bed at the time when he had his visions. God appeared to him, told him that if he stopped drinking he would be permitted to live, also instructed him in what would have to be done in order to make a new and worthwhile society for the Seneca Indians on their reservation. The first radical provision in Handsome Lake's code was that Seneca Indian men become responsible for agriculture. This change was a critical one. Up to that time it was Indian women who were responsible for growing crops. The men regarded this as an effeminate occupation. He was seriously proposing that basic values with regard to appropriate behavior for men and women should be changed. Second, he proposed that the central kinship unit no longer be a matrilineage, with the continuity and responsibility running from mother to daughter, but be the nuclear household – husband, wife, and their children – which would be cultivating a family farm. He demanded that Indians confess publicly various sins, including violations of the code of ethics that he promulgated, and he was so successful in gaining converts not only on his own reservation, but on surrounding reservations, that in fifteen years observers said that they didn't recognize these people at all. It was no longer possible to make Indians drunk at the trading posts, they had good farms, they set up a sawmill, they set up schools for their children, they had better-organized communities in fact than most of the surrounding white people did. Handsome Lake also turned to the surrounding white community for support. He made a personal trip to the capital of the United States to visit President Jefferson, told him that his vision applied to Jefferson as well as to the Indians, and that Jefferson had better pay some attention to it. The President very politely said that he did believe that Handsome Lake had had a valid religious experience, that the white man and the red man must live together peacefully on this continent; he complimented him on the wisdom of his proposals, gave him every kind of good wish and moral support, and ordered the Secretary of War (who was then in charge of Indian affairs) to make the Indians comfortable in their stay and to escort them home. It was a very pleasant, warm, rewarding sort of experience. The Indians went back, preserving the letters from Jefferson and the letter from the Secretary of War, had them framed, and hung them up in the longhouses where the religious meetings were held (copies are still on display). Now this movement, which had warm and sympathetic support from Europeans, remains today as a non-Christian church on a number of Iroquois reservations in the United States and Canada, and the reforms which Handsome Lake instituted were economically important and effective for at least two or three generations. (There is, incidentally, an interesting anti-prophet in the Taiping case, someone named Chinese Gordon, who ran up and down in a gunboat shooting up the Taipings and in other ways was helpful in suppressing them, and who after this successful career in squelching a revitalization movement went to Africa, where he attempted to suppress the Mahdi rebellion in the Sudan. There Chinese Gordon met his match and lost his life in the massacre of the British troops at Khartoum.)

In summary, then, the main thesis is that the prime motivation in revitalization movements and in the revolutions which grow out of them is not an appetite motivation but an identity motivation. The satisfaction of identity motives is tied, in the code of the movement, to the accomplishment of radical social and cultural change. The demand is desperate, it is a cry for salvation, and this demand is the axis around which many of the events of revitalization movements revolve. If an establishment which would have to be overturned in some measure by a movement insists on the *status quo* and ignores the identity needs of the revitalizers, they have no choice at all. The movement must become a revolution in order to destroy the establishment or die in the attempt. Refusal to listen to the identity demands of a revitalization movement, let alone efforts to suppress it, leads directly to increasingly irrational demands, increasing intransigence, and increasing hostility. Furthermore, trying to buy off a revitalization movement by offering bread and bathtubs and improved housing and generally raising the material standard of living does not necessarily contribute at all to the satisfaction of identity needs. A revitalization movement wants to be reinforced in its identity claims. Here, for instance, is what Mills says about Cuba's relationship with the United States in this regard. Rhetorically, the Cuban revolutionary asks,

> At what point has your Government ever said to us: "Look, Cuban, we're very glad about your revolution. We're glad for the same reasons you are – because it's a way out of all the old horror you've lived with, all the poverty and exploitation and waste of Cuban resources and Cuban talent. We're glad because we do want Latin America really to be prosperous and really to be free."

What was important and wanted and not forthcoming, continues the revolutionary, was some statement from the United States which would have reinforced and supported the claims of the Cubans to having a respectable, worthy movement underway with goals that other human beings could regard as admirable and desirable.

Now, deriving applications in foreign policy from this is a relatively simple matter. If a revitalization movement exists in a society and is in danger of becoming or has become a revolution, and the United States is concerned to orient its foreign policy in such a way that that movement does not become increasingly hostile to the interests of the United States, the first matter to attend to is the nature of the identity demands being made in the code of the movement, and the first efforts should be made to support as much as possible the demands for dignity, self-esteem, self-respect, and so on, which these people are making. Obviously, neither simply providing support to the establishment which they are in some measure threatening nor simply attempting to buy loyalty, by demanding that the code be given up in return for various rational economic gains, will be effective. Something like this is probably observable in the course of events of the last several years in Vietnam, in which no amount of rational effort at economic support, social reforms, and other development programs seems to be effective in reducing the hostility of a great many people towards an establishment which we support and towards us personally. In such a situation, then, it will be impossible to contain or suppress or divert or carry out prophylactic measures by pumping in material support calculated on the basis of assumptions to the effect that these people are motivated largely by appetite dynamics. The necessary efforts have to be directed towards identity dynamics. Much of this effort has to be verbal, and as the illustration from Mills shows, one of the simplest and most obvious ways to avoid getting into an identity struggle with people in a revitalization movement is to avoid saying, "You're baddies, and until you reform we won't talk to you or recognize you." It is essential to give support for identity claims; if identity claims are recognized, there will be no necessity on the part of the revitalizers to resort to revolutionary tactics.

In conclusion, then, we can say that revitalization movements and the revolutions they may spawn are a kind of phenomenon to which the old aphorism, at least with regard to the identity matter, applies with peculiar force: "If you can't lick 'em, join 'em." They may be unruly, unreasonable, and destructive, they may profess doctrines which we regard as bizarre, as alien, and as fundamentally faulty, but since the motivation is based on identity considerations and not on rational calculations of economic advantage, or primarily even on rational military questions, the only way in which any kind of cooperative relationship with a revitalization movement can be accomplished, short of Armageddon (which is usually already envisaged in the possibility of the code), is to support claims to identity. This support has to be accomplished in part by explicit statements of respect for these claims, or at least for substantial aspects of them; sympathy must be conceded with goals which are noble despite the inadequacy of the means proposed to achieve them; and finally, it is essential that a public identity struggle with a revitalization movement never be entered into. The history of our relationships with China, with the present Chinese Communists, is a classic example of a country permitting itself to get into a public identity struggle with the leaders of a revitalization movement which happens to have an alien political philosophy, and out of this struggle it is virtually impossible, either for the Chinese or ourselves, to retreat.

U Thant recently made some remarks, apropos of precisely this, in which he said that one can expect the Chinese to be unreasonable, for it is a country suffering from a national sort of nervous breakdown, and understandably so, since for fifteen years this country has been treated as an outcast and a leper. He, too, is saying: what can you produce by perpetuating an identity struggle with people whose peculiar preoccupation is to achieve self-respect, other than to mobilize an antagonism which is intense and to insulate that group from any possibility of negotiating over rational economic and military matters.

8

A Perspective on the Transformation of Political Culture in Cuba*

One of the most significant aspects of the Cuban revolutionary effort is the continuing attempt to transform the cultural matrix of behavior.[1] In the idiom of the revolution's leaders, this is called the creation of "socialist man", but the implications of this attempt for both the theory and the practice of the Revolution are actually more profound than the official label would at first lead one to believe. Creating socialist man in Cuba means no less than a massive restructuring of the context in which public behavior takes place, and it also implies, as we shall see, a theory of mobilization, participation, individual formation and reformation, and culture change. This essay attempts to put this effort into some perspective, first through a codification of Cuban thinking, then through a review of revolutionary practice, and finally through an evaluation of the successes, failures, and potentialities of the first eleven years.

Cuban thinking about individual *formación* and the transformation of political culture after more than a decade of revolutionary experience can be considered in terms of the following five themes: Communism and the interrelation of abundance and consciousness, technology as the motor of abundance and a component of the new man, money as a "bitter and transitory instrument" of exchange and distribution, the promise and importance of youth, and the burden of the past. Although these themes have been talked about in one fashion or another since the beginning of 1959, it has only been since about 1965

* by Richard R. Fagen.

that Castro and others have woven them together into a relatively clear and consistent developmental doctrine.

Communism and the interrelation of abundance and consciousness. In a speech given on 26 July 1968, the fifteenth anniversary of the attack on the Moncada Barracks, Castro outlined in detail what had come to be his basic views on the content and construction of Communism in Cuba. So many key elements of the revolutionary doctrine were brought together in this speech that it is worth quoting at length:

> No human society has yet reached Communism. The paths by which one arrives at a superior form of society are very difficult. A Communist society is one in which man will have reached the highest degree of social awareness ever achieved. In a Communist society, man will have succeeded in achieving just as much understanding, closeness, and brotherhood as he has on occasion achieved within the narrow circle of his own family. To live in a Communist society is to live without selfishness, to live among the people and with the people, as if every one of our fellow citizens were really our dearest brother. . . .
>
> At the very core of Marx's thought [is the idea that] Socialist society and Communist society must be based on a complete mastery of technology, on a complete development of the productive forces, so that man will be able to create enough material goods to satisfy everyone's needs. It is unquestionable that medieval society, with its minimal development of the forces of production, could not have aspired to live under Communism. It is also clear that the old [Cuban] society, with even poorer and more backward forces of production, could have aspired even less to live under Communism. . . .
>
> People aspiring to live under Communism must do what we are doing. They must emerge from underdevelopment; they must develop their forces of production; they must master technology in order to turn man's efforts and man's sweat into the miracle of producing practically unlimited quantities of material goods. If we

do not master technology, if we do not develop our forces of production, we shall deserve to be called dreamers for aspiring to live in a Communist society.

The problem from our point of view [however] is that Communist consciousness must be developed at the same rate as the forces of production. An advance in the consciousness of the revolutionaries, in the consciousness of the people, must accompany every step forward in the development of the forces of production. . . .

[And above all] we should not use money or wealth to create consciousness. We must use consciousness to create wealth. To offer a man more to do a bit more than is expected is to buy his consciousness with money. . . . As we said before, Communism certainly cannot be established if we do not create abundant wealth. But the way to do this, in our opinion, is not by creating consciousness through money or wealth but by creating wealth through consciousness.[2]

The several strains of the doctrine are here brought together as a set of linked propositions. (1) The ideal Communist society is defined as a cultural system in which every man acts as a true brother to every other man. (2) It is not possible to achieve such a cultural system until abundance replaces want as the collective situation of the citizenry. (3) The very process of creating abundance, however, can easily destroy the potential of the abundant society for being a truly Communist society. (4) Thus a society must strive to achieve abundance by creating and nourishing those values and motivations – shared feelings about collective responsibility and gain, and an ethic of societal service – that will one day become internalized as the general character structure of Communist man. Above all, abundance achieved by appealing to individual aggrandizement, by rewarding *egoismo* (self-centeredness), leads inexorably not to Communism but to increased exploitation of man by man, increased individual alienation, and rising levels of social disorganization.[3]

Thus the Cuban insistence on the correctness of moral incentives and social consciousness as the mainsprings of the productive process should not be understood simply as a cynical attempt to keep the workers at the lathes and the peasants in the fields at the lowest possible cost in wages. It is, rather, an integral part of a thought system in which the way men are motivated to create wealth is considered inseparable from the way they will relate to each other in the more abundant society of the future. It is the Cuban variant of a line of thinking that links Castro to radicals otherwise as diverse as Mao and Tito.[4]

Technology as the motor of abundance and a component of the new man. As suggested by Castro's explication of the relationship between Communism and abundance, modern science and technology are seen as playing a very special role in the process of creating wealth. In the most material sense, this is little more than a recognition that in order to develop and compete in the second half of the twentieth century, a nation must draw on, modify, and apply the scientific and technological skills and resources available in the world community. Thus revolutionary leadership is firmly convinced that there can be no dramatic growth in any sector of the Cuban economy unless the productive process in that sector is modernized.[5] This commitment to bringing technology to bear on production is manifested in the sugar industry as an attempt to move toward mechanized planting and harvesting cycles, in the dairy industry as an attempt to introduce controlled breeding and artificial insemination, and in various other sectors of the economy as a series of programs designed to increase productivity by borrowing, modifying, or developing an appropriate scientific style of labor.

The most interesting aspect of this emphasis on technology, however, is how it affects the *formación* of the work force. Since the mid-1960s much attention has been paid to making a scientific attitude part of the equipment of every Cuban. More narrowly conceived, this is seen as a kind of vocational training, the teaching of skills needed to run a more modern and dynamic economy. But more broadly understood, the scientific attitude implies an appreciation for the part science and technology play in the entire developmental process.[6] "What place can the scientifically illiterate man, the technologically illiterate man, possibly have in the community of the future?" Castro has asked on many occasions.[7] The man of the future, the Communist man, will be not only his brother's keeper, but a trained and scientifically sensitive man as well.

This notion of Communist man as a technologically trained and sensitive man is increasingly being linked with the earlier concern for moral incentives. The idea of what constitutes a moral incentive has undergone revision and enlargement. Thus, when speaking at the University of Havana on 13 March 1969, Castro emphasized that work need not inevitably be viewed as duty and sacrifice – that moral incentives need not derive their motive power exclusively from the individual's sense of duty to the collective. Quite the contrary, he continued, whenever technology and science are needed in the performance of a task, there arises the possibility that the work will be done not "with a sense of duty and necessity alone, but rather with pleasure. The work itself will excite enormous interest, and become one of man's most pleasant activities."[7a] Cutting sugarcane or pulling weeds is not work of this sort, but scientific and technological pursuits are. Thus, in the more modern society of the future, the opportunities for integrating work with life, for deriving personal satisfaction from confronting problems and bringing knowledge to bear on their solutions, will multiply. The distinctions between manual and intellectual work will increasingly blur, and both for individuals and for society in general the separation between education and production will be bridged as the former becomes a continuing process without which growth in the latter is impossible. In sum, in the emerging revolutionary vision, technology not only makes possible the advent of abundance, but also contributes importantly to ending alienation by enabling more men to work at callings instead of at jobs.[8]

Money as a bitter and transitory instrument of exchange and distribution.[9] It follows from Castro's attack on material incentives that in the new revolutionary culture increments of cash income should not be used to reward those who contribute most to the productive process or to the construction of Communism. But the feeling against the role of money in society extends well beyond a simple rejection of extra pay for extra work. What is called into question by Castro and his followers is nothing less than the exchange and distributive functions of the monetary system. That is, in the Castroite vision of Communist society, as in much early Marxist thinking, transactions involving the exchange and distribution of most goods and services are not mediated or controlled by concomitant exchanges of cash or credit. Notice that the manipulation of prices in favor of the poorer sectors is not an element in this long-term vision. That is, the argument does not say that in the new society basic goods and services must be brought within the reach of everyone. It says that they must be given, unsullied by the necessity of giving even one *centavo* in return. On the fifteenth anniversary of his attack on the Moncada Army Barracks, Castro articulated this theme in all its starkness:

> In the past, the capitalists slandered revolutionary ideas and reviled Communism. Nevertheless, that society, that way of life – in which no young person had a chance, in which even the sick were forsaken, in which each man was an isolated, desperate human being left to shift for himself in the midst of a society of wolves – can in no way be compared with what a Communist society really means in the realms of human relations and morality. We hope to achieve that Communist society in absolutely all ways some day. Just as books are distributed now to those who need them, just as medicine and medical services are distributed to those who need them, and education to those who need it, so we are approaching the day when food will be distributed in the necessary amounts to those who need it, and clothing and shoes will be distributed in the necessary amounts to those who need them. We certainly aspire to a way of life – apparently utopian for many – in which man will not need money to satisfy his essential needs for food, clothing, and recreation, just as today no one needs money for medical attention or for his education. Nobody takes money to a hospital; nobody takes money to a high school; nobody takes money to a scholarship school; nobody takes money to a sports event.[10]

If the attack on money as a bitter and transitory instrument is a hearkening back to one of the earliest tenets of Marxism, it is also an outcropping of a basic reaction against the pre-revolutionary social order in Cuba. From the very outset the revolutionaries rejected the old (especially urban) culture as inequitable, materialistic, corrupt, and hopelessly oriented toward consumption. Pre-revolutionary Havana, viewed as a city in which sufficient money could get you anything – a high political office, membership in the country club, a blessing from the bishop, a beautiful woman, first-rate medical care, or protection from the law – became the very antithesis of the social order that the revolutionaries wished to construct. It is not just that great inequalities existed in pre-revolutionary Cuba, that senators drove Cadillacs and ate steaks while shoeshine boys went barefoot and hungry; it is that money and the concomitant capacity to buy and consume were the key bases of human differentiation and the final arbiters of human relations. Cuba, in the revolutionary view, did not even have the dubious virtue of being a highly stratified traditional society. Certainly it was not a meritocracy or a technocracy either. It was – at least in the cities – a dollarocracy, the most vulgar, demeaning, exploitative, and uncreative social order imaginable.[11] Dollars and pesos were the measure of both men and things, the universal standard of value. It is thus not at all surprising that the revolutionaries selected money and commercial relations as one of the prime targets of attack in their war on the old order.

The promise and importance of youth. From the days of the Sierra Maestra young people have occupied a special place on the revolutionary stage. Not only did young men and women figure prominently in the struggle against Batista, but since that time they have continually been given important positions and opportunities in the revolutionary scheme of governance. As many observers have pointed out, the Cuban Revolution has been made largely by and for the young people of the island.

The Cuban emphasis on youth, however, should not be confused with the acceptance of youth culture of the kind that has developed in other societies. Neither in theory nor in practice is there any tendency for Cuban revolutionaries to elevate youth culture – with its various contemporary connotations of seeking after individual experience, freedom from conventional constraints, and challenges to established authority – into a life-style to be emulated. Quite the contrary, the values and behaviors considered appropriate for young Cubans are, if anything, almost directly opposed to those usually associated with contemporary youth culture elsewhere. According to official Cuban publications, young people are expected to exhibit personal abnegation, self-discipline, a sense of duty, service to society, and love of country. Not only do these virtues and behaviors emphasize the importance of patriotism, they also signify "the moralization of work", a Cuban revolutionary variant of the Protestant ethic, stripped of its overtones of salvation by means of private accumulation.[12] Like other Marxist and also capitalist prescriptions for youthful behavior, the Cuban doctrine fuses work and societal service into an idealized vision of a clean, hard, and useful life.[13] Clearly such values and behaviors are not now typical of the life-styles either professed or practiced by the trend-setting young in the more developed nations, either Eastern or Western.

What, then, is the meaning of the Cuban emphasis on youth? In part it is a response to the manpower needs of the developmental effort, made even more acute by the exodus of tens of thousands of Cubans. Just when thousands of persons were needed to staff the bureaucracies, schools, factories, and farms created or reorganized by the Revolutionary Government, thousands of professional, white-collar, and skilled blue-collar workers were going into exile. In staffing the developmental effort, the Revolutionary Government often had nowhere to turn except to young people, who had very limited experience but a great deal of energy and enthusiasm. Thus throughout Cuba one finds engineering students supervising highway construction, twenty-one-year-olds running schools, and young workers in charge of factories.

The emphasis on youth, however, is more than a response to manpower needs. It derives from a fundamental belief that, in general, only the young come to the revolutionary experience uncorrupted and pure enough to be formed into true Communists. The "integral man" so celebrated during the Cultural Congress of 1968 can grow only in an environment that has, in the revolutionary view, just begun to be created in Cuba. Although members of pre-revolutionary generations are or can become the best of citizens and militants, only members of post-revolutionary generations can achieve the proper fusion of beliefs and patterns of action that determine the character and the life-style of the new man. Thus young people are valued not only because of their actual and potential contributions to the developmental effort, but also because they are seen as bearing the seeds of the new culture. They have both the opportunity and the responsibility for being better men than their fathers.

The burden of the past. "It is well known that to build Communism we must confront, in the economic sphere, the underdevelopment imposed on us by imperialism and, in the ideological sphere, the extraordinary weight of the ideas, habits, and concepts that society has accumulated for centuries. The past has its claws into the present."[14] One of the developmental lessons the Cubans have been longest in learning is that the inertia of a cultural system is very great indeed. That is, the revolutionary leaders have had to do their best to learn to live with some of the ideas, habits and concepts that were well integrated into the pre-revolutionary way of life. This inertia can be seen in the traditional reluctance of peasant families to send their children to the new schools, in the absenteeism of workers long accustomed to days off after hard nights on the town, and in a slipping back into social isolation on the part of ordinary citizens who feel abused by constant pressures toward participation and public service. The developmental effort is constantly and inevitably slowed down by the persistence of old values and patterns of behavior, even in the bosom of the newest and most disciplined of revolutionary institutions.

There is, of course, nothing surprising about this state of affairs, for no theme in the literature of social change is as frequently underlined as the dialectic between the old and the new. What should be noted, however, is that the revolutionary leaders have recently emphasized the burden of the past more frequently as an integral part of their doctrine. For example, on 1 January

1969, in his speech commemorating the tenth anniversary of the triumph of the rebel forces, Castro underscored the legacies of both economy and political culture against which the revolution still had to do battle.[15] He also repeatedly reminded his audience of how long and tortuous the road out of underdevelopment would really be. The developmental doctrine has thus come to incorporate very explicitly the notion that, while steadfastly moving toward the Communist society, one must never underestimate the tenacity of the old ways or the perverse vitality of the old culture, with its materialism, self-centeredness, and indiscipline. Just as ten years of revolution have taught that only the young can be formed into the citizens of the new order, so the same decade has taught the related though bittersweet lesson that the claws of the past are not easily or painlessly torn from the flesh of the present.

The five themes sketched above organize the doctrine but not necessarily the practice of mobilization and cultural change in Cuba. Without going into the details of various new programs, is it possible to generalize about the institutional manifestations of this doctrine after more than a decade of revolution? Particularly, is it possible to discern the directions mobilization and cultural change are taking?

At the risk of oversimplifying a complex situation, we can say that the main thrust of current practice seems to be toward engaging as many citizens as possible for as long as possible in productive work in rural (and openly anti-urban) environments. Thus for schoolchildren there is the Schools to the Countryside plan, which each year takes tens of thousands of students with their books and teachers to rural areas for forty-five days of study and work. For other young people there is semipermanent residence on the Isle of Pines – renamed the Isle of Youth – with its special emphasis on forming the first generation of true Communists in a setting of equality and sacrifice. For the adults of the capital there is the *Cordón*, or greenbelt around the city, a program to make the urban complex self-sufficient in foodstuffs by bringing adjacent lands under cultivation. Sometimes called the Isle of Youth for the middle-aged, the *Cordón* represents the implementation of the strain in revolutionary doctrine that views agricultural work as essential for liberating the urban masses from their city ways and bourgeois values.[16]

Programs like these all attempt to fuse as intimately as possible the participatory and the learning components of cultural change. That is, they represent an effort to make available to more and more Cubans the integrated, formative experiences seen by the revolutionary élite as central to the radical transformation of men and institutions. Such programs underline the élite's continuing emphasis on the inseparability of attitudinal, value, and behavioral changes. In this view, significant cultural shifts do not depend in linear fashion on changes in attitudes that in turn produce changes in behavior.[17] Rather, the starting point of change is when more and more citizens take part in the right kinds of activities, activities that direct attention away from the self and toward the collectivity, activities that wordlessly but dramatically teach the lessons of development and underdevelopment. The Schools to the Countryside plan, the Isle of Youth, and the *Cordón* are all examples of what the revolutionary leadership considers the right kinds of activities.

Although only slightly more than a decade of the Cuban Revolution has passed, we must ask what kinds of changes in political culture have taken place in the first ten years and how lasting or rooted these changes seem to be. Such an evaluation is tentative not only because the revolution is still in progress, but also because it is difficult to obtain data on the outcomes and consequences of revolutionary programs. Available information serves relatively well for assessing the ideology, organization, and practices employed on behalf of developmental efforts, but we lack the necessary behavioral data on those who are participating in the revolutionary process.

What is clear is that the revolutionary élite has demonstrated an impressive capacity for mobilizing the Cuban citizenry. Mobilization means getting out the troops to do whatever the leadership feels needs to be done. But however impressive this performance, one cannot infer from it the extent to which individual people are being transformed. That hundreds of thousands

of Cubans belong to the Committees for Defense of the Revolu-
lution, that tens of thousands of workers and bureaucrats occasionally cut sugarcane, and that thousands of Cubans passed
through the Schools of Revolutionary Instruction should not be
taken as evidence that their basic values and attitudes have been
transformed, that the "new man" has arrived. Mobilization of
the type and scale achieved in Cuba certainly attests to the
organizational capacity of the leadership and to the place given
to such activity in the system of ideology and action that guides
them. It also demonstrates the extent to which the new politics
have proven workable in Cuba. But the fact remains that
mobilization is primarily an instrument, rather than the consequence, of cultural transformation.

As a starting point for our evaluation of the transformation of
political culture, it should be emphasized that neither the revolutionaries nor outside observers claim that the utopian vision
outlined at the beginning of this essay has been achieved. By no
stretch of the imagination is Cuba a society in which *egoismo*
has disappeared, in which every man sets societal service above
personal gain, in which Communist *conciencia* and the patterns
of behavior commensurate with it characterize the average
citizen. To deny the fulfilment of the utopian vision, however,
is not to deny that profound changes have taken place. Though
it is difficult in the absence of better data to be specific about the
content and scope of these changes, the broad outlines and thrust
of the transformation seem relatively clear. The following four
propositions help to organize speculation about these matters.

*There is a great deal of revolutionary behavior that does not
stem from the internalization of new values or even from political
attitudes and orientations consistent with the behavior observed.*
Revolutionary behavior in this context refers to any behavior
that is deemed proper, useful, or appropriate from the point of
view of the Cuban leadership. Most social psychological perspec-
tives on the relationship between values, attitudes, and political
behavior carry the implicit – if not explicit – assumption that
values and attitudes are rather good predictors of action.[18] For
instance, if we know how a citizen views the political parties in
a two-party system, it is thought that we can predict fairly

accurately how he will vote at election time. Or if we know what kinds of expectations a person has about being able to get access to politicians and bureaucrats, we can hypothesize, it is thought, with some confidence how frequently and in what way he will attempt such contacts. Such models of the nexus between values, attitudes, and behavior are, however, suspect when applied to Cuba.

In a system like the Cuban, in which political institutions and work environments are oriented toward shaping participation, and in which alternative opportunities are limited, a great deal of revolutionary behavior is evoked from persons who if left to their own devices would probably behave differently. We shall return to this theme in more detail later, but it is well to point out here that in this situation, although group and institutional norms have changed under the impetus of revolutionary leadership, many who participate do so not because their values necessarily fit with those of the leadership, but because they have few if any alternatives and are subjected to substantial peer-group pressure. Thus individual values and attitudes may differ from institutional norms without being reflected in differences of individual behavior. This is not to say that revolutionary behavior – and therefore revolutionary institutions – can persist indefinitely in conflict with individual values and attitudes. The point is that the revolutionary environment makes considerable disjunction both possible and probable.[19]

The modification of some aspects of the traditional value system is perhaps the most important long-term consequence of attempts to transform the political culture. Whereas the first proposition emphasized that in a system like the Cuban it is possible to evoke revolutionary behavior from individual persons without prior large-scale changes in their values, here it is suggested that, in fact, some changes *are* taking place. An example will help to make this clear. One of the value dimensions most discussed by theorists of development is what Seymour Lipset calls equalitarianism-élitism. Among other things, this means that "nations defined as equalitarian tend to place more emphasis than élitist nations on universalistic criteria in interpersonal judgments, and ... tend to de-emphasize behavior patterns which stress hierarchical differences".[20] Furthermore, the argument continues, the equalitarian orientation supports developmental efforts by fostering social mobility and the rise of new talents, by facilitating the formation of associations and working coalitions, and by liberating individual energies in a host of other ways while at the same time encouraging collective efforts.

This theme in the developmental literature frequently carries with it an ethnocentric bias. There is a tendency to generalize out of the American experience certain constellations of values that are assumed to be causally related to the impressive economic growth of the United States and, to a lesser extent, of Western Europe. Thus, the argument continues, less well-developed nations, nations that are also characterized by value patterns quite different from those of the United States, will begin to progress economically only as they become more "Western", more oriented toward achievement, more universalistic in evaluating persons and performance, more equalitarian in social relations, and so forth.[21] The most interesting and important aspect of this argument, however, is that it is probably strengthened if stripped of its ethnocentrism. That is, a nation can become more oriented toward achievement and more equalitarian socially without at the same time becoming more like the advanced Western nations institutionally, organizationally, or in terms of other values. In short, it would seem that although shifts in value patterns as outlined by Lipset and others are in fact related to development, and particularly to economic development, there is no reason to assume that the North American way of life is a necessary concomitant or outcome of cultural systems that stress equalitarianism and achievement.

To return again to the Cuban case, there is evidence that the lessons learned on the farm, in the factory, in school, and in the mass organizations have already shifted the cultural center of gravity significantly away from élitism and hierarchy and toward equalitarianism. Furthermore, the environment of material scarcity, coupled with the relative evenness of remuneration, reinforces the dominant anti-élitism of social relations and opportunities. This does not necessarily mean that the lessons of equalitarianism being learned by the Cuban masses will in the long run direct popular energies into exactly those kinds of behaviors desired by the revolutionary leadership. The basic cultural realignments instigated by the Cuban Revolution are open-ended enough to support a variety of political and economic arrangements. But no matter how value changes as basic as the shift toward equalitarianism manifest themselves in the Cuba of the future, a major cultural shift is clearly taking place behind the immediate effort to inculcate specific attitudes and encourage certain kinds of behavior. While the régime devotes most of its attention to the mobilizational and educational objectives deriving from the exigencies of the present, the value constellations of Cuban society are being moved in exactly those directions advocated by many Western theorists concerned with the relationship between culture and national development.[22]

Youth is, in general, the group most exposed to the revolutionary experience. Earlier in this essay it was mentioned that Cuban doctrine on cultural transformation gives special attention to the promise and importance of youth. Not only are young people seen as the hope of the future, they are also given special opportunities to participate, to immerse themselves in revolutionary activities in ways not open to most adults. In fact, such opportunities are characteristically thrust upon them (e.g. in the Schools to the Countryside plan) more directly than any that are thrust upon adults.

It would seem, moreover, that young people are especially available psychologically for being recruited into and affected by the revolutionary experience. They are encouraged by the régime to participate precisely at that stage of life when – as Erik Erikson has emphasized – they are searching for a sense of the self that is relatively unambiguous, action-oriented, and ideological (providing a convincing world image). The formative environments for young people in Cuba seem to be very conducive to ameliorating many of the most profound difficulties and uncertainties that are usually associated with the search for adult identity. In the more extreme instances, environmental exposure and psychological readiness come together in what Erikson calls the indoctrination experience. Although not all youth environments in Cuba can rightfully be thought of as leading to indoctrination, Erikson's formulation of the extreme case remains very relevant to the fusion of personal identity needs and system requirements in revolutionary Cuba:

> It stands to reason that late adolescence is the most favorable period, and late adolescent personalities of any age group the best subjects, for indoctrination; because in adolescence an ideological realignment is by necessity in process and a number of ideological possibilities are waiting to be hierarchically ordered by opportunity, leadership, and friendship. Any leadership, however, must have the power to encase the individual in a spatial arrangement and in a temporal routine which at the same time narrow down the sensory supply from the world and block his sexual and aggressive drives, so that a new needfulness will eagerly attach itself to a new world-image. At no other time as much as in adolescence does the individual feel so exposed to anarchic manifestations of his drives; at no other time does he so need over-systematized thoughts and overvalued words to give a semblance of order to his inner world. He therefore is willing to accept ascetic restrictions which go counter to what he would do if he were alone – faced with himself, his body, his musings – or in the company of old friends; he will accept the *sine qua non* of indoctrination, lack of privacy. . . . Needless to say, good and evil must be clearly defined as forces existing from all beginning and persevering into all future; therefore all memory of the past must be starved or minutely guided, and all intention focused on the common utopia. No idle talk can be permitted. Talk must always count, count for or against one's readiness to embrace the new ideology totally – to the point of meaning it. In fact, the right talk, the vigorous song, and the radical confession in public must be cultivated.[23]

Erikson's formulation implies that the ideological reordering and thus the sense of identity that is communicated to young people must make sense in terms of their own needs, confusions, and tribulations. Adult leadership must provide both personal models and developmental programs consistent with youthful concerns.[24] In this respect the Cuban revolutionary leadership has been exemplary, not only because it is itself relatively young and much admired, but also because its action programs meet quite closely the implied conditions of Erikson's analysis. Not only are the young able to tolerate (and even enjoy) the scarcity, the physical discomfort and dislocations, and the interruptions of routine that accompany mobilization efforts in Cuba, but their sense of self-importance is profoundly reinforced by participating in activities that are clearly of national importance, that result quite rapidly in a palpable transformation of some aspect of the physical environment, and for which they are often given serious responsibilities. Whatever shortcomings the formative experiences of most young Cubans may have, they are seldom irrelevant to the problems at hand, nor do they entail endless postponement of involvement and responsibility. Owing to the closure of debate and self-examination, the channeling of energies into societal service, and the conformism encouraged by the attacks on *egoismo*, Cuban youth may not be growing up with highly developed critical skills – with regard to either themselves or the new social order. But neither are they – in Paul Goodman's phrase – growing up absurd. The possibility of rebelliousness in the face of continuing regimentation exists, and certainly it is too early to predict what the increased leavening of Cuban society with young adults formed under the revolution will bring. But it is already clear that the growing-up experiences of these future adults differ profoundly from those of their parents. They may not turn out to be the "true Communists" prophesied in the developmental doctrine, but many will be "new Cubans" to about as great an extent as sons can ever differ from their fathers.

There is presently substantial fragility in new Cuban patterns of belief and behavior. This proposition is meant to emphasize the importance of environmental supports for new constellations of thought and action. Put briefly, after more than ten years of revolution the emerging Cuban political culture should be viewed as still very dependent on the revolutionary environment itself, rather than on internalized and deeply ingrained values and patterns of behavior. This follows quite naturally from the previous three propositions on the disjunction of behavior and beliefs, the probability of long-term changes in values, and the special exposure and susceptibility of young people. The radical attempt to transform the political culture of Cuba is, after all, only slightly more than a decade old, and no full generation has yet been raised to adulthood in the hothouse of the revolutionary society. A decade is a short time compared with the time spans ordinarily observed in evaluating the internalization of new values and behaviors.

Note that this proposition does not predict the failure of the radical experiment or even its attrition. It simply says that observed and hypothesized changes to date have not become so much a part of the general culture that they can be considered independent of the mobilization environments now sustaining and encouraging them. At one level, this simply says that were the revolutionary leadership to abandon its radical efforts to transform the political culture (if one can imagine that!), much of the behavior now evoked from the citizenry would also cease. Thus any meaningful amount of volunteer labor in Cuba would stop if all the intragroup pressures and organizational encouragements now sustaining it were discontinued. But the proposition also implies something more. Volunteer labor as a continuing pattern of behavior, particularly when the labor involves agriculture, is difficult to imagine in any modern society without intragroup pressures and organizational devices of the kind now arranged by the Cuban Revolutionary Government. Such cultural values as equalitarianism and such political orientations as strong identification with the nation – and the patterns of action related to them – may, however, eventually become independent of the specific contexts in which they were originally practiced and learned. To pick a common example, people who must exercise patience while waiting in line for rationed goods and practice equality while cutting sugarcane will carry consonant attitudes and behaviors over into other situations if, in fact, the original lessons have been well learned. One would expect, and certainly the revolutionary leadership expects, that when the days of cutting cane and waiting in line are over, Cubans will not simply revert to their earlier ways. But it is wise to emphasize that ten years of revolution is a relatively short period in which to accomplish the kinds of fundamental, internalized transformations that the radicals seek. The revolutionary environment thus is still the single most important determinant of states of mind and behavior, even in those domains of thought and action that one would expect to become much more fully internalized during the second decade of the Cuban experiment.

The phrase "the second decade of the Cuban experiment" implies a prediction about the viability of revolutionary institutions and their continuing innovativeness during the 1970s. Neither aspect of this prediction should be allowed to pass unexamined.

From 1959 on, there has been no dearth of persons willing to testify to the imminent collapse of the Castro régime. Economy-watchers have been firmly convinced that mismanagement in general and Socialism in particular would combine to destroy the productive base of the island; society-watchers have been equally convinced that the Cuban people would not long endure the inefficiency, the autocracy, and the mobilization tactics of the Castroites. They have predicted that the Revolutionary Government is doomed – if not directly because of its own incompetence and irrationality, then indirectly because of the massive defection of sub-élites and the estrangement of the general population. But such has not been the case, and there are important lessons to be learned from an examination of why the Revolutionary Government is still quite fully in command despite admitted economic failures and despite the real costs of autocracy and mobilization.

The easy explanation for foes of the régime is that Castro rules by terror. Couched as it frequently is in general and clearly condemnatory language, this charge is so loaded and so vague that it is not easy to refute. If it means that there are people in Cuba who obey because they fear the Revolutionary Government, it is true but nevertheless irrelevant to any reasonable understanding of rule by terror. If, however, the charge is that

Castro rules by bureaucratized and arbitrary exercise of police violence against selected segments of the population (a charge that links the Cuban Revolution with the Stalinist and Hitlerite experiences), then the explanation is demonstrably false.[25] The entire thrust of most serious scholarship and reportage on Cuba testifies that the régime – while harsh and unrelenting at times – is not even a pale approximation of Stalinism or Hitlerism. The rules of the revolutionary game are quite well understood in Cuba; there is little or no arbitrary violence directed against any sector of the population (as opposed to sporadic harassment); and the quasi-coercive shaping of environments to channel citizen energies toward revolutionary activities is relieved by an easiness of interpersonal relationships and a widespread – though often grudging – feeling among the citizenry that all must contribute to the development of the nation.

But if terror does not explain the staying power of the Castro government, what does? A partial explanation is found in the pre-revolutionary integration of Cuban society, the socio-economic potential of the island, the political skill and charisma of Castro, and the rich heritage of Cuban nationalism combined with the peculiarities of the Cold War. As this combination of factors suggests, the Revolutionary Government has had much to work with; and many of its developmental undertakings have been successful because they have fitted relatively well with the resources and potentialities (human, situational, and material) of the island and the historical period. As exorbitant as it may sound both to critics and to some admirers of the Cuban experiment, the leadership has in fact been quite realistic as well as quite audacious in what it has attempted – particularly since 1963. The first eleven years have seen (in addition to hardship, dislocation, and bewildering change) considerable material progress, increased distributive justice, and a veritable explosion of opportunities for education, social mobility, and occupational responsibility; and these positive and palpable achievements go far toward explaining the continuing popularity and viability of the revolution.

There is, however, a still more basic explanation to be made. Over the past decade Cuba has achieved a more rapid rate of political development than that achieved by any other nation in Latin America and perhaps by any nation in Africa or Asia, and this dramatic progress in political development undergirds the above prediction of the continued viability of the revolutionary effort. To understand and delimit the substance of this claim, it is necessary to be clear about the definition of political development being used. Political development, as seen by Huntington, is the "institutionalization of political organizations and procedures" in the direction of adaptability, complexity, autonomy (insulated from the pull and haul of social forces), and coherence (having a distinctive and internally shared spirit and style).[26] The organizations of the Cuban Revolutionary Government have grown rapidly on all of these dimensions over the past decade. Note that this claim does not deny the continuing importance of Castro or the personalistic aspects of his style of rule. Clearly, revolutionary institutions would be deeply affected by his death and would probably move in the directions of rigidity and disunity, the polar opposites of adaptability and coherence. Nor does the definition depend on a high degree of individual freedom being practiced or allowed within the system. In fact, in real political systems – at least in less developed ones – institutionalization probably takes place in part at the expense of conventional democratic practices. What this formulation does emphasize is that the strength of governmental institutions vis-à-vis the society in which they are embedded is critical for predicting the viability of a régime and its problem-solving capabilities. On this score, the performance of revolutionary organizations in Cuba has been impressive indeed, and there are no signs of decreasing capacity.

The prediction of continued innovativeness within the Cuban Revolution is not, however, based primarily on an assessment of the institutionalization of revolutionary rule. More important factors are the personality and style of Fidel Castro and the characteristics of his ideological system. Nothing that is known about Castro or that can be inferred from his behavior to date suggests that he will routinize or otherwise cease to experiment with the process of governance and development. The metaphor Castro chose to express his feelings about the revolution in his interview with Lee Lockwood is very instructive in this regard:

> *Castro:* We love the Revolution as a labor. We love it just as a painter, a sculptor, or a writer may love his work. And, like him, we want our work to have a perennial value.
>
> *Lockwood:* You consider the making of a revolution a work of art?
>
> *Castro:* Yes, I certainly do. Revolution is an art. And politics is also an art. The most important one, I think.[27]

In Castro's view only hack or pseudo-revolutionaries – like hack or pseudo-artists – would cease trying to improve their creations or the genre that they have evolved. The first decade of the revolution is replete with examples of experimentation that can be understood only in the light of Castro's profound personal need to advance the art of revolutionary transformation. Thus, although at times he appears as merely capricious or reactive, the overall level of innovativeness he has displayed is best seen as the consequence of this "urge to create" as manifested in his political personality. In short, an appreciation of Castro's view of himself as both revolutionary artist and revolutionary warrior goes far toward explaining the intensity and energy with which he has sought and continues to seek new strategies for waging the political struggle and new tactics for winning the battle against underdevelopment.

This restlessness and relentlessness in the search for tactics and strategies that work under Cuban conditions has its direct counterpart in the realm of words and symbols. Out of Castro's voluminous production of speeches it is difficult to codify anything approaching an elegant or even wholly consistent doctrine of man, society, politics, and change. Elements of the New Testament, Marx, Martí, Fanon, and a great deal of Fidel Castro are mixed together in what is best described as a set of postures toward a range of issues rather than a philosophical system. But this does not mean that the revolution has no ideology. Quite the contrary, if ideology is taken to mean a symbol system linking particular actions and mundane practices with a wider set of meanings, then the revolution has a well-developed, flexible, and seemingly successful ideology.[28] It is successful precisely because it is personalistic, adaptive, and artful.

When viewed this way, the ideology of the revolution clearly depends for its success not on its literal truth, but on its evocative and motivating power under prevailing conditions. As Clifford Geertz has pointed out, one ought to take the key metaphors of such an ideological system very seriously, not because they are true in some scientific way, or even because they are plans for action, but because (if successful) they multiply meanings and enlarge understanding for the audiences to which they are directed.[29] Castro is a very effective metaphor-maker for large segments of the Cuban population, and developmental programs of many types have been quite successful in translating the citizen energies thus evoked into prescribed patterns of behavior. Thus part of the revolutionary art is the art of making an ideology that fits with the times and the circumstances. For more than a decade Castro has practiced this art with consummate skill, and there is every reason to believe that he will continue to do so.

Yet even practicing the revolutionary arts with consummate skill will not protect Castro and his lieutenants from having to face certain dilemmas during the 1970s. The history of all radical movements – in China, in the Soviet Union, and in the new governments of Africa and Asia – illustrates that the politics of mobilization, scarcity, sacrifice, and enthusiasm cannot be continued indefinitely. Eventually some substitute must be found. Both successes and failures in the economic sphere carry with them potential for eroding or at least calling into question the politics and developmental style of the first decade. Rising productivity and increasing distributive payoff, if sustained for a number of years, will undermine the *ambiente* of emergency, threat, and sacrifice. On the other hand, because a great many promises have been made, failure to increase productivity and ameliorate living conditions must eventually cost the régime dearly in the coin of support and credibility.

The Cuban leaders are well aware that either success or failure

– or even a mixed performance – in the developmental effort will bring critical new problems of governance to the fore. This is one reason why they attach such great importance to linking increased productivity and more equitable distribution to the creation and internalization of new values. A transformed citizenry, they hope, will not turn soft and turn inward when exposed to increased abundance. The vision is of a revolutionary citizenry living under post-revolutionary economic conditions. This is a profoundly radical and even utopian posture. If the economic effort fails, the vision is clearly doomed. But what if the Cubans can manage their economy well enough to make good on a number of their promises of increased goods and services? When the psychology of siege is lifted and goods return to the stores, the true and enduring test of the radical experiment will be precipitated. Will the process of cultural transformation have been profound and widespread enough to withstand the tendencies toward increased *egoismo* and diminished *conciencia*? Can participation, national service, and sense of community be normalized and incorporated into a nonheroic way of life in Cuba; or are such feelings and behaviors inevitably dependent on an environment of *plena revolución*?[30] No definitive answer to such questions can be given. At the least, however, the Cuban leaders have given us reason to believe that they are very serious in their attachment to radical goals. Passionate commitment is not, of course, tantamount to achievement. But in speculating about the future of the Cuban Revolution, one should not lightly brush aside the utopias of the men who have already made the most profound social transformation ever seen in the Americas. Their visions may not be an accurate prediction of the shape of the future, but they are a promise that it will be very different from both past and present.

NOTES

[1] In this essay, the attempt to transform the cultural matrix is called "the transformation of political culture" because the behaviors sought by the leadership are those they associate with the good citizen and the good revolutionary. Thus the effort is essentially political even when dealing with "non-political" domains of behavior such as work habits.

[2] From Castro's speech of 26 July 1968, *Granma*, Weekly Review, 28 July 1968, pp. 3–5. As Joseph A. Kahl has pointed out, there is no easy translation for the word *conciencia* as used by the revolutionaries. It connotes, among other things, "an amalgam of consciousness, conscience, conscientiousness, and commitment". See Joseph A. Kahl, "The Moral Economy of a Revolutionary Society", *Trans-Action*, VI, 6 (Apr. 1969), pp. 30–7.

[3] Although Castro has never publicly criticized Soviet and East European societies in detail, he has often suggested that the bureaucraticized, materialistic, élitist, and essentially conservative and nationalistic way of life of Socialist Europe does not even begin to approximate his vision of what a Communist society ought to be. See, for instance, his speech on the Soviet invasion of Czechoslovakia, *Granma*, Weekly Review, 25 Aug. 1968, pp. 1–4. The only Socialist system that receives unqualified and continuous public approbation from the Cuban leaders is North Vietnam. Vietnamese sacrifices, courage, and skill in resisting the Yankees are the qualities most often praised, but Cuban leaders also express admiration for the country's social and economic equalitarianism.

[4] For a full discussion of the "moral versus material incentives" debate in Cuba, see Carmelo Mesa-Lago, *The Labor Sector and Socialist Distribution in Cuba* (New York, 1968), and the important analysis of Leo Huberman and Paul Sweezy, *Socialism in Cuba* (New York, 1969), esp. chaps. 8–11. A very useful perspective comparing the Soviet Union, China, and Yugoslavia is contained in Richard Lowenthal, "Development vs. Utopia in Communist Policy", in Chalmers Johnson (ed.), *Change in Communist Systems* (Stanford, Calif., 1970).

[5] For a brief official statement, see "La lucha contra el economismo y por la conciencia comunista", *Granma*, 21 Feb. 1968, p. 4. Despite

the title of this article, its main message is that meetings and talk will not build Communism. Only machines and technical knowledge in the hands of men fully aware of their own Communist purposes and destinies can create the material base needed for the new society. For an informed though negative view of the possibilities of rapid growth in the Cuban economy through the methods and investment strategies currently in use, see Carmelo Mesa-Lago, "The Revolutionary Offensive", *Trans-Action*, VI, 6 (Apr. 1969), pp. 22–9, 62.

⁶ Appreciation for science and technology implies respect for the nuts and bolts as well: "Today machinery arrives and, because of ignorance, it is often put into the hands of persons who haven't the slightest notion of what machinery is. They don't know how to take care of it, or what kind of maintenance, fuel, and oil it needs. They know nothing of its countless parts or of all the details that must be attended to. There are those who use machinery, and if a bolt drops out, they put it next to the seat; if a cap falls off, they put that next to the seat; the accelerator is soon no longer an accelerator but instead a wire to be pulled. If a valve gets lost, a makeshift connection is made. And by the time we see it, a new machine that cost twenty or twenty-five thousand in foreign exchange has become a piece of junk." Castro, speaking to graduates of the University of Oriente, *Granma*, Weekly Review, 15 Dec. 1968, p. 3.

⁷ See in particular Castro's speech to graduates of the University of Oriente on 8 December 1968, as published in *Granma*, Weekly Review, 15 Dec. 1968, pp. 2–3, and his speech at the University of Havana on 13 March 1969, as published in *Granma*, Weekly Review, 16 Mar. 1969, pp. 2–5.

⁷ᵃ The speech continued: "And if we want all men to work some day with such spirit, it will not suffice just to have a sense of duty. [That kind of] moral motivation will not be enough. It will be necessary for the marvelous nature of the work itself, work directed by man's intelligence, to be one of the basic motivations." *Granma*, Weekly Review, 16 Mar. 1969, p. 3.

Although Castro seldom if ever uses the word, he is actually discussing the concept of alienation in the Marxist sense. Unlike many other Marxists, however, he views the nature of the task performed as more central to ameliorating alienation than to the prior (and larger) issue of controlling the means of production. Furthermore, as one deeply engaged in struggling against backwardness, he attaches positive value to the technicalization of the productive process at a time when others see it as a prime causative factor in the alienation of contemporary man in the more developed societies, both Socialist and non-Socialist.

[8] The most complete development of these ideas is found in the various documents of the Cultural Congress of Havana, held in January 1968. See the "Final Resolution of Commission II: The Integral Formation of Man", in *Cultural Congress of Havana* (Havana: Instituto del Libro, 1968). Throughout this aspect of the revolutionary rhetoric one can find echoes of the early Marx, particularly the *Economic and Philosophic Manuscripts of 1844*. See, for instance, Loyd D. Easton and Curt H. Guddat, eds. and translators, *Writings of the Young Marx on Philosophy and Society* (Garden City, N.Y., 1967), esp. pp. 283–337. For a very useful comparative perspective on the variety and uses of Marxist thought, see Robert C. Tucker, *The Marxian Revolutionary Idea* (New York, 1969).

[9] The characterization of money as a "bitter and transitory instrument" is taken from Castro's speech of 13 March 1968, at the University of Havana. See *Granma*, Weekly Review, 24 Mar. 1968, p. 7. A key compilation of revolutionary ideas about the role of money in past, present, and future societies is "El dinero a través de su historia", *El Militante Comunista* (monograph), Aug. 1968. The 38 citations in this monograph are distributed as follows: Fidel Castro, 18; Engels, 10; Marx, 7; Raúl Castro, 2; Che Guevara, 1.

[10] *Granma*, Weekly Review, 28 July 1968, p. 4. At the time of this speech, local phone calls and burials, as well as sports events, education, medical care, and some housing, were free in Cuba. The personal experiences of myself and others who have visited the island would seem to indicate that removing such transactions from the marketplace has been extremely well received, even among those who are less than enthusiastic about the revolution.

[11] Not only revolutionaries hold this view. An American Rabbi visiting Havana in 1968 quotes a deeply religious Cuban Jew as follows: "Rabbi, little girls used to walk the streets of Havana as prostitutes, and teenagers sold themselves to Americans for food and we merchants made money, not from prostitutes, God forbid, but from the system, from the atmosphere. Today there are no prostitutes, no vice, no Americans, no business. Which is better, Rabbi?" Everett Gendler, "Holy Days in Havana", *Conservative Judaism*, XXIII, 2 (Winter 1969), pp. 15–24. Contemporary Cuban art and literature return again and again to this theme. See, for instance, *Cuban Poetry: 1959–1966* (Havana: Book Institute, 1967), and the cartoons and graphics that abound in Cuban publications.

[12] See, for example, Susan Sontag, "Some Thoughts on the Right Way (for Us) to Love the Cuban Revolution", *Ramparts*, VII, 11 (Apr. 1969), 6 et seq. On the clash in Cuba between youth culture as defined by the revolutionaries and the *egoismo* implied by other youthful life-styles, see José Yglesias, "Cuban Report: Their Hippies, Their Squares", *New York Times Magazine*, 12 Jan. 1969, pp. 25 et seq. See also Arlie Hochschild, "Student Power in Action", *Trans-Action*, VI, 6 (Apr. 1969), pp. 16–21, 67, on generational differences among young Cubans. For a concise statement of the ideal virtues of revolutionary youth, see "Declaración del estudiantado cubano en la Ofensiva Revolucionaria", *Granma*, Weekly Review, 28 July 1968, p. 2. This declaration was read by a student leader immediately before Castro's speech on 26 July 1968. See also "Orientaciones sobre el ingreso al Partido", *El Militante Comunista*, Aug. 1968, pp. 5–30, for an outline of the ideal characteristics of a Party militant. It is not coincidental that most rank-and-file Party-members in Cuba are quite young.

[13] An interesting perspective on youth culture and revolutionary virtues was given in a Havana radio broadcast of 7 March 1968: "The young boys [of Havana] think that the new man is one who wears tight pants. One sees how these ill-mannered brats talk back to their parents and how they act in their homes, on the streets, and in the schools. They are disrespectful and use improper language. . . . Perhaps not so many of them have taken up their little guitars after Fidel spoke about them, but there are many left. They wear tighter pants every day and they let their bangs grow longer until they look like girls. We could say that these are the new men of a bankrupt universe. They are the ones who like to sing and dance to modern music. . . . What do they call modern music? A Yankee rhythm which is imported so that they can dance their epileptic dances? They themselves say that they are sick, and they are. They need to be cured. They need a radical cure. The coffee plantations are waiting. The mini-skirt, a type of urban bikini, is another of the styles we import with the greatest shamelessness. It is temptation in the middle of the street. . . . Is that the new world? Is that the human being of the coming third world so heralded by the intellectuals? No! . . . Lack of respect and lack of clothes are not qualities which will characterize the new man." Foreign Broadcast Information Service, *Daily Report: Latin America*, 7 Mar. 1968, pp. HHHH 3–4.

[14] "El dinero a través de su historia", *El Militante Comunista* (monograph), Aug. 1968, p. 57. For elaborations of this theme, see Fidel Castro, "Discurso de clausura del Congreso (de la CTC)", *Cuba*

Socialista, No. 62 (Oct. 1966), esp. pp. 43–5; and Fidel Castro, "La esencia de esta hora es la técnica y el trabajo" (address on the sixth anniversary of the CDR), *Cuba Socialista*, No. 62 (Oct. 1966), esp. pp. 12–17.

[15] *Granma*, Weekly Review, 5 Jan. 1969, pp. 2–6. Castro used the expression *cultura politica* to refer to "the organization, discipline, consciousness, and sense of duty" of the masses.

[16] The Schools to the Countryside plan was initiated in the 1965–6 school year in Camagüey; 20,000 secondary students participated. In 1967–8, 160,000 students from all provinces took part. For a brief description of the plan, see *Cuba: Report to the United Nations Educational, Scientific, and Cultural Organization*, UNESCO, 1967–1968 (Havana: no date or publisher), pp. 25–6. For more detail on the Isle of Youth, see the extremely interesting report "Two Weeks on the Isle of Youth", in Elizabeth Sutherland, *The Youngest Revolution* (New York, 1969). The Cordón de la Habana was begun in the spring of 1967. For a map of the area and an outline of the plan, see *Cuba*, Mar. 1968, pp. 3–15. For a brief and enthusiastic eyewitness report, see Timothy F. Harding and Donald W. Bray, "The Green Belts of Cuba", *The Nation*, 19 Aug. 1968, pp. 107–9. Since 1967, all three efforts have been reported in detail in the Cuban mass media.

These aspects of Cuban practice are much closer to Chinese than Soviet patterns of participation and formation. For comparative materials on the Chinese case, see Franz Schurmann, *Ideology and Organization in Communist China* (Berkeley, Calif., 1966), esp. pp. 17–58, and James R. Townsend, *Political Participation in Communist China* (Berkeley, Calif., 1967), esp. chap 4. The Cubans are not nearly as concerned with theory as the Chinese, nor are Cuban justifications for and explanations of action programs nearly as conscious and doctrinaire. Furthermore, the Cuban leaders do not openly draw upon or cite Chinese political thought, and they have occasionally been sharply critical of Chinese policies. Nevertheless, the Cubans have evolved a style of directed cultural change that has important similarities to the Chinese style.

[17] Social scientists concerned with development are beginning to appreciate, albeit somewhat grudgingly and incompletely, the importance of this view. For instance, Albert O. Hirschman, in "Obstacles to Development: A Classification and a Quasi-Vanishing Act", *Economic Development and Cultural Change*, XIII, 4, Part I (July 1965), pp. 385–93, devotes considerable attention to the possible uses of cognitive dissonance theory for an understanding of the attitude-

behavior matrix in development. In brief, Hirschman argues that "Dissonance theory deals with the possibility of replacing the 'orderly' sequence, where attitude change is conceived as the prerequisite to behavioral change, by a 'disorderly' one, where modern attitudes are acquired *ex-post*, as a consequence of the dissonance aroused by 'modern' type of behavior which happens to be engaged in by people with non-modern attitudes." The quoted passage is from p. 392. What the author fails to consider is the role of developmental élites in creating institutional settings and mobilizational practices in which this "disorderly" change can get started. Thus, although disorderly change may enable one to bypass at some stage in the developmental process certain attitudinal and value patterns, élites must still be viewed as first-order obstacles to change insofar as they fail to create institutions that encourage "disorder" in this sense. The failure of many social scientists in the United States to face squarely the logic of such situations would seem to derive in part from their belief that this way of shaping behavior entails unacceptable authoritarian control or infringements on individual liberties. It should also be pointed out that an interaction between behavioral change and attitudinal change might possibly be established right from the outset, thus rendering the "disorder" model (with its reverse linearity) quite inappropriate for understanding the way change takes place – or could take place. Dialectical or cybernetic models that begin with behavioral change certainly seem the most appropriate for representing the attitudinal-behavioral interaction in revolutionary Cuba, as well as in many other situations. See the position taken by Milton Rokeach, "Attitude Change and Behavioral Change", *Public Opinion Quarterly*, XXX, 4 (Winter 1966–7), pp. 529–50.

[18] The distinction between attitudes and values that is being used here is that drawn by Milton Rokeach, "The Role of Values in Public Opinion Research", *Public Opinion Quarterly*, XXXII, 4 (Winter 1968–9), pp. 547–59: "I will define an attitude as an enduring organization of several beliefs focused on a specific object (physical or social, concrete or abstract) or situation, predisposing one to respond in some preferential manner.

"Values, on the other hand, transcend specific objects and specific situations: values have to do with *modes of conduct* and *end-states of existence*. More formally, to say that a person 'has a value' is to say that he has an enduring belief that a particular mode of conduct or that a particular end-state of existence is personally and socially preferable to alternative modes of conduct or end-states of existence." The quotation is from p. 550; italics in the original.

¹⁹ For those who have difficulty accepting this point of view, the analogy of the wartime Army in the United States is instructive. Although military institutions and their norms often seemed in conflict with the values and attitudes of individual soldiers, acceptable military behavior was evoked from most enlisted men during both the Second World War and the Korean War. Furthermore, the soldiers were not generally coerced into this acceptable military behavior except in the sense that members of all closed and authoritarian social organizations are coerced. In both military and revolutionary organizations, the small primary living or working group (itself closely guided by the organizational leadership) would seem to be the most important single factor influencing individual behavior.

²⁰ Seymour Martin Lipset, "Values, Education, and Entrepreneurship", in Seymour Martin Lipset and Aldo Solari (eds.), *Elites in Latin America* (New York, 1967), p. 6. See also Seymour Martin Lipset, *The First New Nation* (Garden City, N.Y., 1967), especially the Introduction and chap. 3. The literature cited in both of these books documents the origins and intellectual underpinnings of the argument.

²¹ The value categories are those of Talcott Parsons as modified by Lipset. See Lipset, "Values, Education, and Entrepreneurship", note 20, pp. 49–50, for the relevant citations to the work of Parsons.

²² It would seem that the entire general syndrome of Hispanic-American upper-class and middle-class values is breaking up in Cuba under the impact of the revolutionary experience. John P. Gillin, in "Some Signposts for Policy", in Richard N. Adams et al., *Social Change in Latin America Today* (New York, 1960), characterized this syndrome as follows: personalism, the strength of family ties, the importance of hierarchy, a variant of materialism (the importance of land), the weight of transcendental values (the *pensador* tradition), emotion as fulfilment of the self, and a sense of fatalism. If these were, in fact, among the dominant values of the national (middle and upper) sectors of pre-revolutionary Cuba, there is little doubt that they are less so now. Contrast the characterization of Cuban values given by Wyatt MacGaffey and Clifford R. Barnett, *Twentieth Century Cuba* (Garden City, N.Y., 1965), chaps. 2 and 4, with the descriptions contained in Elizabeth Sutherland, *The Youngest Revolution* (New York, 1969).

²³ Erik H. Erikson, *Young Man Luther* (New York, 1962), pp. 134–5. See also Erik H. Erikson, *Identity: Youth and Crisis* (New York, 1968), esp. chaps. 1, 5, and 6.

[24] In an extreme statement and generalization of Erikson's position, Lucian Pye, in *Politics, Personality, and Nation Building* (New Haven, Conn., 1962), p. 288, has characterized one path to national development as follows: "The first approach is that of the grand ideological solution in which some leader, out of the depths of his own personal experience, is able to give his people an understanding of the new sentiments and values necessary for national development. This would be a solution according to the Eriksonian model of the relationship between ideology and personality which suggests that the struggle of the ideological innovator to find his own personal sense of identity may provide a vehicle for an entire people to find their collective sense of identity. If such a leader can fully and honestly face the problems of his times as they emerge in his own personality, he can give powerful and meaningful expression to new attitudes and values which can in turn inculcate in a people the feeling of a new order of legitimacy and redirect their feelings of trust and distrust, of aggression and anxiety, of repudiation and commitment." To the extent that any case has approximated this model during the past twenty years, it would be Fidel Castro and Cuba.

[25] Rule by terror is defined and discussed in Hannah Arendt, *The Origins of Totalitarianism* (New York, 1958), esp. chap. 13, "Ideology and Terror", and in Carl J. Friedrich and Zbigniew K. Brzezinski, *Totalitarian Dictatorship and Autocracy* (New York, 1963), esp. section IV, "The Psychic Fluidum: Propaganda and the Terror". Although the models developed differ in emphasis, neither is applicable to Cuba.

[26] Samuel P. Huntington, "Political Development and Political Decay", *World Politics*, XVII, 3 (Apr. 1965), pp. 386–430. See also Samuel P. Huntington, *Political Order in Changing Societies* (New Haven, 1968), esp. chaps. 1 and 5. In a similar vein, Lucian Pye earlier suggested that "it may be fruitful to think of the problems of development and modernization as rooted in the need to create more effective, more adaptive, more complex, and more rationalized organizations." Pye, p. 38.

[27] Lee Lockwood, *Castro's Cuba, Cuba's Fidel* (New York, 1967), p. 180.

[28] Herbert L. Matthews, in *Fidel Castro* (New York, 1969), elaborates this point at length and quite convincingly. Matthews, along with many others, calls this ideology Fidelismo and argues that it is Communist only because its author so designates it. See also Lockwood.

[29] See Clifford Geertz, "Ideology as a Cultural System", in David E. Apter (ed.), *Ideology and Discontent* (New York, 1964), esp. pp. 57–60. For example, if Cuban rhetoric concerning the new man is taken as a design for an action program, then the appropriate measures of success and failure are "before and after" tests of the modalities of individual values and social behavior. However, if the rhetoric is also seen as metaphor, then the appropriate measures of success and failure involve the evaluation of the understandings of self and society that are achieved by, and the political and organizational consequences attributable to, the multiplication of meanings. Obviously, the accounting scheme needed to capture the results of a metaphor that is "working" are extremely complex. As Geertz has indicated, many social scientists tend to evaluate ideological systems as if they were either blueprints or descriptions, rejecting them as foolish or unimportant when they find them to be unworkable or untrue. To do this in the case of the Cuban Revolution and Fidelismo is to run the risk of misunderstanding the significance of the ideology while at the same time underestimating its capacity to be regenerated by Castro as circumstances change.

[30] Certain critics see the continuance of revolutionary behavior outside the revolutionary environment as possible only with the establishment of tyranny. A variant of this position is taken by Eric Hoffer in *The Ordeal of Change* (New York, 1963), p. 33: "Much has been said by all manner of people in praise of enthusiasm. The important point is that enthusiasm is ephemeral, and hence unserviceable for the long haul. One can hardly conceive of a more unhealthy and wasteful state of affairs than where faith and dedication are requisite for the performance of unmiraculous everyday activities. The attempt to keep people enthusiastic once they have ceased to believe is productive of the most pernicious consequences. An enormous effort has to be expended to maintain the revivalist spirit and, inevitably, with the passage of time, the fuels used to generate enthusiasm become more crude and poisonous."

Notes on the contributors

RICHARD R. FAGEN
Associate Professor of Political Science, Stanford University. Writings include *Cuba, The Political Content of Adult Education; Politics and Communication; Enemies in Politics; Cubans in Exile.*

ANDRE GUNDER FRANK
Visiting Professor of Economics and History, Sir George Williams University, Montreal. Writings include *Capitalism and Underdevelopment in Latin America; Underdevelopment or Revolution.*

JOHN GERASSI
Writings include *The Great Fear in Latin America: The Reconquest of Latin America by Latin Americans.*

GINO GERMANI
Professor of Social Relations, Harvard University. Writings include *Politica y Sociedad en una Epoca de Transición; Sociologia de la Modernización; La Sociologia en la America Latina: Problemas y Perspectivas.*

IRVING LOUIS HOROWITZ
Professor of Anthropology-Sociology, Washington University. Writings include *Radicalism and Revolt Against Reason; Three Worlds of Development: The Theory and Practice of International Stratification; Revolution in Brazil: Politics and Society in a Developing Nation; Latin American Radicalism.*

IVIN ILLICH
Director of Cento Intercultural de Documentación, Cuernavaca, Mexico. Writings include *Bolivia y la Revolucion Cultura.*

HELIO JAGUARIBE
Visiting Professor, Harvard University, founder of ISEB and Brazilian Institute for Studies in Development. Writings include *Economical Development and Political Development.*

ANTHONY F. C. WALLACE
Professor of Anthropology, University of Pennsylvania. Writings include *Culture and Personality; Religion: An Anthropological View.*